From
Spare Oom
to
War Drobe

From Spare Oom to War Drobe

Travels in Narnia with my
Nine Year-Old Self

KATHERINE LANGRISH

First published in 2021 by
Darton, Longman and Todd Ltd
Unit 1, The Exchange
6 Scarbrook Road
Croydon CR0 1UH
editorial@darton-longman-todd.co.uk

This new edition published by Herne Books of the same address.

This product conforms to the requirements of the European Union's
General Product Safety Regulations (GPSR).
EU Authorised Representative for GPSR:
Easy Access System Europe –
MustamAAe tee 50, 10621 Tallinn, Estonia
gpsr.requests@easproject.com

© 2021 and 2025 Katherine Langrish

The right of Katherine Langrish to be identified as the
Author of this work has been asserted in accordance with the
Copyright, Designs and Patents Act 1988.

ISBN: 978-1-917665-04-9

No part of this book may be used or reproduced in any manner for the
purpose of training artificial intelligence technologies or systems.

A catalogue record for this book is available from the British Library.

Printed and bound in India by Replika Press Pvt Ltd.

*To the memory of my parents,
who brought me up in a house full of books.*

Contents

Foreword: In Search of Narnia	9
Introduction	15
The Magician's Nephew	33
The Lion, the Witch and the Wardrobe	65
The Horse and His Boy	104
Prince Caspian	133
The Voyage of the Dawn Treader	162
The Silver Chair	202
The Last Battle	229
Afterword	275
Appendix 1: Orphans in Narnia	279
Appendix 2: Of a Narnian Fish	285
Appendix 3: The Picture Portal in The Voyage of the Dawn Treader	289
Acknowledgements	295
Bibliography	297

Foreword

In Search of Narnia

I have a confession to make. When I was ten years old, I believed fervently in the existence of the land of Narnia – *as a reality* – and tried very hard to get there. I laid my plans: waiting until my parents were out of the house, I went into their bedroom, climbed inside their big, double-fronted, wardrobe, pulled the door to – but not quite shut, because Mr C. S. Lewis had strongly advised against it.

Of course, I knew the wise Professor Kirke had told the four Pevensie children that no one ever enters Narnia by the same route twice but, since *I* hadn't previously tried the wardrobe route, it seemed worth a go. So, there I sat, in the moth-balled closeness, my eyes screwed tight shut, willing the backboard to the wardrobe to melt away so that I might feel the silent kiss of falling snow on my face and, on opening my eyes, might find myself in a winter world, walking towards a lamppost just as Pauline Baynes had depicted in her entrancing illustrations. I should like to be able to say that that is what happened but, alas …

This confession is prompted by reading Katherine Langrish's superb Narnian travelogue with its passionate recollections of childhood reading that chimes so completely with my own memories and, I am sure, with those of a great many other readers. In re-viewing these perennial classics through the dual prism of her young and adult self, the author re-lives and re-evokes the enduringly powerful imagery of a place redolent with all the familiar forms, textures, sounds and aromas of our own natural world — but also re-appraises those stories with the experience gained from literary knowledge and spiritual understanding.

There is no shortage of books about C. S. Lewis, his life, work and beliefs — *too many*, it could well be argued! — but *From Spare Oom to War Drobe* is an indispensable companion to the seven 'Chronicles of Narnia'. Katherine Langrish writes with a freshness untainted by the prevalent and awesome weight of Lewis hagiography, whilst even-handedly engaging with vociferous contemporary critics of the Narnian creation.

As a result, we have here a work that deserves an honoured place among Lewis scholarship — all the more so, because this is not a stuffy, academic analysis of a bookish phenomenon (for that is what it is with its unflagging sales figures and popular translations for stage, screen, television and radio) but a volume that also, rather miraculously, captures the fragile ghosts of youthful reading with its vivid excitements, puzzlements, even occasional disappointments that comes with being a nose-in-book-and-lost-to-the-world child!

As for me and my relationship with the country beyond the wardrobe: sixty years older (though not much wiser) I still believe in the existence of a place called Narnia, much as I believe in the existence of Middle-earth, Wonderland, Moominland, Never Land and other fantasy realms — only with a sense of wonderment and yearning that becomes more 'true' as I grow ever closer to that shadowy day when I may be able to say, like the Unicorn in *The Last Battle*: 'I have come home at last! This is my real country! I belong here. This is the land I have been looking for all my life, though I never knew it till now... Come further up, come further in!'

Now, come further up and further in and join this fine seven chronicled exploration of the world of the Lion ...

BRIAN SIBLEY

began," the King, "What brings you—" The stag interrupted him.

"Lord King— news. A galleon has come from the Lone Islands to say that the Islands are rampaged by a dragon that breathes fire and kills men. They want you to kill it, and promise the Islands in return." Gale frowned. "A dragon, eh?" "Yes, Sire. And—" Gale sprang to his feet. "Go you to Cair Paravel, prepare me a galleon, Chervie. I will follow. The men from the Lone Islands can be told to go back, and tell also them that I am coming." "With a good will, Sire— and—" "What is it Chervi?" "Shall I tell them that they must get ready the 'Splendour Hyaline, or the—" "Splendour Hyaline." "I go, Sire." There was the flash of a white stern amongst the trees, and Chervie was gone. "Come, Diamond," said Gale, "We too, must be going. Can'st take me on your back, friend? For we must be fast, or never there at all." "With a good will, Sire." said Diamond, "But you had ~~betted~~ better gird on your sword." So the king put on on his sword, and sprang onto Diamond's back. Diamond spread his wings, and they were off. In about half an hour, they could see Cair Paravel shining on the ~~egde~~ edge of the Eastern sea. Its many towers were glistening in the sunshine, and the effect was lovely. Diamond glided downwards, and landed in the middle of a crowd of Talking Beasts, Fauns, Centaurs, Unicorns, and the like, who had made room for them. "Where is the

Introduction

When I was nine years old I wrote a book called *Tales of Narnia*, and I still have it. In spiky blue ink, written in my best handwriting with only occasional crossings-out and spelling mistakes, it runs for eighty-six numbered pages and fills an old hard-cover notebook from front to back. There's a list of contents (as all proper books should have), five short stories, three poems, several illustrations and two maps: 'Narnia and adjoining lands' and 'The Lone Islands', copied from the ones by Pauline Baynes. I covered the notebook with a paper wrapper which I painted dark blue, and stuck a poster-paint picture I'd made of Aslan on the front. He looks very stiff, very yellow, and rather cross.

It was a labour of love. I was proud of it, though it makes comic reading today. In my opening tale, 'The Story of King Gale', the king sails for the Lone Islands to fight a dragon: a story sketched out by Jewel to Jill in *The Last Battle*. This posed me a problem. Only two Narnian ships are ever named, King Peter's *Splendour Hyaline* and Caspian's *Dawn Treader*. It couldn't be the *Dawn Treader*, since Gale is a much earlier Narnian king than Caspian. I thought he might have inherited Peter's ship (though truth to tell, he may be earlier than Peter), but I felt strongly that a king ought to have a *choice* of ships. So the talking stag who brings news of the dragon asks King Gale:

'Shall I tell them to get ready the *Splendour Hyaline*, or the —'

'*Splendour Hyaline!*' the king snaps decisively, covering the fact that I hadn't for the life of me been able to think of any other ships' names ... My characters all keep saying, 'With a good will, Sire!' and 'By the Lion's Mane!' — and clearly feeling Lewis' description of Cair Paravel 'shining on the edge of the eastern sea' lacked something, I added, 'Its many towers were glistening in the sunshine and the effect was lovely.'

I'd read and re-read all of the Seven Chronicles and I longed, *yearned* to read more, but C. S. Lewis was dead (he'd died about three years earlier). There wouldn't be any more Narnia stories, so the only thing to do was to try and write some of my own. I enjoyed myself, but discovered in the process that there's a difference between the way you believe in a story you are reading and in one you are writing. As writer, you can't abandon yourself to it in the same way. You are on the outside, making it; not inside, living it — and I wanted to *live* in Narnia more than almost anything else. Exploring her own relationship with Narnia in *The Magician's Book*, the American writer Laura Miller remembers the same childhood longing to visit this non-existent country and wishing desperately to get there: 'For the rest of my life,' she writes, 'I will never want anything quite so much again.'[1]

It's impossible to exaggerate the effect the Narnia

---

[1] Miller, Laura, *The Magician's Book*, 3

INTRODUCTION

stories had on me. I loved them deeply, jealously, selfishly: was so possessive about them that when my mother suggested she might read *The Lion, The Witch and the Wardrobe* as a bedtime story to me and my brother, I vetoed it. Aslan would have growled, but I wanted to keep Narnia all to myself. (My brother read them anyway.) Another time I remember saying tentatively to my mother, 'It almost feels as if Narnia is real', when what I meant was, 'Narnia *has* to be real', because the alternative – that it had no existence except between the pages of a book – was unbearable. My mother didn't spoil anything for me by telling me that Aslan 'is' Christ. She just replied quietly, 'I think you're meant to feel that way.'

Philip Pullman, one of Narnia's most outspoken critics, has suggested children enjoy the series because they lack discrimination.

> Why the Narnia books are popular with children is not difficult to see. In a superficial and bustling way, Lewis could tell a story, and when he cheats, as he frequently does, the momentum carries you over the bumps and potholes. But there have always been adults who suspected what he was up to.[2]

It's true that children are generally inexperienced readers, but that doesn't mean they're not sensitive ones. I couldn't have explained it very well when I was nine, but I knew there was a qualitative difference between the pleasure I got from

---

[2] Pullman, Philip, *The Dark Side of Narnia*, The *Guardian*, October 1, 1998, originally found at *The Guardian* URL at http://reports.guardian.co.uk/articles/10/1/p-24747.html and widely available on the internet

reading the adventure stories of Enid Blyton, say, and my far deeper love of the Narnia books. Yes, I enjoyed Lewis's storytelling, but the real enchantment lay in the rich silence of the Wood Between the Worlds, the black sky of the city of Charn, the almost unbearable light of the Eastern Sea, the bleak, gusty heights of Ettinsmoor, and the stars falling like prickly silver rain near the end of *The Last Battle*. These were the things I loved about Narnia, the things that drew me back again and again. When eventually I noticed the Christian messages in the books, they seemed unimportant by comparison.

Then decades passed. The books sat on my shelves. Except for reading a couple to my own children, who were more interested in Harry Potter, I didn't return to them even though I write for children myself. Had they simply become so familiar that I didn't feel the need, or had the charm faded? What might they mean to me now?

I thought I would read them again, remind myself of what had once enchanted me and discover if it still had the power to do so. Over a period of about eighteen months I re-read all the Seven Chronicles, and this too became a labour of love: a personal journey hand in hand with my nine year-old self, tracing as many paths as we could through Lewis's thick forest of allusions not only to Christianity, but to Plato, fairy tales, myths, legends, medieval romances, renaissance poetry and indeed to other children's books. There were many things I hadn't noticed when I was nine, but you don't have to know where a thing comes from before you can enjoy it. I never connected the cold queenliness of the White Witch with Hans Andersen's Snow Queen, nor did I realise that, as Queen Jadis, she owes even more to the Babylonian Queen in Edith Nesbit's

INTRODUCTION

The Story of the Amulet. Even though I'd read those stories, they remained separate for me. I saw differences where now I see similarities, and both are important. The Lady of the Green Kirtle was fixed in my imagination well before I met the courtly, dangerous, green-clad queen of fays riding down from the Eildon Tree on her milk-white steed in the ballad of *Thomas the Rhymer*:

> Her shirt was o' the grass-green silk,
> Her mantle o' the velvet fine.[3]

In fact the land of Narnia owes its character, richness and depth to precisely the heterogenous mix of mythologies and sources of which Tolkien disapproved. It is like *The Waste Land*, for children.

Writers borrow from older literature all the time and it's what they make of it that matters: what they add, their own take or twist, variations on the theme. The Wood Between the Worlds is in some ways similar to the Wood Where Things Have No Names in Lewis Carroll's *Through the Looking Glass*, but Lewis's conception of it as an 'in-between' place is very different and in its turn has influenced later writers. In Diana Wynne Jones' *The Lives of Christopher Chant*, the eponymous young hero gets into a multiverse of related worlds, which he calls 'Anywheres', via 'The Place Between': an unsettling 'left-over piece of the world', full of 'formless slopes of rock' with a 'formless wet mist'[4] hanging over everything: no place to linger in. Lev Grossman's more recent '*Magicians*' trilogy, a magnificently

---

[3] Oxford Book of Ballads, 7
[4] Wynne Jones, Diana, *The Lives of Christopher Chant*, 8

inventive adult fictional homage to Narnia, presents yet another place of in-between potential: a timeless, empty city rather like Charn, with marble fountains in place of pools.

I enjoyed re-reading the Narnia books. I found plenty of the old magic, and rediscovered how very good Lewis is at giving his readers something to think about. I also found things I disliked. Some of these were things I'd disliked as a child as well; my love of Narnia had been passionate but never entirely uncritical.

Philip Pullman is by no means the only critic of the Narnia stories but he is one of the best-known, and may speak for many when he accuses the Narnia books of sending the message: 'Death is better than life; boys are better than girls; light-coloured people are better than dark-coloured people; and so on'.[5] He is a fine writer whose opinions are always worth considering, and on the last point I agree with him: Lewis's portrayal of Calormen culture and of most individual Calormenes is indefensibly racist and there will be more to say about it later. I can't agree that the Narnia books are sexist, though, and I claim personal experience. When I was a little girl in the 1960s it was clear to me that many authors automatically assumed their reader would be a boy. In order to armour myself against routine slights such as 'cry like a girl', 'run like a girl,' 'behave like a girl', etc., I would mentally swap genders and read *as if* I were a boy. (I've often wondered if this enforced identification with the Other is why girls are usually said to be more able readers than boys.)

---

[5] Pullman, Philip, *The Dark Side of Narnia*, *The Guardian*, October 1, 1998

INTRODUCTION

This stratagem was never necessary with the Narnia books. Polly, Lucy, Aravis and Jill are strong characters and I could tell that Lewis liked them. I revelled in Lucy's integrity, Aravis's lordly glamour, Polly's practical common sense, Jill's courage and ability. As for Susan, 'the problem of Susan': yes, I was furious about that and I now think it an artistic mistake as well. In the two books in which she actually appears, Susan is cautious, conscientious, responsible, the sort of child who works hard at school: a plodder perhaps, but definitely a tryer. She is one of the two most interesting characters in *Prince Caspian*, and at the end of that book she appears to reach a mature balance which ought to be a good foundation for life in our world. She doesn't seem to me to have the makings of the silly, flighty person Lewis hints at in *The Voyage of the Dawn Treader*, the book in which he begins to betray her.

Lewis can be unfair. He can be thoughtless and nasty. The slurs cast at little girls with fat legs in *Prince Caspian*, and the snide singling out of a woman head-teacher in *The Silver Chair* — I notice these now, though back then they passed me by. The fat-legged little girls are balanced by a set of pig-faced little boys, which seemed to me even-handed, and though I'd had four highly effective women head-teachers by the time I was eleven, children don't generally feel much sympathy for head-teachers of whatever sex. I stick to my opinion that in general, Narnia is an equal-opportunities fantasy land.

As for Philip Pullman's accusation that the Narnia books teach 'death better than life', if it is directed at the entire series, then I disagree. However I think Pullman is talking about the end of *The Last Battle*, where the Christian message becomes explicit and final and we find out that the children have died. I always disliked that ending very much, partly because of Susan and partly for the same reason that I disliked the ending of John Masefield's *The Box of Delights* where Kay's marvellous, magical adventures turn out to have been only a dream. 'The term is over: the holidays have begun,' Aslan tells the children. 'The dream is over: this is the morning.' Lewis intends this to be uplifting, but in fact it dashed me down. It still does.

Stories are important, as Lewis was well aware. In one of his essays he complains of an illustration in his 'nursery copy' of *The Pilgrim's Progress,* of the moment Christiana crosses the river to the Celestial City waving a cheerful farewell to her friends. Rather than depicting the events of the story, the artist plumped for a heavy-handed literal interpretation of the *allegory,* illustrating the story with a picture of an old woman on her death-bed. 'If Bunyan had wanted a literal death-bed scene,' Lewis comments, 'he would have written one.'[6]

The ending of *The Last Battle* is the equivalent of that picture. Never mind the story: this is what it was *really* about ... Then why have a story at all? If it's no more than a superficial disguise to be cast aside, why write it? Especially since in another essay, recalling how difficult it was for him as a child to feel 'as one was told one ought to feel about God or the sufferings of Christ', Lewis explains how one of the impulses to write the Narnia books occurred when it came to him:

> ... that by casting all these things into an imaginary world, stripping them of their stained-glass and Sunday

[6] Lewis, C. S., The Vision of John Bunyan, *Selected Literary Essays,* 149

school associations, one could make them for the first time appear in their real potency ...[7]

Well, quite. Story is king. It enriches our perceptions and is valuable in itself, and Lewis is usually very good at it. I think Philip Pullman gets things back to front when he complains of:

> The colossal impertinence, to put it mildly, of hijacking the emotions that are evoked by the story of the Crucifixion and Resurrection in order to boost the reader's concern about Aslan in *The Lion, The Witch and the Wardrobe*.[8]

When anyone says 'to put it mildly' they always mean to put it strongly. I don't doubt Mr Pullman's outrage, but he sees it this way because he first read the book as an adult. When I was nine I didn't *have* any deep feelings about the Crucifixion and Resurrection. It was the other way around. If I'd connected those events with Aslan's story they would have detracted from my emotional engagement, not boosted it. Aslan's death and resurrection moved me *more* than the story of Jesus, and Lewis is most successful when he works within the framework of his imaginary world, not when he tries to break out of it. *The Voyage of the Dawn Treader* is full of adventures which I am now able to interpret as vivid, imaginative accounts of spiritual experiences. One is the Dark Island. Another is Eustace's rebirth as a boy

---

[7] Lewis, C. S., *Sometimes Fairy Stories May Say Best What's To Be Said*, On Stories and Other Essays on Literature, 47
[8] Pullman, Philip, *The Dark Side of Narnia*, The Guardian, October 1, 1998

after his transformation into a dragon, and another is the light-washed sea and sky of the Eastern Ocean which, like those of the Irish voyage tales it echoes, seem brimming with purity and holiness. Such images lose their power when they are made explicit.

At the beginning of *The Pilgrim's Progress*, John Bunyan explains how he came to write the book. While engaged upon a different work about the spiritual life, Bunyan 'fell into an allegory' and saw how he could represent it as the physical journey of the Saints to Glory. Ideas began to multiply in his head 'like sparks that from the coals of fire did fly'.[9] In an essay on Bunyan, Lewis suggests that in this coalescence of adventurous quest and spiritual journey we can see Bunyan's earnest Christianity coming together with his boyhood delight in old wives' tales and chivalric romances: 'The one fitted the other like a glove,' he remarks. 'Now, as never before, the whole man was engaged.'[10]

Now, as never before, the whole man was engaged — Lewis might be talking about himself. The Narnia books are a fusion of his life-long love of literature, his Christian faith and the experiences of his own childhood: the latter most obviously in *The Magician's Nephew*, where Digory's wish to save his sick mother derives its poignancy from the death of Lewis's own mother in his early boyhood. There is even more to it than this. In *The Lion, the Witch and the Wardrobe* the Professor's big house, full of book-rooms and passages and unexpected places, sounds a lot like Lewis's childhood home Leeborough House, or 'Little Lea', a big house on

---

[9] Bunyan, John, *The Pilgrim's Progress*, 135
[10] Lewis, C.S., *The Vision of John Bunyan*, Selected Essays, 147

the outskirts of the city of Belfast[11] to which his family moved in 1905 when he was only seven and before his mother fell ill. In *Surprised by Joy* he describes it with love:

> The New House is almost a major character in my story. I am a product of long corridors, empty sunlit rooms, upstair indoor silences, attics explored in solitude, distant noises of gurgling cisterns and pipes, and the noise of wind under the tiles. Also, of endless books.[12]

The New House *is* a major character in Lewis's stories. An imagery of labyrinthine houses, passages, secret rooms and doorways into Elsewhere recurs throughout the Narnia series. I will look at these in detail later, but here are some examples: the attics of *The Magician's Nephew*, and the palace-city of Charn; the Professor's house and the wardrobe itself in *The Lion, the Witch and the Wardrobe*, which 'contains' the whole land of Narnia; there's Aravis and her friend Lasaraleen losing themselves in the dangerous maze of the Old Palace of Tashbaan, and the Pevensie children exploring the ruins of Cair Paravel in *Prince Caspian* and discovering the treasure chamber; there's Lucy tiptoeing along the creepy, sunlit passages of the Magician's House in *The Voyage of the Dawn Treader* – the City Ruinous and the Dark Castle of Underland in *The Silver Chair* – and the stable in *The Last Battle*, arguably the last and greatest doorway of all.

Not coincidentally, I think the triumphal cry from the end of *The Last Battle* – 'Farther up and farther in!' –

---

[11] McGrath, Alister, *C.S. Lewis: A Life*, 14
[12] Lewis, C. S., *Surprised by Joy*, 17

is consciously or unconsciously borrowed from George MacDonald's adult fantasy novel *Lilith* (1895), another book set in a vast, rambling house with portals to other dimensions. In Chapter 3, the protagonist Mr Vane rushes after the figure of a mysterious Mr Raven, chasing him up many stairs into unfamiliar attic regions and a garret furnished only with a mirror. Vane stumbles through the frame into a wild, visionary landscape, and is told by Mr Raven that he has come into this strange land through a door.

> 'I never saw any door,' I persisted.
>
> 'Of course not!' he returned; 'all the doors you had yet seen — and you haven't seen many — were doors in; here you came upon a door out. The strange thing to you,' he went on thoughtfully, 'will be, that the more doors you go out of, the farther you get in.'[13]

'The more doors you go out of, the farther you go in' is almost certainly what Lewis also means us to understand: an exit from the narrowness of selfhood which paradoxically leads to an expansion and enrichment of apprehension.

This imagery of an 'endless' house isn't restricted to Narnia. It comes from somewhere deep, turning up in Lewis's Christian apologetics as well, and even in his literary criticism. 'In my Father's house there are many rooms,' said Jesus (John 14:2). In the preface to *Mere Christianity*, Lewis describes the basic Christian faith as a hallway, out of which doors open into different rooms representing different denominations: 'The hall is a place to wait, a place from

---

[13] MacDonald, George, *Lilith*, 10

INTRODUCTION

which to try the various doors, not a place to live in.'[14] In its function, this hall sounds surprisingly like the Wood Between the Worlds – another 'in-between' place that opens into many dimensions: a place of potential, not a place to stay.

In his memoir *Memories, Dreams, Reflections*, Carl Jung records a personal dream of exploring an ancient house. It began somewhere on an upper floor, in a richly furnished rococo-style salon hung with fine old pictures. Going downstairs, he found the ground floor furnished in an older, medieval style with a red brick floor. Everything seemed 'rather dark.' Exploring room after room, he came across a heavy old door and behind it, a stone staircase leading further down into an even more ancient, vaulted room:

> My interest was now intense. I looked more closely at the floor. It was of stone slabs, and in one of these I discovered a ring. When I pulled it, the stone slab lifted and again I saw a doorway of narrow stone steps. These too, I descended and entered a low cave cut into the rock [where] I discovered two human skulls, obviously very old ...[15]

The story that follows this is worth repeating. Jung recounts how he took the dream to Freud and asked for his opinion of its meaning. Focussing almost entirely on the two skulls, Freud decided they must represent a death-wish – an interpretation which the newly and happily married Jung felt

---

[14] Lewis, C. S., *Mere Christianity*, II,12
[15] Jung, Carl, *Memories, Dreams, Reflections*, 182-3

was quite wrong. He had his own ideas about the meaning of the dream, but fearing to offend Freud and damage their friendship he pretended to agree and told Freud the death-wish must be directed at his new wife and sister-in-law.[16] Freud seemed 'greatly relieved' by this admission, Jung comments with a twinkle.

Jung's own interpretation was that the house was 'a kind of image of the psyche', and that in descending through the various levels he was descending from the conscious mind into the unconscious.

> The ground floor stood for the first level of the unconscious. The deeper I went, the more alien and the darker the scene became. In the cave, I discovered remains of a primitive culture, that is, the world of the primitive man within myself – a world which can scarcely be reached or illuminated by consciousness.[17]

Building upon this reading, Jung later came to form his theories of the collective unconscious and of 'archetypes' or symbols common to the human mind.

Writing with a touch of humour, Lewis acknowledged the emotional and poetic power of Jung's theory of archetypes. Even if it should turn out to be poor science, he commented, it was still 'excellent poetry' of a mythic character. The concept of the archetype as something old, meaningful, hidden, deeply buried but gradually coming to light made him feel like 'Schliemann digging up what he believed to be the very bones of Agamemnon, king of men'

---

[16] 'I had to name someone whose death was worth the wishing!' Jung adds.
[17] Ibid, 184

INTRODUCTION

— or 'my own self, hoping, as a child, for that forgotten, that undiscovered room.'[18]

Maybe most children hope to find a hidden room: still, in expressing this desire, here is Lewis returning again to the same potent image. If Jung and Freud could disagree over the interpretation of Jung's dream, perhaps there's a chance for me to speculate that for Lewis the archetypal house symbolised the security of his childhood before his mother's death. After that event, Little Lea became gradually intolerable to him. While his father was dying he described it in a letter as a place where he had never experienced freedom — yet he added, 'I have never been able to resist the retrogressive influence of this house which always plunges me back into the pleasures and pains of a boy.'[19]

> 'Into my heart an air that kills
> From yon far country blows ...'[20]

The house which sheltered the happiness of Lewis's early childhood had long vanished into that land of lost content, the far country of the past: but in imagination he was a constant visitor, exploring passages and tiptoing into rooms, searching for the doorway through which he might pass into joy.

---

[18] Lewis, C. S., *Selected Literary Essays*, 297-298
[19] Letter to Owen Barfield, 9 Sept 1929, *Letters of C. S. Lewis*, 350
[20] Housman, A. E., *Poetry and Prose: A Selection*, 86 [*A Shropshire Lad XL*]

A note on the order of the Narnia stories:

In what order to read or discuss the Narnia books is a riddle in itself. I saw four possibilities: the order in which the books were written, the order of their publication, the order of the internal history of Narnia, or the order in which I first read them. The last wouldn't do at all: it was quite haphazard. The first Narnia book I ever read was *The Silver Chair*, which I was given for Christmas 1965, when I was eight. Over the next couple of years I read them out of sequence, ending with *The Voyage of the Dawn Treader*: it all depended what I received as presents, bought with my pocket money or could borrow from the local library. (This random order made no difference at all to my enjoyment of the series!)

Order of publication might seem sensible. That would mean beginning with *The Lion, The Witch and the Wardrobe* – but then *The Horse and His Boy* comes after *The Silver Chair*, and *The Magician's Nephew* immediately precedes *The Last Battle*. To complicate matters further, the order of publication is different from the order in which the books were actually written. For example, Lewis wrote *The Voyage of the Dawn Treader* before *The Horse and His Boy*, and he began *The Magician's Nephew* in 1949 soon after he had finished *The Lion*: it might have been the second of the Narnia stories but was put aside twice (the second time in 1951, on Roger Lancelyn Green's advice) and Lewis did not finally return to it until 1954 after completing *The Last Battle*. Writing is not a tidy process.

Since difficulties emerge in no matter what order the series is arranged, I have decided to follow Lewis's own preferred order as expressed to Walter Hooper.[21]

---

[21] Lancelyn Green, Roger, Hooper, Walter, *C. S. Lewis, A Biography*, Revised and Expanded Edition, HarperCollins 2002, 320

INTRODUCTION

1. *The Magician's Nephew*
2. *The Lion, the Witch and the Wardrobe*
3. *The Horse and His Boy*
4. *Prince Caspian*
5. *The Voyage of the Dawn Treader*
6. *The Silver Chair*
7. *The Last Battle*

This order makes narrative sense of Narnian history, but still leaves a number of anomalies such as Mr Beaver's account in *The Lion* of the White Witch's descent from Lilith and the giants, which contradicts her extra-terrestrial origin as found in *The Magician's Nephew*. I have done my best to indicate when these occur.

The Magician's Nephew

This is a story about something that happened long ago when your grandfather was a child. It is a very important story because it shows how all the comings and goings between our world and the land of Narnia first began.

In those days Mr Sherlock Holmes was still living in Baker Street and the Bastables were looking for treasure in the Lewisham Road ...[22]

The Magician's Nephew is unique among the Narnia stories in that a large proportion of the narrative — just over half, in fact — takes place *outside* Narnia. (This may be why in the second sentence Lewis gives the possibly impatient child reader an assurance that the book will eventually get there.) First he locates the story in the real past 'when your grandfather was a child', and immediately after in the fictitious past of Sherlock Holmes and the Bastable children. Why both?

Partly it's shorthand. Any child who'd read E. Nesbit's

[22] *MN*, 9

books, and in the 1950s and 60s, many of us had,[23] would feel instantly at home in the London parts of the narrative. There are obvious similarities between *The Magician* and Nesbit's 1906 novel *The Story of the Amulet* which Lewis read and loved as a boy. 'It first opened my eyes to antiquity, the "dark backward and abysm of time"', he wrote in his autobiography *Surprised by Joy*. 'I can still re-read it with delight.'[24] The similarities between the books are not restricted merely to period and style. Both involve the use of magical tokens to travel into other worlds — time travel in *The Amulet,* and travel between universes in *The Magician*. Lewis even borrows and re-interprets Chapter 8 of *The Amulet* in which Nesbit's children struggle to entertain and control a Babylonian Queen in Victorian London. More of that later.

In spite of this, *The Magician's Nephew* is a very different kind of book from E. Nesbit's. The world of her characters is essentially safe: no matter what scrapes they get into, it's impossible to imagine anything truly bad happening to them. In her 1899 book *The Story of the Treasure Seekers*, the Bastable children have lost their mother as Digory fears to lose his. However it's a *fait accompli* that does not affect the reader, and Oswald Bastable gets it briefly out of the way: 'Our mother is dead, and if you think we don't care because I don't tell you much about her you only show that you do not understand people at all.' *The Story of the Treasure Seekers* is not about loss. The Bastables' emotions are not on display.

'Happy, but for so happy ill secured' runs the epigraph from Milton that heads the first chapter of *Surprised by Joy*.

---

[23] Most remained in print, and were re-issued as paperback Puffin editions throughout the late fifties and sixties.
[24] Lewis, C. S., *Surprised by Joy*, 21

The chapter ends:

> With my mother's death all settled happiness, all that was tranquil and reliable, disappeared from my life. There was … no more of the old security. It was sea and islands now; the great continent had sunk like Atlantis.[25]

'Like Atlantis' — the metaphor is striking and strange. Could it, I wonder, be drawn from Chapter 9 of *The Amulet* in which the children visit Atlantis, and barely escape as a great wave swamps the city and the mountain bursts into flame? Their friend the 'learned gentleman' looks back through the arch of the Amulet and sees 'nothing but a waste of waters, with above it the peak of the terrible mountain with fire raging from it.' If this passage made a deep impression on Lewis's childhood imagination (and what was he reading while his mother lay dying?) it's no wonder *The Magician's Nephew*, which engages so closely with the trauma of his mother's illness and death, borrows so much from *The Amulet* in imagery and style.

This is the book in which Lewis remembers, rewrites, reclaims his own past. It is a myth of healing, a poetic re-imagining, a fairy tale in which the universe turns out not, after all, to be impersonal and unkind. Its emotional core is not the wondrous creation of Narnia but Digory's approaching personal tragedy. He is in tears when we meet him: his happiness is ill secured. The line comes from Book 4 of *Paradise Lost*, when Satan arrives in Eden and views Adam and Eve in their short-lived innocence:

---

[25] Ibid, 27

> Ah! gentle pair, ye little think how nigh
> Your change approaches, when all these delights
> Will vanish, and deliver ye to woe —
> More woe, the more your taste is now of joy:
> Happy, but for so happy ill secured
> Long to continue ...[26]

The Magician's Nephew works so well because Digory's grief is truly felt. But it's possible that Lewis's first-page references to the world of Sherlock Holmes and the Bastables deliver a sub-textual, maybe even unconscious warning. This is a story like theirs: this is *fiction*. For young Jack Lewis and his mother there was no miracle. The things that will happen to Digory Kirke are not the sort of things that happen in real life.

For those who came to *The Magician's Nephew* as I did, after reading several of the others first — this would include most of its original readers — there is a brisk, fresh energy to the narrative with its new characters and new setting. The first four pages (three, minus the illustrations) form a brilliantly economical bit of scene-setting and tell us everything we need to know about Polly and Digory, and Digory's Uncle Andrew, mad Mr Ketterley. Within another page or so Polly is showing Digory her den in the attic, a dark place behind the cistern where she keeps a box containing various personal treasures, a story she's writing, and of course provisions: apples, and bottles of ginger beer which make the den look satisfactorily like a smugglers' cave.

Polly is tough, practical and confident, with a strong sense of self-respect. (And she is the only character in all

---

[26] Milton, John, *Paradise Lost*, Book 4, lines 366-371

the Narnia stories who is a *writer*. I wonder what she wrote about?) She is an excellent partner for the impulsive and more emotional Digory. In his 1998 article for *The Guardian*, 'The Dark Side of Narnia', Philip Pullman has complained that in the Narnia books Lewis is guilty (among other crimes) of sending the message 'boys are better than girls.'[27] Possibly it's not fair to take someone to task for an opinion in a newspaper article written so long ago, and some of Pullman's accusations are justifiable, but hardly this one. I cannot see it and never have. To base an accusation of sexism on 'the problem of Susan' alone is to ignore the strength of such different characters as Polly, Lucy, Aravis and Jill – all gallant, courageous and memorable. I do wonder how recently Mr Pullman had read the books.

A little girl myself, I certainly didn't feel excluded or denigrated. The easy, bickering comradeship between Polly and Digory was just what I was used to in Nesbit's books. Moreover, Polly sounded like me: *I* wrote secret stories! With my brother, I loved to make dens – in hedges, cupboards, in corners of the playground, in barns, attics, sheds and lean-to's, in patches of waste ground, on building sites. (Pacing stilt-like, ten feet up, across the open floor-joists of a half-completed house, my brother fell across and through them, badly scraping his ribs. We didn't confess.)

Just as the Bastable children in *The Treasure Seekers* play detectives and spy on the empty house next door, Polly and Digory explore further down the attic tunnel, hoping to come out in the abandoned house next-door-but-one. They try to calculate how far they will have to go, and I don't

---

[27] Pullman, Philip, *The Dark Side of Narnia*, The Guardian, October 1, 1998

notice any nonsense about boys being better than girls: the children are equally and endearingly erratic with their sums, getting different answers, trying again, and even then not getting it right. Their mistake leads them to emerge in the wrong house. Pushing open a little door in the rough brick wall, they see not a barren attic, but a comfortably furnished room — lined, of course, with books. Everything is silent. No one seems to be here. Full of curiosity, Polly puffs out the candle-flame and steps through the door.

Following Polly's lead, we look around. Bookshelves everywhere. A fire is burning in the grate. A high-backed armchair faces it, with its back to us. On a bright red wooden tray is a collection of shiny yellow and green rings, in pairs. The room is almost quiet, except for a clock ticking — and a faint humming sound:

> If Hoovers had been invented in those days Polly would have thought it was the sound of a Hoover being worked a long way off — several rooms away and several floors below.[28]

Lewis's asides to the reader never divide us from the narrative, they pull us in. We're there, holding our breath, listening to the quietly ticking clock, which is ordinary — and to the almost sub-acoustic humming which is *strange*. The comparison of the sound to a vacuum cleaner being run 'a long way off' creates unease in two ways: it can't *be* a vacuum cleaner (in Victorian England), and it directs our attention to the remoteness of this attic room at the top of the house, its distance — rooms and floors away — from the

---

[28] *MN* 17

safe and ordinary world of cleaners and household tasks. It's an almost cinematic build-up of tension, and in classic horror-film style Lewis allows us and his characters to take one breath before springing the trap. Just as Polly declares that there's no one there, the chair in front of the fire is suddenly shoved back, and out of it leaps Uncle Andrew, 'like a pantomime demon coming out of a trap door'.

> Digory was quite speechless ... Polly was not so frightened yet; but she soon was. For the very first thing Uncle Andrew did was to walk across to the door of the room, shut it, and turn the key in the lock. Then he turned round, fixed the children with his bright eyes, and smiled, showing all his teeth. 'There!' he said. 'Now my fool of a sister can't get at you!' [29]

This is truly frightening; in fact I think it frightens me more now than it did when I was nine. With his clean-shaven face, sharply-pointed nose and tousled mop of grey hair, tall thin Uncle Andrew – who behaves in ways, as Lewis puts it, 'dreadfully unlike anything a grown-up would be expected to do' – now strikes me as a kind of ur-Jimmy Savile. Compare the situation in *The Story of the Amulet*, where the children consult the elderly scholar who lives upstairs about the inscription on their Amulet.

> 'There's a poor learned gentleman upstairs,' said Anthea, 'we might try him. He has a lot of stone images in his room, and iron-looking ones too – we peeped in once when he was out.'[30]

---

[29] *MN* 18
[30] Nesbit, Edith, *The Story of the Amulet*, 41

There are no horrid surprises and their 'learned gentleman' is no threat. Not so here. Though it wasn't spelled out to me in the 1960s just *why* you should never get into cars with strange men — and I doubt C. S. Lewis intended anyone reading this passage to think 'child-molester' — there is no doubt at all that Digory and Polly are in serious and as yet unspecified danger. The cloud of possibilities is terrifying.

Digory is more frightened than Polly, in this passage — and Polly is more easily fooled. Is this because she *is* a fool? No. The difference between the children, here and right through the book, is that Polly possesses the as-yet-untested confidence of an ordinarily happy childhood. There is something pathetically innocent about her plea to Uncle Andrew: 'Please, Mr Ketterley. It's nearly my dinner time and I've got to go home. Will you let us out, please?' But Digory has already been hurt by life. His mother is dying, he knows that awful things can and do happen: *his* plea acknowledges the danger and answers it with a threat: it really is dinner time, so if they don't turn up soon, the other adults in their lives will be looking for them. 'You must let us out.'

Uncle Andrew appears to capitulate. For Polly, this is the universe righting itself after an alarming wobble. He offers her one of the pretty yellow rings and she is ready to trust him, but Digory doesn't like the avid expression on his uncle's face. He shouts a warning, but it's too late. The moment Polly's fingers touch the ring, she vanishes.

All that in just the first chapter, perhaps eleven pages all told.

It's been strong stuff. At this point in the narrative Uncle Andrew is far scarier than the White Witch or the

Green Lady, or even Queen Jadis — and the reason is because he is so much more plausible. Children don't expect to meet Witch Queens, but eccentric adult relations are two a penny. This must be why through the rest of the book, Lewis transforms Uncle Andrew from a nightmare Jack-in-the-box to a drenched and muddy figure of fun a child can only laugh at. As soon as Uncle Andrew embarks on justifications of his behaviour, though pompous, selfish and manipulative, he becomes less frightening. When he emotionally blackmails Digory to go after Polly into the unknown, Digory loses his fear and delivers a searing rebuke. He didn't ever believe in magic before, he says, but now he sees it's real. In which case perhaps all the fairy tales are real as well, and in all fairy tales, wicked magicians come to bad ends, and so will Uncle Andrew, and it will serve him right.

Digory has taken the moral high ground and got the upper hand: his words are an implicit promise that good will prevail. From now on Uncle Andrew will be more of a nuisance than a bogeyman.

The Wood Between the Worlds is a marvellous creation. It isn't Aslan's country; it's not at all like the high, wooded mountain top of *The Silver Chair* with its bright birds and clear air, or the vast mountains behind the wave at the edge of the world in *The Voyage of the Dawn Treader*. 'It was the quietest wood you could possibly imagine', a place of no names, of infinite potential and zero accomplishment: an eternal, 'dreamy, contented' place in which if you linger, you are in danger of losing your identity. When the children see one another they have already forgotten who they are and how long they have been here.

The Wood may owe something to Tennyson's poem *The*

Lotos-Eaters, where stranded sailors drowse for ever 'with half drop't eyelid' on a languid, fertile shore, lost to ambition; but if The Wood Between the Worlds has a single literary antecedent it is surely 'the wood where things have no names' in *Through the Looking Glass*:

> [Alice] was rambling on in this way when she reached the wood: it looked very cool and shady. 'Well at any rate it's a great comfort,' she said as she stepped under the trees, 'after being so hot, to get under the — under the — under *this*, you know!' putting her hand on the trunk of the tree. 'What *does* it call itself, I wonder? I do believe it's got no name — why, to be sure it hasn't! ... And now, who am I? I *will* remember, if I can.' ... [But] all she could say, after a great deal of puzzling, was 'L, I *know* it begins with an L'! [31]

Wandering on, Alice meets a Fawn. As neither can recall its own identity, they walk trustfully together, Alice's arms around the Fawn's neck, until they reach the end of the wood where they regain their names and memories and the Fawn flees in fear. It's a very short passage, but as a fable of prelapsarian, Edenic innocence it comes with a troubling, perplexing taint: the struggle to remember has a nightmarish flavour, and the trust between Alice and the Fawn is rooted in ignorance rather than innocence. A tree may not need to 'call itself' anything, Carroll seems to be saying, but without names *we* are hardly human. The relief of rediscovery, even with a sting of loss, is palpable.

Though so peaceful, the Wood Between the Worlds too

---

[31] Carroll, Lewis, *Alice's Adventures in Wonderland and Through the Looking Glass*, 210

is no place for humans. It is a place where one could drowse forever like the Lotus-eaters: and though Digory is here to 'rescue' Polly, it is she who sticks to the knowledge of what she's seen and done. When Digory announces that he has 'been here forever' she contradicts him; she's just seen him emerge from the pool, and she has a feeling they may possibly have met before. This extinguishing of memory and identity might also be nightmarish, but it doesn't last long. The children see the guinea pig with the yellow ring on its back, and are reminded of who they are and what has happened.

Aware now of the danger of the place, Polly insists they must leave. But Digory has a new idea. What if the Wood isn't any kind of world, but an 'in-between place' — like the tunnel in the attic that leads between all the houses in the row at home? Perhaps all the pools in the Wood are doors to other worlds and if so, why shouldn't they visit one? In making this comparison, Digory explicitly connects the exploration of old houses with the exploration of other worlds, an imagery which recurs in all of the Narnia books, as we shall see.

Before testing his theory, the children want to be certain the green rings will actually take them home and we are given a marvellous description of how they turn about, half-way back to London. Whirling through space they see stars, and Jupiter with its moons, and then the roofs of London, and St Pauls, and Uncle Andrew through the wall of his house, getting nearer and clearer ... Changing their rings they rise through the pool back into the Wood where, eager to test his theory, Digory is ready to jump straight into a nearby pool chosen at random. 'Stop!' shouts Polly. 'Aren't we going to mark *this* pool?'

I've always loved this 'gasp' moment as Polly prevents catastrophe. The pools are all alike, the trees are all alike:

without marking *their* pool, how would they ever find it again? How would they ever get home? Shock provokes a brief squabble, after which they jump into the new pool and discover by experiment the difference between the yellow and green rings. (The yellow rings draw you towards the Wood. The green rings send you away from it.) On the second try, they find themselves standing in a dull, reddish light, under a black sky, in the ruined city of Charn.

The children have already quarrelled about the pools. Now they begin to do so again. Pragmatic Polly wants to leave Charn almost at once, on the grounds that there's nothing interesting to see, and Digory suggests she's scared: what's the good of owning magic rings that take you into other worlds if you're too frightened to explore them once you've arrived? During this chapter Digory is recognisably his uncle's nephew — manipulative and driven by the desire to *know*. Just like young Jack Lewis, Digory Kirke will grow up to become a Professor, famously learned. The question is what sort? Scientist, scholar or magician?

Lewis can hardly disapprove *per se* of the desire for knowledge, but he asks us to consider the price of it and who pays. Uncle Andrew, when he was attempting to justify his actions to Digory, recounted the story of how he made the yellow and green rings. On her deathbed his old godmother Mrs Lefay (clearly a *fairy* godmother, and not a nice one; was her first name Morgan?) had asked him to find a little box and promise to burn it after her death, unopened. Instead, he broke his promise and opened it, an action Digory describes as 'rotten'. This is something Uncle Andrew cannot understand, and he embarks on his own selfish apologia: the rules are for the little people. Keeping one's promises and things of that kind are all very well for children, servants, women and other lowly, ordinary folk, but —

> '... can't possibly be expected to apply to profound students and great thinkers and sages ... Ours, my boy, is a high and lonely destiny.'[32]

Lewis has an extraordinary ability to engage his child readers in philosophical and moral questions at a level appropriate to their understanding and without talking down. Children are interested in ethics: much of childhood is spent testing and negotiating the rules. They also have a strong sense of justice. Uncle Andrew's credo as a Magician is the credo of all those prepared to waive the rules in their own favour, make special exceptions of themselves, and treat 'lesser' people as commodities. It is a fault not limited to magicians: examples can found in the pages of any newspaper. Digory sees right through it.

But his behaviour in Charn demonstrates that he too can be selfish in pursuit of his own way. Exploring the dead and deathly city with its dry fountains and labyrinth of hallways, rooms, arches and stairs — a quest that like the exploration of the attic will lead to a hidden room and a revelation — the children come at last to the gold doors of the Hall of Statues.

Again Polly takes the lead, just as it was she who stepped first into Uncle Andrew's attic room. One of the many things I like about this book is the children's equal agency in the taking of decisions. Polly wants to see the magnificent clothes in which the figures are dressed, and Lewis makes it

[32] *MN* 23

plain these are well worth looking at. I find Polly's interest in the clothes realistic rather than stereotypical; intelligent too, as her first remark demonstrates:

> 'Why haven't these clothes all rotted away long ago?'
> 'Magic,' whispered Digory. 'Can't you feel it? I bet this whole room is just stiff with enchantments. I could feel it the moment we came in.'[33]

Yes! And the enchantments are preserving far more than just clothes. There follows the memorable progression of the faces of the 'statues' sitting in their stone chairs: a marvellously succinct way of presenting the degeneration of an empire, or even perhaps of an individual over time. As the children walk through the room, they see kind, wise faces changing to ones they like less: 'strong and proud and happy, but they looked cruel.' The expressions degenerate further until the faces are full of cruel despair, as if those to whom they belonged have endured and committed terrible things. It should therefore be hardly necessary for Digory to exclaim that he wishes he knew the story behind it all. His curiosity leads him to examine a golden bell and a hammer set in the centre of the hall with a provocative inscription.

> *Make your choice, adventurous Stranger;*
> *Strike the bell and bide the danger,*
> *Or wonder, till it drives you mad*
> *What would have happened if you had.*[34]

---

[33] *MN* 47
[34] *MN* 50

Now the children have their most serious quarrel. Digory badly wants to strike the bell, so he persuades himself that he *must*, that he has no choice: the magic is already working, he'll be forever tortured by not knowing what would have happened. Polly disagrees. She says he's 'putting it on' (that lovely childish taunt) and accuses him — tactlessly but tellingly — of looking 'exactly like your Uncle'.

Aslan often tells people they will never know *what might have been*: he says it twice to Lucy, once in *Prince Caspian* and once in *The Voyage of the Dawn Treader*. This scene may be read as a version of the Fall: a temptation acted upon by a boy in a ruined city near the end of a world, rather than by a woman in a garden near the beginning of one. Both cases result in expulsion, ruin, and the need to atone. The children's quarrel becomes physical. Digory grabs Polly's wrist and strikes the bell. The note strengthens and strengthens until the whole room is vibrating unbearably and the roof falls in. Shocked, sobered, they think it's over. They are wrong. Jadis, the last Queen of Charn and last of the statues, awakes.

Tall and terrifying, she leads the children through the collapsing city. Again it's Polly who sees Jadis clearly for what she is: dangerous and terrible, 'strong enough to break my arm with one twist'. To Digory the Queen seems brave and magnificent; he admires her as she blasts the palace doors to dust with her magic, and they emerge into open air to see a weary red sun hanging low over the ruined horizon. This, the Queen tells them, is Charn (a name with strong undertones of 'charnel house'), once the greatest city of the world or even, she adds in her pride, of any worlds, which was destroyed in an instant by one woman, herself: 'I, Jadis, the last Queen, but the Queen of the World.'

Here is one of the first parallels Lewis draws between Queen Jadis and Milton's Satan, who declares in *Paradise Lost*:

> 'To reign is worth ambition, though in Hell.
> Better to reign in Hell than serve in Heaven.'[35]

'To reign is worth ambition': the title is everything, even if it's an empty crown. Jadis shares Satan's blindness: she is unable to see that to be Queen of a dead world is to be Queen of nothing. Pride, deceit, selfishness and power are some of the themes *The Magician's Nephew* examines, and though the Deplorable Word spoken by Jadis to destroy the world of Charn may sound like an enchantment out of *Le Morte D'Arthur*, it is an unmistakeable metaphor for the atom bomb: towards the end of the book Aslan delivers a warning to the children that makes the parallel explicit. It's not that Lewis can't appreciate the excitement and wonder of scientific research. Here is Uncle Andrew talking marvellously about the dust in Mrs Lefay's box, dust from another world:

> '... another Nature – another universe – somewhere you would never reach even if you travelled through the space of this universe for ever and ever – a world that could be reached only by Magic – well!'[36]

The thrill is authentic. But can the end justify the means? It depends. What *are* the means? What is the price of this knowledge? When Digory objects to his uncle's experiments on live guinea pigs, some of which exploded (Lewis never

---

[35] Milton, John, *Paradise Lost*, Book I, lines 262/3
[36] *MN* 25

spoke of vivisection without abhorrence), Uncle Andrew is unable to see there could even *be* an ethical problem. The guinea pigs were his, so he could do what he liked with them. He progresses from breaking a promise, to experimenting on animals, to experimenting on Polly. For him, the guinea pigs are not living, sentient creatures but a commodity to be used — and so are the children.

Scientists don't get a great press from Lewis. Uncle Andrew is as much scientist as magician, and the scientists Weston and Devine in Lewis's adult trilogy *Out of the Silent Planet, Perelandra,* and *That Hideous Strength* are an appalling duo. But before we accuse him of simple prejudice we should remember that in Lewis's lifetime science had produced horrors like mustard gas and machine guns, and in 1945, only ten years before *The Magician's Nephew* was published, nuclear bombs had wiped out the cities of Hiroshima and Nagasaki. The Deplorable Word is the no-first-use, last-resort weapon of Charn. Even the Queen herself protests that she *had no choice*, had tried all other methods first. Lewis undoubtedly has in mind Milton's famous condemnation of Satan, who 'with necessity,/The tyrant's plea, excused his devilish deeds'.[37] Jadis claims she was forced to this extremity: she did not use her power until all of her soldiers were dead, and her sister and rival (who sounds just as bad!) was close upon her, claiming the victory.

> '"Yes," said I. "Victory, but not yours." Then I spoke the Deplorable Word. A moment later I was the only living thing beneath the sun.'[38]

[37] Milton, John, *Paradise Lost*, Book IV, lines 393,394
[38] *MN* 60

Digory is horrified by the thought of all the people she has killed, but it's not until Jadis echoes Uncle Andrew's words of exculpation, 'Ours is a high and lonely destiny', that he realises for the first time that in spite of being impressively beautiful she is as wicked as his uncle. He is correspondingly dismayed when she announces that she intends to come with them, assuming his uncle to be a great enchanter who has fallen in love with her across the worlds and wishes her to be his consort. Isn't that so?

> 'Well, not *exactly*,' said Digory.
> 'Not exactly,' shouted Polly. 'Why, it's absolute bosh from beginning to end.'[39]

Why does Digory temporise? Is he tempted by Jadis' mistake, so much more flattering to both his uncle and himself than the truth? Polly's outburst puts an abrupt end to it. The Queen grabs her by the hair, and is drawn after the children as they vanish back to the Wood. Here the Queen turns sick and faint and can barely breathe. The children have the upper hand and are about to jump into their own pool, when the Witch pleads for mercy, begging them not to leave her here to die. Polly is unimpressed.

> 'It's a reason of State,' said Polly spitefully. 'Like when you killed all those people in your own world. Do be quick, Digory.'[40]

But Digory falters, feeling pity, and his hesitation gives the Witch the chance to seize his ear and be towed down into

[39] *MN* 63
[40] *MN* 66

their own world, where Uncle Andrew is about to meet more than his match.

Spiteful or not, it's hard not to feel that Polly is exactly right. ('Reasons of State': 'Necessity, the tyrant's plea'.) If only they had left the Witch (as she is now more and more frequently called) in the Wood, she could have done no more harm in any world. Yes, Polly's being spiteful but doesn't the Witch deserve it? And don't we enjoy hearing it? What are we supposed to think?

I think Digory's pity is tainted with admiration. Beside the Witch's fierce beauty, Uncle Andrew is a poor creature, losing all terror. '*Him* a Magician!' Digory thinks. 'Not much. Now *she's* the real thing.' It's a boy's version of Uncle Andrew's 'dem fine woman'. If his admiration for the Witch were to continue, he might end up no better than his Uncle. Digory is in a muddle.

Polly is clear-sighted. She quite reasonably blames first Uncle Andrew for the mess they're in, and then Digory, and when Digory wants to know what he's done wrong she makes no bones about telling him.

> 'Oh, nothing of course,' said Polly sarcastically. 'Only nearly screwed my wrist off in that room with all the waxworks, like a cowardly bully. Only struck the bell with the hammer, like a silly idiot. Only turned back in the wood so that she had time to catch hold of you before we jumped into our own pool. That's all.'[41]

The surprised Digory makes a genuine apology and pleads for her help; it's his Mother he really cares about: what if the

[41] *MN* 72

Witch invaded her room and frightened her? Polly sees the point of this and relents. Changing her tone, she agrees to call it 'pax' and promises to come back when she can. Polly is the Hermione Granger of Narnia.

Next comes the comic whirlwind of a chapter in which Queen Jadis wreaks havoc in the London streets. It's closely related to Chapter 8 of E. Nesbit's *The Story of the Amulet* where Nesbit's children try desperately to control and entertain an Ancient Babylonian Queen on the loose in London. Nesbit's Queen causes chaos – she is thrown out of the British Museum as she attempts to claim her own ancient property from the glass cases; but she is fundamentally well-intentioned. Nesbit even gets in a little Fabian satire.

> '[H]ow badly you keep your slaves. How wretched and poor and neglected they seem,' she said as the cab rattled along the Mile End Road.
>
> 'They aren't slaves, they're working people,' said Jane.
>
> 'Of course they're working. That's what slaves are. Do you suppose I don't know a slave's face when I see it? Why don't their masters see that they're better fed and better clothed?'[42]

Lewis takes this episode and ramps it up into something far more dramatic. With Uncle Andrew for her slave and lieutenant, Jadis rampages through London on top of a hansom cab, ambitious to become Empress of our world and hampered only by the fact that she's lost her power of turning people to dust. The children know they must stop

---

[42] Nesbit, Edith, *The Story of the Amulet*, 148

her, but Polly's mother has sent her to bed in disgrace and Digory sits alone by his window, watching anxiously for the Witch. This is when he overhears his aunt talking about his mother and saying that only the fruit of the land of youth could help her now, for nothing in this world can. For Aunt Letty it's a sentimental metaphor, but Digory is filled with desperate hope. He knows there really are other worlds, to be reached through every pool in the Wood. Surely in one of them he can find the fruit to make his mother better — make everything right again? 'And oh, oh ...'

In *Surprised by Joy*, Lewis describes his own struggle with hope. Like many Christian children he had been brought up to believe that if he had faith, God would answer his prayers. (You may remember that when Huckleberry Finn is told this, he prays for fish-hooks, doesn't get them, and decides there's nothing in it.) Of course the thing Jack Lewis most wanted was for his mother to recover, and he convinced himself that if he prayed hard enough, God would grant it.

> When nevertheless she died, I shifted my ground and worked myself into a belief that there was to be a miracle ... [God] was, in my mental picture of this miracle, to appear neither as Saviour nor as Judge, but merely as a magician; and when he had done what was required of him I supposed he would simply — well, go away.[43]

I understand what he's saying: that an interest in God generated solely by a desperate desire to *have* something is worthless. That a view of God as a *magician* is worthless

---

[43] Lewis, C. S., *Surprised by Joy*, 26

might be counted one of the primary themes of this book. But, compared with the tenderness with which he explores Digory's emotions, Lewis's account of himself is stiff and critical — too detached from the youthful self whose anguished efforts I find heartbreaking. Little Jack Lewis may not have loved God but he certainly loved his mother, and so does Digory, and the love is true.

Before Digory can act on his impulse, life interrupts in the form of the Witch, splendidly and crazily balancing upright on the roof of a hansom cab while driving it full tilt through the streets, pursued by a crowd of comedy Cockneys who are delightfully unimpressed by the Empress Jadis in her splendour. The Cabby tries to calm his maddened horse, Uncle Andrew totters out of the wreckage, Jadis wrenches the cross-bar from an iron lamp-standard and fells a policeman — and Polly arrives in the nick of time. The children join hands, Digory grabs the Witch's heel, Polly touches her yellow ring, and with children, Witch, Cabby, horse and Uncle all stuck together like the characters in the fairy tale of the Golden Goose, they rise into the Wood Between the Worlds. A moment later, Strawberry the cab-horse steps into a nearby pool to have a drink, and the entire party sinks into the darkness of an unborn world.

There is an unnerving simplicity about it. If the Wood Between the Worlds is a place of rich vegetable growth and enervating drowsiness, this is a flat emptiness offering nothing but the basics: somewhere to stand and air to breathe. It is a sheet of blank paper waiting to be drawn or written upon. The children don't know it, but this no-place will become Narnia — and we are just over halfway through the book.

The Cabby takes charge — not the only adult here, but the only decent one. While he raises the children's spirits by starting up a hymn, Uncle Andrew sneaks and schemes. A far-off Voice begins a wordless singing and is suddenly joined by the massed voices of the stars as they leap into existence. A dawn wind springs up, and as a new sun joyfully rises the humans see they are standing in a bare valley of coloured earth and rock — 'fresh, hot and vivid' — adjectives expressive of vibrant youth and life. Finally the owner of the Voice comes in sight, and it's a Lion.

As the Lion paces up and down, singing grass and trees and flowers into existence, each character responds individually and revealingly. The Cabby is enchanted by Aslan and his music. The horse drops his head to tear up mouthfuls of the new grass. Polly is intrigued by the correspondences between the Lion's song and the things it creates. Digory becomes nervous as the Lion draws nearer — Uncle Andrew is terrified — and the Witch hurls the iron bar she tore from the London lamp-standard straight at the Lion's head. It glances harmlessly off. She screams and runs, and the iron bar begins to grow where it has fallen into the lamp-post that will one day greet Lucy Pevensie's eyes and give its name to Lantern Waste.

The soil of Narnia is fertile indeed. On witnessing this phenomenon, Uncle Andrew's reaction is to dream of filling Narnia with scrap metal. Digory, though, realises this may truly be the land of youth and becomes desperate to speak to the Lion. Meanwhile the Narnian soil bubbles up with animals, and Aslan breathes consciousness into his chosen creatures: 'Love, think, speak. Be walking trees. Be talking beasts. Be divine waters.'

There follows a fair bit of slapstick to lighten the

solemnity. I wasn't a child who enjoyed comedy much, so I wasn't terribly keen on this, though I'm sure there must be many who find it delightfully funny. The First, Second and Third Jokes left me cold (and still do), and I've never been sure how the Elephants fit into Narnia; in Pauline Baynes' illustration there are even two giraffes. Perhaps they wandered off southwards. It all has a fabulous feel to it, by which I mean it feels like a fable: there's a flavour of Kipling's 'The Crab that Played with the Sea':

> Before the High and Far-Off Times, O my Best-Beloved, came the Time of the Very Beginnings; and that was in the days when the Eldest Magician was getting Things ready. First he got the Earth ready; then he got the Sea ready; and then he told all the Animals they could come out and play. And the Animals said, 'O Eldest Magician, what shall we play at?' and he said, 'I will show you.' He took the Elephant — All-The-Elephant-There-Was — and said, 'Play at being an Elephant,' and All-The-Elephant-There-Was played.
>
> ... [The Eldest Magician] went North, Best Beloved, and he found All-The-Elephant-There-Was digging with his tusks and stamping with his feet in the nice new clean earth that had been made ready for him.
>
> *'Kun?'* said All-The-Elephant-There-Was, meaning, 'Is this right?'
>
> *'Payah kun,'* said the Eldest Magician, meaning, 'That is quite right' ...[44]

---

[44] Kipling, Rudyard, *Just So Stories*, 157-159

While the Eldest Magician shows all the Animals how to play at being themselves, and sets the Man, whom he addresses as 'Son of Adam', in charge of them, Pau Amma the Crab runs off into the sea and only the Man's best-beloved little girl-daughter notices ...

Back to Narnia: in the middle of all this creative fun Lewis provides a serious and characteristically clear exposition of Uncle Andrew's thought processes: he will not, and consequently soon *cannot* understand the Talking Beasts: 'the trouble about trying to make yourself stupider than you are is that you very often succeed.' Deliberate blindness is a sin to which Lewis will return in *The Last Battle*.

I'm afraid that the Council which Aslan calls to deal with the threat of the Witch's presence in Narnia is, with the exception of the female raven, exclusively male – Aslan calls specifically on the He-Owl and the Bull-Elephant, though the She-Elephant has, arguably, a more important narrative role in planting and copiously watering the unconscious Uncle Andrew. It's probable that Lewis did think of males as the most natural councillors, but all the real fun happens without them. And look how Digory, hoping for a cure for his mother, is brought to confess to Aslan that it's *his* fault that the Witch came to Narnia. Digory, not Polly, is Narnia's Eve. When Digory suggests he and Polly somehow just 'met' the Witch, or that she 'woke up', Aslan won't let him equivocate, and he's driven to admit that he actively woke her by striking the bell:

'Polly didn't want to. It wasn't her fault. I – I fought her. ... I think I was a bit enchanted by the writing under the bell.'

'Do you?' asked Aslan; still speaking very low and deep.

'No,' said Digory. 'I see now I wasn't. I was only pretending.'[45]

As Digory sheds his protective layers of self-deceit, as he comes closer to honesty about himself and his motives, he gets further away from the person he might have become — his Uncle. If you're a child reading this, you appreciate that Digory is owning up to what he did wrong — that he needs to be honest with Aslan. If you're a Christian, you probably think in terms of confession and repentance. If you're an atheist you may feel sickened by a deity callous enough to ignore Digory's urgent need in order to rake over his faults. But atheists sometimes take a more literal view of God than is necessary. Except perhaps for fundamentalists, God is always a metaphor seen through a glass, darkly. Digory needs to be honest with *himself*.

Young Jack Lewis needed to be honest with himself too. He needed to stop using magical thinking. He needed to see that it wouldn't be his fault if his mother died. He needed to realise that he had no ability to save her and wasn't responsible. 'I think I was a bit enchanted ...' No, he was just pretending. And the pretence was an agonising waste of effort.

Digory finally understands. He can't 'do' anything for his mother, but he can shoulder his real responsibilities and face the next task. That doesn't mean an end to pain. Even though he's ready now to help undo the evil he has brought into Narnia on its first day, he can't help thinking about his mother and how much he had hoped to cure her, and how these hopes are now dashed:

[45] *MN* 125/6

and a lump came into his throat and tears in his eyes, and he blurted out, 'But please, please — won't you — can't you give me something that will cure Mother?'[46]

If prayer is a heart-felt plea thrown out into the universe, we all pray. The only answer we can hope for is love and a shared knowledge of grief. This, Aslan provides, and no false promises.

How I adored the next bit, in which Aslan turns Strawberry the cab horse into Fledge the flying horse! — a transformation enchantingly rendered by Pauline Baynes. 'Is it good?' asks Aslan. 'It is very good', Fledge responds, echoing the Eldest Magician as well as Genesis. And clinging to Fledge's back, the children fly off on their quest to find the paradisal garden in the far West, Narnia lying fresh and unexplored below them — on what is still the very first day of this world.

There are delightful and sinister episodes *en route*. I love how Lewis plays with the possibilities of the newly-created Narnia's fruitful soil — the solution to the children's hunger as they plant the toffees from Polly's pocket (tearing the paper bag off the sticky toffees) and wake next morning to find a toffee tree with soft brown fruit and whitish, papery leaves. Then there's a creepy disturbance in the night and a glimpse of a 'tall dark figure gliding away' — the Witch, who has overheard them talking. Now she knows where to go, and when the children arrive she will already be there.

This part of the book is full of Miltonic resonances. In fact it's fair to say that Lewis borrows his description of the tall green hill in the snowy mountains wholesale from the passage in *Paradise Lost* when flying towards Eden, Satan sees

[46] *MN* 131

Paradise: 'an enclosure green' crowning the head 'of a steep wilderness' overgrown with forest trees.

> ... Yet higher than their tops
> The verdurous wall of Paradise up-sprung ...
> And higher than that wall a circling row
> Of goodliest trees, loaden with fairest fruit,
> Blossoms and fruits at once of golden hue
> Appeared, with gay enamelled colours mixed.
> ... One gate there only was, and that looked east ...[47]

With the children on his back Fledge glides down to the green hill, and alights on the slope. The children fall into the grass, pick themselves up and climb to the top, where they find that the wall around the garden is made of 'green turf' — Milton's 'verdurous wall', reminiscent of a prehistoric hill fort — and is closed with high, golden gates facing east. Trees grow luxuriously over the wall, their green, blue and silver leaves stirring in the wind. 'You never saw a place which was so obviously private.'

Here at the entrance to this Hesperidian paradise of apple trees, the children find a second challenging verse in the same form as the one they found in Charn — but in this new and innocent world the warning is clearly prohibitive rather than provocative.

> *Come in by the gold gates or not at all,*
> *Take of my fruit for others or forbear.*
> *For those who steal or those who climb my wall*
> *Shall find their heart's desire and find despair.*[48]

---

[47] Milton, John, *Paradise Lost,* Book IV, lines 142 *et seq*
[48] *MN* 146

This time Digory gets it right, albeit with help. The gates open at a touch. The garden is full of quiet life, with a fountain and a tree loaded with 'great silver apples' at the centre, like Milton's 'Tree of Life ... blooming ambrosial fruit/Of vegetable gold'[49]. Digory picks one for Aslan and then, tempted by the delicious smell, wonders briefly whether to pick another for himself. He considers ignoring or reinterpreting the words of warning at the gates: perhaps it was just a bit of advice, and after all nobody ever listens to advice ... Then he notices a bird, a phoenix, watching slit-eyed from the branches just as Milton's Satan sits in the Tree of Life in the form of a cormorant: but Lewis's bird is a guardian, not an intruder, in this enclosed, secret garden.

Would Digory have resisted the temptation to steal if he hadn't seen the bird? Lewis indicates not, but leaves room for some doubt. In any case, Digory is about to be subjected to a much harder test. Half hidden in the leaves he sees the Witch, who has just eaten one of the forbidden apples, in the act of throwing away the core. She looks 'stronger and prouder than ever, and even, in a way, triumphant: but her face was deadly white, white as salt.' She has ignored the gate and climbed over the wall like Milton's Satan:

> Due entrance he disdained, and, in contempt,
> At one slight bound high overleaped all bound
> Of hill or highest wall, and sheer within
> Lights on his feet.[50]

Now fully identified with Satan, she strikes hard at Digory's weakness. The apple could save his mother, so why not take

[49] Milton, John, *Paradise Lost,* Book IV, lines 219, 220
[50] Ibid, lines 179-183

it to her at once? Where does his loyalty lie? What does he owe the Lion, a wild animal in a strange world? What would his mother think if she knew Digory *could* have saved her, and wouldn't? (Was this the thought which got young Jack Lewis out of bed and on to his knees in the middle of the night?) A single mouthful would cure her. He could be happy again, like any ordinary boy.

It is still agonising to watch Digory struggle. The Witch reproaches him with her own sins: he is cruel, she tells him. Pitiless. She draws power from his own dark side as he turns inward, fighting his own guilt. So he made a promise? What does that matter when his mother is so much more important? He can banish her pain, give her 'sweet, natural sleep, without drugs'. His mother would disapprove of his theft? Then don't tell her. Don't tell anyone! In fact, why not leave Polly behind? Then no one in his own world can ever know anything about it ... And with this, the Witch overreaches herself. Shocked at the idea of abandoning Polly, Digory sees past his self-absorption and knows the Witch cannot be trusted. He repudiates her: 'Why are *you* so precious fond of *my* Mother all of a sudden? ... What's your game?'[51]

It's a victory, but no easy one. As the subdued children and Fledge set off eastwards with the apple, the Witch – no longer mortal – heads north to reappear, Narnian centuries later, in *The Lion the Witch and the Wardrobe*.

Narnia is protected meanwhile by the great Tree which springs up to mature grandeur after it's been planted in the magically fertile soil of the riverbank. And Digory learns from Aslan that though the stolen apple would indeed have healed his mother, it would have been at a terrible price:

[51] *MN* 152

'... not to your joy or hers. The day would have come when both you and she would have looked back and said it would have been better to die in that illness.'[52]

It is strong and solemn stuff to read that there can be 'things more terrible than losing someone you love by death', yet it seemed to me as a child to be true, and it still does. Lewis has demonstrated by the examples of Uncle Andrew and Queen Jadis that personalities or relationships founded on deceit and selfishness are unlikely to turn out well. If there are no happy endings, there may still be a choice of unhappy ones and it may be true, as Socrates said, that it is better to suffer evil than to do it. In a way, the whole book is about how Digory *ceases* to be the Magician's Nephew.

'Happy, but for so happy, ill-secured' might be the epigraph to *The Magician's Nephew* as well as to the first chapter of *Surprised by Joy*. It is Satan's comment on the precarious condition of humankind: it is Lewis's comment on the sudden disappearance of the stability and happiness of his childhood: it is anybody's comment who looks clear-sightedly at the world. The happy ending of *The Magician's Nephew* doesn't erase what's happened before. Digory is not the person he would have been if his mother had never been ill.

But this is a children's fairy tale and in fairy tales there is always a reward for those who triumph over adversity. Digory has fought himself and won. Now he deserves the apple Aslan gives him to take home to his mother and make her truly better.

---

[52] *MN* 163

The brightness of the Apple threw strange lights on the ceiling. Nothing else was worth looking at: indeed you couldn't look at anything else. And the smell of the Apple of Youth was as if there was a window in the room that opened on Heaven.

'Oh darling, how lovely,' said Digory's Mother.[53]

It still makes me cry.

---

[53] *MN* 167

THE LION, THE WITCH AND THE WARDROBE

The Magician's Nephew was the last of the Narnia books to be completed and *The Lion, the Witch and the Wardrobe* was the first, and it shows. Technically, *The Magician* is a better book: the characters are better drawn, the narrative is more sophisticated. As a child I loved *The Lion* more though, and it's easy to say why. Of all the Narnia stories this is the one in which Aslan plays the greatest part, and Aslan is a child's ultimate dream friend — a golden, lordly, playful, talking Animal who lets you ride on his back and in whose comforting mane you can bury your face.

On top of that, the death of an animal is often the first real grief a child has experienced. I was six when our pet dog was killed by a car and I had no idea what to do with my feelings or even what they were, so I bottled them up and announced out loud I didn't care — and felt miserable guilt whenever I thought of it. Just a few years later when I read this story of Aslan's death, it took me on a tremendous emotional journey. Catharsis works for children too.

> Once there were four children whose names were Peter, Susan, Edmund and Lucy.

It's not the most gripping of first sentences, but in the dedication to his god-daughter Lucy Barfield, Lewis describes *The Lion, The Witch and the Wardrobe* as a fairy tale. Well, fairy tales begin with 'Once upon a time', and get on with the story. So here. In one brisk, workmanlike paragraph we meet the main characters: Lucy the youngest, Edmund, who is going to be difficult, Peter the authoritative eldest, and dutiful Susan, trying to stand in for Mother. Fairy tales are all about what you set out to find, not what you leave behind, so Lewis disposes of the reason the children are sent away from London — the Blitz — in half a sentence, and the adventure begins once they arrive at this house 'in the heart of the country'. Exactly where doesn't matter: the story directs us inwards, not outwards: in the heart of the country there is a house, inside the house there is a room, inside the room there is a wardrobe, inside the wardrobe there is Narnia ...

Just like Polly and Digory — and for the same reason, because it's raining outside — the Pevensie children set out to explore the indoor world of a house 'full of unexpected places': many spare bedrooms, a room filled with pictures and a suit of armour, a room tapestried in green with a harp standing in one corner, odd flights of steps leading up and down, hallways, whole suites of rooms lined with books —

> And shortly after that they looked into a room that was quite empty except for one big wardrobe; the sort that has a looking-glass in the door. There was nothing

else in the room at all except a dead blue-bottle on the window sill.[54]

The armour, the harp, the roomfuls of old books, the green hangings: the house already hints at chivalry and magic, though the really important room seems unpromising. And of course, the description is reminiscent of Lewis's childhood home, which was also full of books:

> There were books in the study, books in the drawing room, books in the cloakroom, books (two deep) in the great bookcase on the landing, books in a bedroom, books piled as high as my shoulder in the cistern attic … In the seemingly endless rainy afternoons I took volume after volume from the shelves.[55]

In this portrait of Jack the boy, alone and happily lost in the corridors and 'endless rooms' of the big house and escaping into a world of books, we find the real-life version of Polly's attic in *The Magician's Nephew* and of the Professor's house in *The Lion*. That Lewis regarded books as doorways to other worlds is confirmed by a passage in *An Experiment in Criticism* where he describes literature as 'a series of windows, even of doors. One of the things I feel after reading a great work is "I have got out". Or from another point of view, "I have got in".'[56]

This pervasive imagery of rambling old houses has yet another root in the many fairy tales which tell of houses and castles with a secret room or forbidden chamber.

[54] *LWW* 13
[55] *Surprised by Joy* 17
[56] *An Experiment in Criticism* 138

Some, like the Bloody Chamber in *Bluebeard*, contain horrors: 'mad' Uncle Andrew owes something to this, jumping out at Polly and Digory like a wicked Jack-in-the-box in the attic room they've been told not to enter, and so does the coming-to-life of the Witch in the Hall of Statues. On the other hand, a doorway or stair may lead to something marvellous: the soldier-hero of the Grimms' tale *The Twelve Dancing Princesses*[57] follows the eponymous princesses through an opening beneath a bed and down a stairway to a fabulous underground kingdom where there are trees of silver, gold and diamond. This land is neither good nor bad (though one senses the tale disapproves of it) but magical: Other – as tempting perhaps as the deep land of Bism which Golg the gnome describes in *The Silver Chair*, where the trees grow edible rubies and diamonds.

And of course there's Princess Aurora, the Sleeping Beauty, who follows a stairway up to the top of a tower where she finds a little room where an old woman sits spinning ...

In a very early draft of *The Lion, the Witch and the Wardrobe*, cited by Walter Hooper and Roger Lancelyn Green in their biography of C. S. Lewis, the story begins, 'This book is about four children whose names were Ann, Martin, Rose and Peter. But it is mostly about Peter who was the youngest.'[58] Only a fragment, it may date back to September 1939 when some evacuee children were billeted at The Kilns, Lewis's Oxford house. Lewis abandoned this attempt, but ten years later began again and this time the youngest child, the one whom the story is going to be 'mostly about' is a girl: Lucy.

Why the change? He may simply have found the

---

[57] Properly known as *The Shoes that were Danced to Pieces*, KHM 133
[58] *C. S. Lewis: A Biography*, 303

character worked better as a girl: unless they're behaving badly like Edmund or Eustace, Lewis's boys are less interesting than his girls. And he may have named her after his god-daughter, Lucy Barfield. But in a letter of 10 September 1947,[59] writing to an American couple who'd asked his views on the 'moral dimension' of children's stories, Lewis replied by claiming that many fairy tales contain a spiritual dimension and cited as examples *The Sleeping Beauty* and George Macdonald's *The Princess and the Goblin* and *The Princess and Curdie*. He added that he himself had tried his hand at writing a children's fairy tale, but that it had been so bad, he had destroyed it.[60]

Destroying a bad draft doesn't mean a writer stops thinking about the story. I feel certain the character of Lucy Pevensie was inspired by eight year-old Princess Irene, the heroine of George MacDonald's *The Princess and the Goblin* who one rainy day, unable to play outside (sounds familiar?), gives her nurse the slip and sets off up a 'curious old stair of worm-eaten oak' to explore the old house in which she lives.

> Up and up she ran – such a long way it seemed to her! – until she came to the top of the third flight. There she found the landing was the end of a long passage … full of doors on each side. There were so many she did not care to open any but ran on to the end, where she turned into another passage, also full of doors … All those doors must hide rooms with nobody in them! That was dreadful! Also the rain made a great trampling sound on the roof …[61]

[59] Ibid
[60] Ibid
[61] MacDonald, George, *The Princess and the Goblin*, 6

Climbing still higher like the Princess Aurora, little Irene arrives at a small landing with three doors. Hearing a low, sweet humming from behind one of them, she opens it to find a bare room in which her magical great-great-grandmother sits spinning. Unlike the malevolent fairy of *The Sleeping Beauty*, Irene's ancestress is a power for good, though a little frightening too; and she isn't always visible. She requires Irene to have faith in her, and not to deny her existence. This is soon put to the test when the little princess tells her nurse about the beautiful grandmother with long white hair she has seen in the attic.

> 'Did you expect me to believe you, princess?' asked the nurse coldly. 'I know princesses are in the habit of telling make-beliefs, but you are the first I ever heard of who expected to have them believed ...'[62]

Irene sticks to her story with a princess's poise and dignity. Here are many elements also to be found in *The Lion, the Witch and the Wardrobe*: the rain that keeps the children indoors, a truthful little girl exploring a rambling old house, a door that opens into Elsewhere, a benign Power who rules there, beautiful and alarming – and the disbelief which greets both Irene and Lucy's accounts of their adventure.

This has been a long digression. Back to Lucy! Alone in the empty room with the wardrobe, and curious about what's inside, Lucy opens the door to find rows of fur coats. She likes the 'smell and feel of fur,' so she steps in to stroke them and rub her face against them.

I well understood Lucy's impulse. When I was that same

---

[62] Ibid, 18

age my mother kept spare blankets in a big camphor-wood chest which stood in the hall. She kept a little white rabbit-fur cape and muff in it, too, which I was sometimes allowed to try on. Decades before the anti-fur movement I didn't consider the animal it had come from. I loved the glossy richness of the fur, and the strong, spicy camphor-wood smell that clung to it; and what I notice now is that Lucy discovers Narnia via a process first of curiosity, and then of sensuous delight — all without a hint of disapproval. As she pushes in, the fur changes texture under her touch to something prickly, like 'branches' ('*fir* branches' in fact). A moment later something cold and soft is falling on her and she's '... in the middle of a wood at night-time with snow under her feet and snowflakes falling through the air.'

The transition is beautiful, grading so naturally from one world to the next that — as mothballs crunching underfoot turn into crisp snow — neither Lucy nor the child reading the story can tell where one world ends and another begins.

Lucy's passage through the confined dark space of the wardrobe, pushing through the furs into the cold world beyond, is undoubtedly open to a Freudian interpretation, but Lewis didn't much care for Freudian interpretations of literature. He took issue not with their validity or invalidity, but with what he saw as their tendency to reduce things to a naked common denominator. If a garden is 'really' (in some way beyond metaphor) a woman's body, then where does that leave our love of gardens? Why can't we appreciate both? Turning again to an imagery of rambling old houses, he writes that his dislike of Freudian explanations is not because he feels repulsed by them, rather, he finds them uninteresting — boring.

> It is not as if we had drawn back an embroidered curtain and found earwigs behind it: it is as if we had drawn it expecting to find a whole new wing of the house and found merely a door that led back into the old familiar dining room. Our feelings would ... demand ... the disappointed grunt, 'Oh! so that's all.'[63]

In other words, of course you may interpret Lucy's arrival in Narnia as some form of parturition, but births are common and passages through wardrobes to fantastical lands are few. Let's focus on the individual story in all its rich clothing.

Just how different the 'same' story can be in the hands of different writers can be shown by a glance at *The Aunt and Amabel*,[64] a short story by E. Nesbit which Lewis may have read in boyhood. Spending a day in disgrace in her aunt's spare room, Amabel climbs into a 'large wardrobe with a looking glass' which opens into the magical railway station of '*Bigwardrobeinspareroom*', where she catches a train to '*Whereyouwanttogoto*'. This story is the likely source for Lucy's wardrobe: on meeting Mr Tumnus, she explains that she came into Narnia 'through the wardrobe in the spare room', and Tumnus' comic misapprehension underlines the association:

---

[63] *Psycho-Analysis and Literary Criticism*, Selected Literary Essays, Cambridge University Press 1969, 294

[64] Nesbit, Edith, *The Aunt and Amabel*, The Magic World, E. Nesbit, 1912. The short story was originally published separately in Blackie's Christmas Annual 1909. According to his biographers Walter Hooper and Roger Lancelyn Green, Lewis had forgotten it until he was later reminded.

'Daughter of Eve from the far land of Spare Oom where eternal summer reigns around the bright city of War Drobe, how would it be if you came and had tea with me?'[65]

Other than the wardrobe-as-portal and the little girl protagonist, however, the stories are far apart in detail and tone. The magic in Nesbit's story utilises an urban imagery of railway stations and porters, refreshment carriages, mayors and silver bands, and her world beyond or within the wardrobe has a cloying, claustrophobic feel, worlds away from the cold wilderness of snowbound Narnia.

Tumnus provides Lucy with a delicious tea and entertains her for hours with stories of nymphs, dwarfs and dryads; but like Snow White in the cottage of the seven dwarfs, Lucy soon discovers that the apparent safety of his house is compromised by the power of a dangerous queen. When at last she rises to leave, Tumnus breaks down and confesses. Between sobs he explains that he's an informer who has taken service under Narnia's ruler the White Witch. He has promised the Witch that if he ever meets a human child in the woods, he will kidnap 'it' for her. Now that abstraction 'a human child' has become a reality: little Lucy sitting in his nice cave eating his toast and honey and iced cakes. 'Of course I can't give you up to the Witch,' he weeps, 'not now that I know you.'

When I was a child, Tumnus' repentance seemed simple enough: he did something naughty but he's nice really, and now he's sorry! But there's a serious message here

[65] *LWW* 18

about how 'nice' people can end up doing dreadful things. Tumnus agreed to the Witch's demand more easily because he had never met a Human and could dismiss them as Other. As well as its insight into complicity and prejudice, the passage demonstrates Lewis's rather touching faith in the ability of ordinary people to act with decency towards others *once they have actually met them*. In letter VI of *The Screwtape Letters* (published in 1942, during the War), the elder devil Screwtape complains of the 'fanciful' hatred of the English for enemies they have not met:

> They are creatures of that miserable sort who loudly proclaim that torture is too good for their enemies and then give tea and cigarettes to the first wounded German pilot who turns up at the back door.[66]

Mmm. Unfortunately this also means that fanciful hatreds can continue to fester so long as the 'enemy' — German pilots, immigrants, whoever — remains faceless; I fear Screwtape may have been flattering us. Tumnus, however, does the right thing. Having realised that the creature he'd agreed to turn in is a *person*, he lets her go, although he knows there will be consequences: in her anger the Witch is quite likely to cut off his tail and horns, or she may even turn him to stone, with no hope of ever coming back to life again unless the four thrones at Cair Paravel are filled — a possibility that despite Lucy's arrival seems so remote to Tumnus, he doubts if it will ever happen at all.

Lewis never forgets who he is writing for. The potential terror of Lucy's predicament is modified by Tumnus'

---

[66] Lewis, C. S., *The Screwtape Letters*, 36

distressed repentance, along with comic reassurance as she adopts the grown-up role of scolding and calming him: 'You ought to be ashamed of yourself, a great big Faun like you!' The danger to *her*, once recognised, is already over. For Tumnus the danger is imminent, but I could tell this was the kind of story in which good characters ultimately prevail. Anxiously — afraid that even some of the trees may be about to report him — he escorts Lucy back to the lamp-post, from which she can spy English daylight beyond the wardrobe door. (No other portal into Narnia remains open like this, or gets used more than once.) Scrambling back into the spare room she calls excitedly to her brothers and sister, and tries to tell them about her adventure.

Like Irene's nurse, they *don't believe her.*

I would regularly become furious at this point. It was so *unfair* — and gets even more unfair when Edmund actually lies about it! Poor Lucy sticks to her story over several days, enduring Peter and Susan's wordless disapproval of what they consider her silly make-believe, but Edmund actively teases and bullies her — and he is about to become much worse. Almost beginning to doubt herself, Lucy revisits the wardrobe for another look and Edmund follows her in, hoping for another chance to torment her. Closing the door behind him he shuts himself up in the dark — a symbolic action — loses his sense of direction, panics, and emerges into the cold daylight of the Narnian woods.

Lucy is out of sight. Uncomfortable on his own, Edmund shouts an apology to her, though only for his disbelief, not for his behaviour. Then with a jingle of bells the White Witch arrives in a sledge drawn by white reindeer and driven by a dwarf. Dressed in furs from head to foot, she carries a gold wand and wears a golden crown, which would sound lovely, except that Lewis undermines it by giving her a face as white as 'snow or paper or icing-sugar', and by contrast, a vividly scarlet mouth.

The forerunner to the White Witch is Hans Christian Andersen's Snow Queen who steals little Kay away to her icy palace: and Kay is another little boy who has begun to go wrong. After glass splinters from the Devil's broken mirror have pierced his eye and heart, he taunts and teases Gerda just as Edmund taunts and teases Lucy. It's their hardness of heart and their selfishness which renders both boys vulnerable to the blandishments of Snow Queen and White Witch.

Whiteness generally symbolises purity, but Lewis knows that a truly white face is something inhuman. He links the whiteness of the Witch's skin with the coldness of snow, the barrenness of blank paper and the intense, choking, powdery sweetness of icing sugar — a sinister mix. (We have seen that in *The Magician's Nephew* after biting into the stolen apple in the paradisal garden, the Witch's face becomes 'white as salt' — a substance which is bitter on the tongue and in which nothing can grow. No child could be tempted by a spoonful of salt.) Icing sugar is the stuff Turkish Delight is smothered in, and it's this sticky sweetmeat, plus a sweet, hot, foamy, creamy drink which one of my friends insists on calling 'SEXY MAGIC OVALTINE' that the Witch conjures for Edmund from drops of some dubious liquid she lets fall hissing to the snow.

Thus Edmund's first encounter with a denizen of Narnia is the mirror of Lucy's. Tumnus the Faun and the Witch both lure the children with offers of shelter and food. Neither offer is what it seems, but where Tumnus repents and Lucy retains truth and integrity, Edmund is suborned and becomes a liar and traitor. Learning that he has a brother and two sisters, the Witch falsely promises to make him a Prince and eventually a King – if he will bring them to her house. Edmund consents, and the Witch drives off with a final warning to keep silent about their meeting. Moments later, Lucy reappears. She's seen Mr Tumnus! He's safe!

He soon won't be, now that the Witch knows about him, but Edmund says nothing. Already more than half on the Witch's side, he simply discounts Lucy's description of how she turns people to stone and has made it always winter in Narnia, but never Christmas. Still, only selfish spite could prompt him to do what he does next. Back in the Professor's house, as Lucy happily urges Edmund to tell the others that her story is true and he too has been to Narnia, he says they've only been playing that her country in the wardrobe is real, and there's nothing there.

His betrayal does him no good. Peter gives him a sharp telling-off for teasing Lucy and encouraging her fantasies. Then, feeling the matter is becoming too serious for them to handle, the two eldest children take their worries to the Professor. After listening to them carefully, he asks why they should assume Lucy's story isn't true?

Adults in children's books are not usually open-minded about the possibility of magic. Generally they react like Princess Irene's nurse, or like the 'poor learned gentleman' in *The Story of the Amulet* who even travels to Atlantis with the children but explains it to himself as a marvellous dream. The Professor cannot *know* about Narnia; Lewis hadn't begun writing Digory's story yet – but the Professor is Lewis's avatar, and Lewis is the man who in *Mere Christianity* writes of 'a door behind which, according to some people, the secret of the universe is waiting for you'.[67] Schooled in Plato as well as the Gospels, he believed the world we live in to be a shadowland, a screen through which we sometimes glimpse bright gleams of the greater Reality immanent in the fabric of everyday life. No wonder this Professor thinks other worlds are likely to exist and in Lucy's defence puts forward a form of one of Lewis's theological arguments, framed as a set of logical propositions ('if that: then this'):

> 'There are only three possibilities. Either your sister is telling lies, or she is mad, or she is telling the truth. You know she doesn't tell lies and it is obvious that she is not mad. For the moment then and unless any further evidence turns up, we must assume she is telling the truth.'[68]

Shaken but unconvinced, Peter objects that there was nothing in the wardrobe when he and Susan looked in it, and 'if things are real, they're there all the time', to which the Professor merely responds, 'Are they?' Susan tries another tack, pointing out that there simply wasn't time for all the things Lucy has described to happen: 'It was less than a minute, and she pretended it had been hours.'

In answer to this, the Professor claims that the very unlikeliness of Lucy's story is an indication of its truth: she could not have *invented* anything as improbable as her visit to Narnia taking no time in our world. (Of course this is not logic, but supposition.) Then he dismisses the children

---

[67] Lewis, C. S., *God in the Dock*, 112
[68] *LWW* 48

with the brisk suggestion that they should mind their own business.

These are remarkable concepts to find in a story for young children and I was very much impressed by them, especially since in the context of the story I *knew* Narnia to be real. I did not see that the flaw in the Professor's argument is his declaration that only three options are available: liar, lunatic or truth-teller. Yet faced with a child who insists on the existence of an invisible friend or an imaginary land, most wise adults regard it as it a phase in the child's developing imagination, not that she or he is mad or deliberately lying. The same flawed argument appears in *Mere Christianity:*

> A man who was merely a man and said the sort of things Jesus said would not be a great moral teacher. He would either be a lunatic – on a level with a man who says he is a poached egg – or else he would be the Devil of Hell. You must make your choice. Either this man was, and is, the Son of God: or else a madman, or something worse.[69]

In my early teens I was as impressed by this argument as I had been with the Professor's: the logic seemed stark and inescapable. My current objection is not merely to the deliberately polarising rhetoric (poached egg/Devil of Hell) but that once again Lewis arbitrarily limits his options to three choices when in fact there are more. The present Dalai Lama, a figure of great moral stature, believes himself the fourteenth incarnation of the first, as well as an emanation of the Bodhisattva of compassion. Non-

---

[69] Lewis, C. S., *Mere Christianity*, 52

Buddhists may not agree, but so far as I know no one has suggested this must mean he is insane or wicked. Human beings are complicated.

I still appreciate very much, though, that Lewis thought it worthwhile to introduce logical argument into a 'fairy tale' for children. He presented a method of thinking that was quite new to me, in so simple a way that aged nine or so, I could instantly grasp it. It was as if he had made me a present of a box of tools and shown me how to use them. And I never learned it in any of my schools, he was right there.

Back to the Pevensies. A day or two later, trying to avoid a party of sightseers taking a tour of the house, the four children are driven to hide in the wardrobe. They huddle there, cramped, and then cold — and then wet — and then all four of them are standing in winter daylight with a snow-covered wood in front of them, and fur coats dangling from pegs at their backs.

Another seamless transition. And the practical difficulty of keeping warm in this winter world is easily dealt with: the children simply borrow the fur coats, which as Susan says, no one can object to, since, 'we shan't even take them out of the wardrobe' — a neat metaphysical point.

The children set out into the wood, and quite soon Edmund suggests a change of direction 'if we are aiming for the lamp-post' — which gives away that he has been here before; and lied about it, and made Lucy seem the liar. Peter calls him 'a poisonous little beast', and with Edmund resentfully meditating revenge they steer for Mr Tumnus' cave, only to find his cosy home in ruins, the door violently smashed in, the floor covered in drifted snow mixed with charcoal and ashes from the dead fire:

Someone had apparently flung it about the room and then stamped it out. The crockery lay smashed on the floor and the picture of the Faun's father had been slashed to shreds with a knife.[70]

This is strong stuff for young children – strong stuff for anyone. Remember this book was published only five years after the end of the War, and in Russia, Stalin was still in power. Narnia under the Witch is literally a police state. It is no small achievement to be this frank, this clear about spite and violence and hate – confirmed by the denunciation on the door signed 'MAUGRIM, Captain of the Secret Police' – in a book for young children which most of us remember as full of magic and delight.

Understandably rattled, Susan wishes to go home, but Lucy cries that they have to help Mr Tumnus, in trouble only because he saved her from the Witch. Peter and Susan agree, but how to begin? A robin leads them to a clearing where Mr Beaver beckons them from behind a tree. In token of trust he shows the handkerchief Lucy had lent to Mr Tumnus. Fearing arrest, Tumnus had given it to him with the warning that if he were taken, the Beaver must look out for any reappearance of Lucy and her siblings. The children have fallen into the hands of the Narnian Resistance and things are happening at last. D-Day is approaching. 'Aslan is on the move'!

It isn't a moment for long explanations. Without telling us who Aslan is, Lewis builds him up by describing the effect his mere name has upon the four Pevensies. Peter feels brave, Susan experiences sensuous delight, Lucy feels

[70] *LWW* 56

the happiness of a child waking up on the first day of the holidays – a metaphor Lewis uses over and over to convey divine joy and freedom. Only Edmund's experience is negative: he feels a creeping sense of horror. (In *The Last Battle* this will translate into a final parting of the ways as each Narnian creature looks in Aslan's face and either loves or rejects him.)

A welcome domestic interlude follows. Mr Beaver leads the children to his frozen dam (from whence Edmund spies the two small hills which mark the Witch's house). In the warmth and safety of his cosy lodge they are greeted by motherly Mrs Beaver and given a dinner of fried fish, potatoes and butter, with 'a great and gloriously sticky marmalade roll' for dessert. English comfort food at its best, and there's probably no more point asking how the Beavers can find butter, milk, or oranges for marmalade in snow-bound Narnia than there is in asking how the Water Rat fills a hamper with:

'coldtonguecoldhamcoldbeefpickledgherkinssalad frenchrollscresssandwichespottedmeatgingerbeer lemonadesodawater – '[71]

For the moment we're in Animal Land, where Mrs Beaver's sewing machine is no more out of place than Peter Rabbit's jacket or Mrs Tiggy-Winkle's ironing board. At least, as a child I took it so. All the same, Animal Land isn't quite Narnia, and I confess these things rather stick out for me now. Lewis may have come to feel the same way; he avoids the mistake, if it is a mistake, in other books. In *Prince Caspian*

---

[71] Grahame, Kenneth, *The Wind in the Willows*, 8

when the animals offer food to the young prince, they bring things they might conceivably naturally obtain: the Bear gives him honey, the Squirrel nuts, while the Centaurs provide a classical yet subtly horsey repast of oatcakes and apples, wine, herbs and cheese.

Dinner over, the children hear from Mr Beaver that Mr Tumnus has been taken away to the Witch's house and likely turned to stone, and that the best way to help him is to join forces with Aslan – the great Lion, lord of the wood, who has not been seen in Narnia for generations but is now returned and will soon, it is felt, deal with the White Queen. They are to meet him tomorrow at the Stone Table to fulfil an old prophecy:

> *When Adam's flesh and Adam's bone*
> *Sits at Cair Paravel in throne,*
> *The evil time will be over and done.*[72]

When two Sons of Adam and two Daughters of Eve sit on the four thrones at Cair Paravel, the Witch's reign will come to an end, along with her life. The Witch herself (Mr Beaver explains) is not human, coming on one side from Adam's first wife Lilith, 'one of the Jinn', and on the other side from the giants. This genealogy links the Witch to the mythology of our own world in a way not really consistent with her otherworldly origin in *The Magician's Nephew* (nor is it clear how Mr Beaver would know any of this), but Lewis hadn't yet written *The Magician's Nephew* and if he'd stuck to this particular sketch of the Witch's history, he never would.

---

[72] *LWW* 77

In any case the Narnian world is nothing if not permeable. In the course of the seven books, visitors from other worlds total: eight children, Uncle Andrew, Frank the London cabby and Helen his wife, Strawberry the cabhorse, Jadis of Charn, and the pirates from whom the Telmarines of *Prince Caspian* are descended. It is inhabited by naiads and dryads from classical mythology, giants and dwarfs from the Norse legends and German fairy tales, and talking animals out of English children's books. It borrows Green Ladies from medieval romances and mystical islands from Celtic voyage tales and, in this one first book, it has Father Christmas ... Tolkien didn't like it, but without this heterogenous mix Narnia would not be Narnia. To compare it with a closed system like Middle-Earth is to miss the point.

Close on the heels of Mr Beaver's description of the Witch's inhuman ancestry comes his splendidly sinister warning about 'things that look like humans and aren't':

> [T]ake my advice, when you meet anything that's going to be human and isn't yet, or used to be human once and isn't now, or ought to be human and isn't, you keep your eyes on it and feel for your hatchet.[73]

This unspecific warning evokes the possibility of moral as well as physical regression, so it's significant that just moments later Lucy notices Edmund is missing, and Mr Beaver confesses he has doubted him from the moment he saw him, for there was something wrong about his face and eyes. 'He had the look of one who has been with the Witch

---

[73] *LWW* 78

and eaten her food,' he says perciepiently. In great dismay they realise Edmund has gone to the Witch's house to betray them. To go after him would be disastrous and to stay here is now impossible. They must get away — fast! There isn't a moment to lose.

Edmund meanwhile is having a deservedly terrible time. Wet and freezing he scrambles through trackless snowdrifts, keeping himself going by planning what he will do as King. All the 'bad' male characters in the Narnia books — even the ones who later reform, like Eustace Scrubb and Edmund himself — indulge in fantasies of technology and modernisation. Edmund plans how many cars he will have, and 'his private cinema, and where the principal railways would run'. Finally the moon comes out and he sees the Witch's house: a small castle, all towers and spikes which throw strange shadows on the snow. It's scary. Edmund has to creep right around the building before he finds an archway with iron gates standing open and unmanned. Or is it?

> Just inside the gate, with the moonlight shining on it, stood an enormous lion crouched as if it was ready to spring.[74]

It is an image drawn from a passage in Malory's *Le Morte d'Arthur*.[75] On the quest for the Grail, Lancelot arrives at the rear of a castle where he finds a postern gate '... open without any keeping, save two lions kept the gateway, and the moon shone clear'.[76] As Lancelot draws his sword to

[74] *LWW* 88
[75] And quoted by Lewis in *An Experiment in Criticism* as an example of 'spare' good writing (33).
[76] *Le Morte d'Arthur*, Book XVII Ch. 15 p.354

fight the lions a mystical voice rebukes him for trusting in arms rather than in God, and in response Lancelot sheathes his sword, crosses himself, and passes the lions without hurt.

Edmund doesn't do so well. Initially terrified, he gradually realises the lion is motionless and that snow lies on its back. In fact it is one of the victims the Witch has turned to stone and in growing glee he thinks it must be 'the great Lion Aslan they were all talking about.' Now comes a real low point: he scribbles a moustache and spectacles on its face with a bit of lead pencil. It's very much the sort of thing a little boy might do, and Lewis describes the act as 'silly and childish', but it's still a desecration: this lion used to be alive! I could well see this was more like scribbling on a gravestone than on an ordinary statue – and very obviously Something You Should Not Do.[77]

Edmund tiptoes through the courtyard past the spookily still images of the Witch's victims. At the top of the castle steps, what he supposes to be a stone wolf lying across the threshold springs suddenly up to challenge him. It is Maugrim, Chief of the Witch's Secret Police, who brings Edmund into a gloomy pillared hall where the Witch receives him angrily for arriving alone. Still imagining he's going to be made a prince Edmund pleads that he's done his best, and tells her that his brother and sisters are hiding with Mr and Mrs Beaver in their house on the dam. Hearing this and the news he has brought about Aslan, the Witch immediately calls for her sledge.

Meanwhile back at the dam, the other children and the

---

[77] This episode is a variation on a passage in Lewis's adult novel *That Hideous Strength*, in which Mark Studdock halts his moral downward slide by refusing to insult a crucifix.

Beavers bustle to make their escape, the tension both heightened and amusingly undercut by Mrs Beaver's cool insistence on a careful and extensive packing of provisions such as ham, tea, sugar, bread and handkerchieves. *'Hurry, hurry!'* I thought — really anxious, yet at the same time amused (Mrs Beaver is funny) and reassured (Mrs Beaver is a mother figure and if she's not scared, neither need I be). Mr Beaver locks the door and they set off along the river bank through moonlit snow, keeping among the trees at the bottom of the valley where the Witch cannot bring her sledge. Tired out at last, they find refuge in a hole in the river bank: a hiding place for beavers in times of trouble. 'If you hadn't all been in such a plaguey fuss when we were starting, I'd have brought some pillows,' says Mrs Beaver, magnificently ignoring the crisis and sustaining the general tone of a family outing.

Sleigh-bells wake them. Is it the Witch? Mr Beaver dashes out to reconnoitre, then calls excitedly for them all to come out and join him. It isn't the Witch — and her power must be crumbling! There *is* a sledge, and it *is* being pulled by reindeer with bells on their harness — but the driver is someone quite different, and instantly recognisable.

> He was a huge man in a bright red robe (bright as hollyberries) with a hood that had fur inside and a great white beard that fell like a foamy waterfall over his chest. ... He was so big, and so glad, and so real, that they all became quite still.[78]

Many readers have disliked this appearance of Father Christmas. I've never minded it, though I think Lewis

---

[78] *LWW* 100

was wise not to invite him back. After all, when a writer has come up with a lovely phrase like *'Always winter and never Christmas'* — well, what is he to do? The hollyberry comparison reminds me of the Green Knight, Bertilak, who rides into Arthur's hall with a holly branch in his hand (the 'greatest in green when groves are bare') and combines pagan giant and courteous Christian in a single figure. I'm also reminded of Grandfather Frost in Russian fairy tales, the white-bearded old spirit of the snowy woods who may, if you address him politely enough, give you gifts rather than freezing you to death. Father Christmas in Narnia is a lot easier for me to accept than the facetious reference to golf in *The Hobbit* — where Tolkien relates how Bilbo's ancestor Bullroarer Took knocked off the head of the goblin king Golfimbul. 'It sailed a hundred yards through the air and went down a rabbit hole, and in this way the battle was won and the game of Golf invented at the same moment.'[79] Conscious flippancy of this kind was one of the things I disliked about *The Hobbit* as a child. It jolted me out of the world of the book in just the same way people complain of here.

Appropriately or not, Father Christmas *is* here, and his presence is a sign of the Witch's power failing, and he proceeds to do exactly what you'd expect. He distributes presents — presents to be used, 'tools not toys'. Peter receives a sword and a silver shield with a red lion on it: 'a very serious kind of present'. Susan is given a bow and arrows and an ivory horn which, whenever she blows it, will call help to her side. Lucy receives a dagger (which we never hear of again) and a little diamond bottle reminiscent of Galadriel's gift

---

[79] Tolkien, J. R. R., *The Hobbit*, 17

to Frodo; it contains a cordial that will heal all hurts, 'made from the juice of one of the fire flowers that grow in the mountains of the sun'.

It used to annoy me that the girls are warned by Father Christmas not to get involved in any fighting; when Lucy objects that she thinks she could be brave enough, he tells her that 'battles are ugly when women fight'. What about Joan of Arc, I thought, and aren't battles ugly in any case? It still seems a lapse into pseudo-chivalric woolly thinking. As *pièce de résistance,* Father Christmas now whips out an entire tea-tray laid with cups and saucers, sugar bowl, cream jug and teapot — cracks his whip crying 'Merry Christmas! Long live the true King' — and is gone. Like him or not, you have to admit he makes a proper job of it.

While the children and the Beavers enjoy a breakfast of hot cups of tea and ham sandwiches, Edmund begs for Turkish Delight and is given dry bread and water. Having ordered Maugrim the Wolf to race to the house of the Beavers and kill them, or, if they have already left, to meet her secretly at the Stone Table — the Witch sets off on her sledge in another direction, the dwarf driving, and Edmund shivering coatless and miserable at her side. Too late, he sees that he's been deceiving himself about the Witch. She isn't good, she isn't kind, and she isn't going to make him king. He's chosen the wrong side, and wishes desperately that he could be back with his brother and sisters again.

Next comes a truly upsetting episode. Coming across a happy little woodland party of fauns and animals sitting around a table, eating plum pudding and drinking wine, the Witch halts her sleigh in scandalised anger and wants to know where such a feast came from? Who gave it to them?

A terrified Fox tries to appease her but finally stammers out that they have seen Father Christmas, which of course is the worst news the Witch could hear: her endless winter explicitly bans Christmas! 'Say you have been lying!' she storms at the frightened creatures – and one of the baby squirrels loses it.

> 'He has – he has – he has!' it squeaked, beating its little spoon on the table. Edmund saw the Witch bite her lips so that a drop of blood appeared on her white cheek.[80]

Though Edmund yells at her to stop, she turns the whole little group to stone. Then, striking Edmund to punish his plea for mercy, she drives on; but for the first time in the story Edmund is sorry for someone other than himself and his inward compassion almost undoes that callous scribble on the stone lion's face:

> It seemed so pitiful to think of those little stone figures sitting there all the silent days and all the dark nights, year after year, till the moss grew on them and at last even their faces crumbled away.[81]

It's the more poignant because this outlined future seems so final: we never do find out if this little group is found and restored to life. I used to try and comfort myself by thinking that *of course* Edmund tells Aslan and he rescues them, but Lewis never says, and artistically it feels right. Not every wrong will be undone, even in a fairy tale. To this day it troubles me.

[80] *LWW* 109
[81] Ibid

As compassion enters Edmund's heart, the long winter ends. Imperceptibly at first, then unmistakably, the snow thaws to slush and mud. The sledge is abandoned. Water flows, flowers rise, birds begin to sing. With hands roped, Edmund is forced to hurry through woods unfurling fresh green leaves. A bee buzzes by, and the dwarf suddenly stops in his tracks to exclaim that this isn't just a thaw, it is *spring* — and it must be Aslan's work. The Witch deals with this unwelcome comment by threatening Edmund and the dwarf with death, should either of them ever again speak Aslan's name.

Meanwhile Edmund's brother and sisters, with the Beavers, are climbing the hill of the Stone Table. Reaching the open top they find wide views and the glitter of the far-off sea, while in the centre stands the Stone Table itself, a grim slab supported on four uprights carved with strange figures, mysterious as a neolithic tomb. Pitched nearby is a silk pavilion with crimson cords, the lion banner of Narnia flying over it, and here in royal state stands Aslan the Lion amid a half-circle of Dryads, Naiads, centaurs and Talking Beasts, the chivalry of Narnia gathered to his side.

> There was also a unicorn, and a bull with the head of a man, and a pelican, and an eagle, and a great Dog. And next to Aslan stood two leopards of whom one carried his crown and the other his standard.[82]

Some of these creatures seemed to me quite odd, especially the man-headed bull which I pictured as scary and ugly and

---

[82] *LWW* 117

wondered why it was on Aslan's side. In fact it must be the benign *lamassu* or guardian spirit of Assyrian mythology, though such a creature never appears in Narnia again outside this book. I see this gathering now as a piece of deliberate iconography or pageantry: the creatures have meanings. Because of the medieval belief that it fed its young on its own blood, the pelican symbolises Christ's sacrifice. The crown-and-standard-bearing leopards signify royalty. The unicorn stands for purity, but as it's also the lion's traditional enemy, its presence here symbolises peace. The Dog represents faithfulness. As for the all-seeing eagle — well, there's this passage in Revelation 4:6-7 which describes the throne of God surrounded by strange creatures:

6: And before the throne there was a sea of glass like unto crystal: and in the midst of the throne and round about the throne were four beasts, full of eyes before and behind.

7: And the first beast was like a lion, and the second beast was like a calf, and the third beast had a face as a man, and the fourth beast was like a flying eagle.

With the man-headed bull, the eagle and the Lion himself, we're close to having all four of the visionary animals of Revelation in this tableau. It seems possible Lewis was slipping in hints of Aslan's divine nature for anyone who might notice. That would explain the presence of some otherwise pretty random critters. None of this was remotely visible to me as a child and I wouldn't have thanked you for telling me.

Aslan welcomes the three children and the Beavers

and asks where is their brother — the fourth child? They explain, and Lucy — of course it is Lucy — dares ask if anything can be done to help Edmund? Aslan assures her that 'All shall be done' — *all*, not just anything — but adds that 'it may be harder than you think'. For of course nothing will be held back; he will give himself. And he falls silent and looks sad, as well he might. As a child, on second and third readings I assumed Aslan was sad because he knew what was going to happen to him. I now sense his sadness may be for Edmund too: for the human frailty which necessitates such sacrifice.

Dryads escort the girls towards the pavilion and Aslan leads Peter to the hill edge to show him a far-off view of Cair Paravel where he will be King. Suddenly Susan's horn sounds, blowing for help. Maugrim the Wolf is attacking the crowd on the hilltop! Susan swings herself into a tree to escape the wolf's charge, and prompted into action by Aslan, Peter draws his sword for the first time and rushes to the rescue.

The fight with the Wolf is violent and vivid. Peter's first wild slash misses, but by reflex rather than skill he manages to thrust his sword deep into the beast's chest.

> Then came a horrible, confused moment like something in a nightmare. He was tugging and pulling and the Wolf seemed neither alive nor dead, and its bared teeth knocked against his forehead, and everything was blood and heat and hair.[83]

The horror is very physical — neither can get free of the other

[83] *LWW* 122

— and intensified by that detail of the Wolf's teeth 'knocking' Peter's forehead as if it's still trying to get to him even after it's dead. In the emotional aftermath Peter and Susan are both deeply shaken, with 'kissing and crying on both sides', and Lewis makes a point of telling us that 'in Narnia no one thinks any the worse of you for that'. Brother and sister both cry, both embrace. It's strong, truthful and real.

After cleaning his blade, 'smeared with the Wolf's hair and blood', Peter is knighted by Aslan. Meanwhile the Witch has decided the simplest way to prevent the four thrones at Cair Paravel from being filled is to kill Edmund. She would prefer this to happen on the Stone Table where such sacrifices have customarily been performed — a glimpse of a dark past — but with Aslan there, that's not possible. At this moment Maugrim's fellow Wolf rushes up with news of the happenings at the Stone Table. Sending him off to gather an army of Narnia's most evil creatures, the Witch turns to the task in hand, ordering the dwarf to prepare Edmund for ritual sacrifice. In the nick of time a rescue party dashes up of Aslan's swiftest troops: centaurs, unicorns, deer and eagles who have been pursuing the Wolf. They release Edmund but in the confusion they miss the Witch.

Edmund is safe, reconciled and forgiven. But there is a debt still to be paid and next morning the Witch sends her dwarf to demand a meeting with Aslan. He sends the two leopards back as heralds. As so often, a comic touch lightens the tension. Lucy worries that the Witch may turn the leopards to stone - and so do the leopards, who set off with the fur rising on their spines, and bushed-out tails. However, they are unharmed. The Witch approaches Aslan and calls upon the Deep Magic inscribed on the Stone Table — the magic written on the fire-stones of the Secret Hill and the sceptre of the Emperor-beyond-the Sea

— 'the magic which the Emperor put into Narnia at the very beginning' — which states that the blood of a traitor is forfeit to her. Edmund's blood is her due. Hearing this, the man-headed Bull at Aslan's side bellows out a challenge for her to come and get it! The Witch turns on him savagely. Force cannot wrest her rights from her, she cries, for the Deep Magic cannot be denied and his master, Aslan, knows it, for '... unless I have blood as the Law says all Narnia will be overturned and perish in fire and water'.[84]

It couldn't be more serious. Aslan and the Witch move aside to talk alone and everyone waits in terrible suspense. The talks go on and on. At last Aslan announces that the matter is settled. The Witch has relinquished her claim to Edmund's blood.

There is a great deal of blood in Narnia, in contrast to *The Lord of the Rings* which remains bloodless even when Wormtongue cuts Saruman's throat. Legolas may resharpen his long knife at Helm's Deep after slaying two dozen orcs,[85] but there's no messy blood and hair to clean off the blade such as Peter finds after slaying Maugrim. No blood spurts from the neck of the Nazgul's winged steed when Éowyn strikes its head from its body. The wound in Frodo's shoulder pains him as if 'a dart of poisoned ice' has been driven into it, but rapidly closes to 'a small white mark' and never seems to bleed.[86] Gimli kills forty-two orcs, and the minimal signs of the carnage are a notch in his axe and 'a linen band stained with blood'[87] around his head. It's as though — I say it with affection — Tolkien felt graphic

---

[84] *LWW* 132
[85] Tolkien, *The Two Towers*, 140
[86] Tolkien, J. R. R., *The Fellowship of the Ring*, 208, 216
[87] Tolkien, J. R. R., *The Two Towers*, 148

descriptions of blood and wounds would be in poor taste: G. R. R. Martin he was not. Wounds in Middle-Earth cause spiritual, not physical damage, and it's the same in the films: any amount of slashing and almost no gore.

Blood in Narnia is always highly charged and significant. A single drop of red blood rolls down the Witch's white skin as she bites her lip in fury. Aslan's claws carve bloody stripes on Aravis's back to pay for the stripes inflicted on the back of the maidservant she deceived. A foot-long thorn driven into Aslan's paw releases the drop of blood that resurrects dead King Caspian. Philip Pullman accuses Lewis of a 'sado-masochistic relish for violence that permeates the whole cycle',[88] a charge not to be dismissed out of hand. In the case of Aravis's punishment, I incline to agree. More often though, I would simply say Lewis takes violence and bloodshed seriously and writes about its physical cost in a way that used to be, though no longer is, unusual in books for children.

Edmund is safe. Everyone ought to be breathing sighs of relief. But the Witch is departing with an expression of 'fierce joy' on her face, and Aslan's mood is quiet, almost dull. No one likes to ask. He advises Peter on strategy for a likely battle but gives no assurance he will be there himself. During the night the girls are uneasy and get up to look for Aslan. Out in the moonlight they spot him walking away into the wood. They follow: he sees them, and allows them to come with him so long as they promise to stop when he tells them, and let him go on alone. Thus begins a close, tender relationship between Aslan and the girls, especially Lucy, for they can see that something is very wrong. Lewis

[88] Pullman, Philip, 'The Dark Side of Narnia', *The Guardian*, October 1, 1998

emphasises Aslan's physicality: the heaviness of his head, his slow, plodding walk, his sudden involuntary moan. Full of love and pity the girls ask if he's ill, and he tells them that he isn't ill, he is simply sad, lonely, and in need of physical comfort. He wants their touch. So Susan and Lucy bury their cold hands in his 'beautiful sea of fur' and walk with him till the Stone Table comes in view. Telling them to stop now and keep out of sight, Aslan walks out alone on to the top of the hill, where a crowd of evil creatures waits for him with burning torches.

I didn't know what was coming. I had no idea that this passage between Aslan and the children was a version of the Garden of Gethsemane. Thank goodness for that. A child should read a book whole-heartedly, not raise her eyes from the page to draw comparisons with some parallel story. To read this book and try to keep in mind that Aslan 'is' Christ is to flit between two worlds and inhabit neither. Children immerse themselves in a book and take what they read at face value. They don't come up for air and think as adults do, 'What is this author trying to tell me?' I'd gone to church and Sunday school, I'd read my book of children's Bible stories, I'd enjoyed singing the Easter hymn that begins 'There is a green hill far away', but it never occurred to me to associate any of that with Aslan. They were different stories — just as Lucy's adventures through the wardrobe are different from Mabel's.

In fairy tales, innocent characters who die are often brought back to life. In the Grimms' tale *The Juniper Tree*, a murdered boy is transformed into a beautiful bird which rewards the good and destroys the wicked before turning back into a living child. Resurrections occur in myths and in fairy tales because there, if anywhere, good can prevail over evil. Lewis came to regard the incarnation, death and resurrection of Christ as a myth which really happened. We don't have to follow him all the way, but we can still be moved, and what happens to Aslan is almost unbearably moving.

Only three pages, yet they're still difficult to read. Aslan offers his enemies no resistance. In passive resignation he allows them to bind his paws, making no sound even as the cords cut into his flesh. The crowd ('of Cruels and Hags and Incubuses, Wraiths, Horrors, Efreets, Sprites, Orknies, Wooses and Ettins', a catalogue of bogymen all the creepier for not being described) begins to drag him towards the Stone Table. The Witch halts them and orders him to be shaved. Aslan's gorgeous mane falls to the earth in 'masses of curling gold'. They jeer at him, muzzle him, hoist him on to the Table and tie and tighten more cords. ('The cowards! The cowards!' sobs Susan. 'Are they *still* afraid of him, even now?') The Witch bares her arms, whets her stone knife. She bends over Aslan as he gazes quietly and sadly at the sky and tells him in a voice of quivering triumph that he is dying for nothing. When he is dead she will kill Edmund too, and Narnia will be hers forever. 'In that knowledge, despair and die.'

> The children did not see the actual moment of the killing. They couldn't bear to look and had covered their eyes.[89]

Deep breath.

Thing is, as a child I was right there with Susan and Lucy, crouching in the bushes watching these terrible

[89] *LWW* 144

things being done to this wonderful, noble, infinitely lovable Lion. 'How *can* they?' cries Lucy. 'The brutes, the brutes!' The wild mob of evil creatures comes sweeping past the girls' hiding place on their way to war. Let them go! All I wanted was to creep out into the silent moonlight with Susan and Lucy, and see poor dead Aslan, and stroke his face, and cry. 'Sado-masochistic relish for violence'? I think not.

I don't remember what I thought would happen next, if I thought at all. I was only nine, and the way I read stories then could be best described as 'travelling hopefully'. I knew that in most books, even if you couldn't see how, things would come right in the end (if only in a perfunctory 'with one bound, Jack was free' sort of way). That's not how this works, because Aslan's pain and suffering has been made so real it cannot be discounted. Even after he comes to life again, his death continues to count. 'Oh chestnut-tree, great-rooted blossomer ...' I felt it, I couldn't have explained it. Life and death and life again: an organic whole.

The girls get the horrible muzzle off Aslan's face but can't untie the knots that bind him. Later in the night, kind little fieldmice gnaw the cords away, as they do for the lion in one of Aesop's fables. Birds begin to sing, dawn comes. Stiff and cold, the girls walk on the eastern edge of the hill. The sun comes up, and with a loud noise 'as if a giant had broken a giant's plate' – the Stone Table has cracked in two. Running back they find Aslan's body gone, and for a second, like the women at the tomb of Jesus on the third day, they fear someone has taken him away. But no! There's Aslan right behind them, alive and real. Is it magic? 'Yes!' says Aslan, and tells them of the Deeper Magic that the Witch did not know: when an innocent victim willingly died in a traitor's place, 'the Table would crack and Death itself would start working backwards'.

Of course the Christian message is there, and of course Lewis means it. All the same it's perfectly possible for a child to read *The Lion, The Witch and the Wardrobe* and to see Aslan as no more and no less than the literal account makes him: a wonderful, golden-maned, heroic Animal. I know, because that's how I read it, and that is why I loved him. Aslan's death and resurrection is indeed 'deep magic from the dawn of time', it resonates as a myth as well as a Christian parable. An icy white queen: a fiery golden lion. 'When he shakes his mane, we shall have spring again ...' Of course Aslan comes back to life! Who can kill summer?

Now? Playtime! Rejoicing in life and strength, Aslan and the girls chase one another around the ruins of the Stone Table until they fall together in a laughing heap. Then with a great roar the Lion announces it's time to go, and climbing on his back the girls set off on a ride so marvellous I could only sigh with longing:

> ... right across Narnia, in spring, down solemn avenues of beech and across sunny glades of oak, through wild orchards of snow-white cherry trees, past roaring waterfalls and mossy rocks and echoing caverns, up windy slopes alight with gorse bushes, and across the shoulders of heathery mountains and along giddy ridges and down, down, down again into wild valleys and out into acres of blue flowers.[90]

[90] *LWW* 152

Rushing towards the Witch's house, Aslan jumps the high castle wall and the girls tumble from his back into the courtyard of statues.

The first thing he does is breathe on the stone lion – then dashes from statue to statue, breathing on them so they all come alive. In a lovely simile, just as flame creeps along the edge of a lighted newspaper, so a tiny streak of gold creeps along the stone lion's back until 'the heavy stone folds' of his mane 'ripple into living hair'. The courtyard fills with colour – and comedy too, as the newly freed creatures rush joyfully about the castle to find and rescue others. This kangaroo is unexpected and preposterous, which is surely the point:

> 'Oh! I say. Here's a poor kangaroo. Call Aslan – Phew. How it smells in here. Look out for trap-doors ...' ... But best of all was when Lucy came rushing upstairs shouting out, 'Aslan! Aslan! I've found Mr Tumnus. Oh do come quick.'[91]

Soon all are freed, and the urgent thing is to 'defeat the Witch before bed-time' (a nicely child-centred phrase) and come to the aid of Peter and Edmund, busy fighting a desperate battle against her and her evil army. The battlefield is dotted with statues, but right now the Witch is only using her knife. As the reinforcements arrive Aslan flings himself upon her and in amazed terror she goes down. Once she's dead the battle is over in minutes, but Edmund who has fought brilliantly and smashed

---

[91] *LWW* 158

the Witch's wand, is terribly wounded. Peter takes Aslan and Lucy to find him behind the lines, and again Lewis pulls no punches about the physical cost; he's 'covered in blood, his mouth was open, and his face was a nasty green colour'.

Lucy's cordial helps, but is not instantaneous, and after a rebuke from Aslan, 'Must *more* people die for Edmund?' she leaves him and goes to attend the other wounded. On her return Edmund is fully healed and looking as he'd used to look before he went to his 'horrid school' where he began to go wrong. (The first but not the last time in the Narnia stories that Lewis will take a crack at schools.)

Now comes the coronation of the four children at beautiful Cair Paravel by the sea, where as the waves break on the beach and the mermaids and mermen sing in honour of the new Kings and Queens, Aslan utters the splendidly reassuring promise: 'Once a king or queen in Narnia, always a king or queen.'

A brief coda follows, describing how well the children reign, and how much good they do in Narnia (such as 'liberating young dwarfs and satyrs from being sent to school', though exactly who might have been sending them there is left untold) and defeating the giants on the northern border. They grow up; of course they do. They become Peter the Magnificent, Susan the Gentle, Edmund the Just and Lucy the Valiant. But one day after the fashion of a medieval romance they hunt a White Stag deep into the forest, till he vanishes into a thicket too dense for the horses. So they follow him on foot and come to the lamp-post — which they barely remember — and agree to go further and take whatever adventure shall befall. And the trees become coats and they tumble out of the wardrobe, children again, and no time has passed. Will they ever return to Narnia? Of course, but not through the wardrobe. The Professor, to whom they tell their story, advises them not even to try. It'll happen. One day when they're least expecting it, they'll get there ...

And so will we.

THE HORSE AND HIS BOY

This, the fifth Narnia book in order of publication, was written after *Prince Caspian* and before *The Voyage of the Dawn Treader*, but it fits in here because it all takes place in Narnia's Golden Age, in the reign of Peter, Susan, Edmund and Lucy. Oddly perhaps, considering that next to Narnia, ponies were my passion, it wasn't a particular favourite of mine. I enjoyed it, but I didn't love it the way I loved some of the others.

This may be because it's the least complex, least layered of the Seven Chronicles. It's a straightforward adventure story with appealing characters, obnoxious villains, touches of humour, an arduous journey and a nick-of-time rescue. What it doesn't offer, alone among the Narnia books, is much in the way of emotion, wonder or awe. Nothing to match the moment when the Stone Table cracks in two, or when Reepicheep's coracle vanishes over the crest of the wave at the eastern edge of the world, or when Jill sees the brilliant birds fluttering in the trees at the top of Aslan's holy mountain. These were the things I really read the books for. To use Lewis's own term, there's no 'stab of joy' in *The Horse and His Boy*, at least for me. I was entertained and amused, but seldom moved.

It is also the only one of the Narnia stories seen throughout from the point of view of characters native to Narnia rather than our own world. The hero, Shasta, has grown to the age of perhaps twelve believing himself the son of Arsheesh, a poor fisherman in the southern land of Calormen, a country which will remind most readers of the Persia of the Arabian Nights. And at once there is a difficulty: the dark-skinned Calormenes are depicted in a way that strikes me now as at best naively Orientalist, at worst worryingly racist.

True, the polytheistic Calormene religion is nothing like Islam, but the culture is recognisably that of a medieval caliphate — the coins are even called 'crescents' — and Lewis leaves us in no doubt that Calormene society is morally inferior to that of Narnia. One has only to look at the relationship between Shasta and his foster father Arsheesh to see how he tips the scales. The folktale motif of a child cast adrift (in objects such as chests, baskets, boxes and boats) is found world-wide,[92] from Moses, to Perseus, to Perdita of *The Winter's Tale*, and in numerous fairy stories like the Grimms' *The Devil with the Three Golden Hairs* in which (attempting to forestall a prophecy) a king casts a poor man's baby into a river. Throughout these stories the person who finds the child, whether humble fisherman or noble princess, rescues and raises it with unselfish tenderness. Lewis inverts that tradition. Arsheesh self-servingly claims he took the boy in out of compassion after the boat containing the child and his

[92] Aarne-Thompson motifs S141, 'Unnatural cruelty': exposure in boat, and LIII.21 'Reversal of Fortune': future heir found in boat.

dead guardian floated ashore, but the Tarkaan impatiently interrupts; it is clear to him that Arsheesh sees Shasta purely in terms of cheap labour.

Overhearing this exchange and realising that Arsheesh is going to sell him to the Tarkaan, Shasta is simply relieved to learn that he's not the fisherman's own flesh and blood, for he has never felt for him as a son should. It's rather an anaemic reaction: he feels no regret, no wish that their relationship had been different or that Arsheesh might have loved *him*. Shasta's life is an emotional blank. Ambition stirs, but no longing. He wonders if he might be the son of someone important – a Tarkaan like this one, or the Tisroc himself, or even a god! And he dreams that 'the lordly stranger on the great horse might be kinder to him than Arsheesh'. Lewis soon dispels this dream, leaving an adult reader in some discomfort as to *why* this Tarkaan has taken a sudden fancy to buy Shasta, for it seems the boy is good looking – 'fair and white like the accursed but beautiful barbarians who inhabit the remote north.'

Admiration for despised beauty is never a good sign. When Bree the Talking Horse warns Shasta against the Tarkaan in the strongest terms ('Better be lying dead tonight than go to be a human slave in his house tomorrow'), I used to assume this meant hard work and beatings. Now I wonder.

Orientalism is a subset of racism which views Eastern cultures as irredeemably mysterious, 'inscrutable' and other. Recalling the sexism and racism prevalent in children's books during the first half of the twentieth century, Lewis's younger contemporary Geoffrey Trease illustrated it with a toe-curling extract from a story he himself wrote as a schoolboy in 1923:

'The white dog!' hissed the Arab leader, and his scimitar grated against my cutlass ... [L]ike a flash I ducked, and striking upwards with my left hand, administered a thoroughly British uppercut. And, because an Oriental can never understand such a blow, he reeled back, a look of almost comical surprise on his face. Ere he could recover, I lunged out with my cutlass and stretched him dead upon the ground.[93]

As an adult writer, Trease set out to combat the prejudice he'd parroted as a boy. His historical novels for children such as *The Red Towers of Granada* are deliberately respectful of other cultures such as those of Judaism or Islamic Spain, but in spite of his efforts the range of literature available to me growing up in the sixties was still crammed with dodgy foreigners: cunning, comic, cowardly or cruel. I didn't question it. I took it for granted. And the Calormenes fitted right into the same mould.

Adults often give children the books they remember from their own childhood, and books are durable physical objects that may sit for decades on dusty shelves, to be pulled out by voracious young readers. This is how I came to gobble down the jingoistic novels of G. A. Henty, published eighty to a hundred years before I was reading them in the 1960s. I doubt many children read them now:[94] but the seventy year-old Narnia stories are still very much with us. Henty's

[93] Trease, Geoffrey: 'The Revolution in Children's Literature,' *The Thorny Paradise, Writers on Writing for Children*, ed. Edward Blishen
[94] Although according to Deirdre McMahon in *'Quick Ethel, Your Rifle': Portable Britishness and Flexible Gender Roles in G. A. Henty's Books for Boys*, they apparently remain popular among right wing and conservative Christian homeschoolers: muse.jhu.edu/article/392764 retrieved 12 August 2019.

prejudices may no longer matter, but those of C. S. Lewis do, and I can't help feeling he should have known better.

And more is going on. Where Narnia is a child's paradise of happy magical creatures and talking animals, Calormen is a grown-up country. It has farms and roads, a religion and a class structure, a bureaucracy, a literature, slaves, soldiers and cities. Despite its supposed Arabian Nights exoticism, from a child's perspective Calormen is a dull place. Where are the flying carpets, magical rings, terrifying jinni, sorcerers and enchantresses with which Scheherezade fills *The Thousand and One Nights*? Lewis ditched the lot. He borrowed the trappings but left out the magic: Shasta's village is so boring that the boy is not even interested in going there.

> In the village he only met other men who were just like his father — men with long, dirty robes, and wooden shoes turned up at the toe, and turbans on their heads, and beards, talking to one another very slowly about things that sounded dull.[95]

Lewis makes Calormen sound like a bad nineteenth-century European travelogue of a journey in rural Turkey, and his description of life in a poor village isn't even fair. Where are the women, where are the children? Are there no other boys to play with? Is Shasta the only one for miles around?

It's not as if the Narnia books never bear us away to foreign lands. The wilds of Ettinsmoor, the depths of Bism, the numinous islands of the Eastern Sea — these belong, these fit within the Narnian world. Calormen doesn't. It

[95] *HHB* 11

exists to oppose Narnia's every quality. Lewis could have incorporated peris and griffins, flying carpets and sphinxes into this story, but he didn't. Not even the ghouls of the Tombs are 'real'.

In a fantasy series which happily blends classical and Norse mythologies, medieval legends and talking animals, why did Lewis instinctively (I doubt he thought about it) strip all the magic from the Arabian Nights? Where else in the Narnian world does this failure of enchantment occur? In the least interesting episode of *The Voyage of the Dawn Treader* where the Calormenes trade for slaves on the unmagical Lone Islands, that's where – and in King Miraz's Narnia, a regime of schools, towns and bridges which Aslan overthrows with the help of the personified powers of nature: a destruction significantly presented as a restoration. Narnia at its most Narnian is a place of natural freedom where rules are not needed because no one *wants* to do anything bad. It has no villages like Shasta's, no cities, no roads. Cair Paravel is a stand-alone fairy tale castle with no city around it. King Lune's castle of Anvard in Archenland is similarly isolated.

Unlike the threats posed by the magical White Witch and the Green Lady, the threat to Narnia from Calormen and from the Telmarine rule of Miraz is a divorce from magic. Their rule would destroy Narnia, substituting an order of economics, progress, trade, politics, scepticism and other unromantic things which Lewis didn't like and didn't want in his fairy paradise. The Calormenes only represent these values, however, because Lewis chose they should. No doubt at the back of his mind was the medieval clash between Islam and Europe – the Song of Roland, the Battle of Lepanto – but historically it is the west which has imposed its industrial and political values upon the rest of the world.

I think deep in his bones Lewis disliked the magic of *The Thousand and One Nights*. He found it foreign, inimical. So he left it out, but his depiction of the Calormenes raises all sorts of questions. They are human, which ought to mean they, like Peter, Edmund, Susan and Lucy, are 'sons of Adam and daughters of Eve'. Where have they come from? When Aslan sang Narnia into existence in *The Magician's Nephew*, did he create the land of Calormen too? And their gods, Zardeenah, Azaroth and Tash? There'll be more to say about these questions when we come to *The Last Battle*.

One of the best things about *The Horse and His Boy* is the relationship between Shasta and Bree the Talking Horse, kidnapped from Narnia as a little foal and pressed into the Tisroc's army. Bree, or to give him his full name, Breehy-hinny-brinny-hoohy-hah, is a superb character. I loved and still love the comedy of his good-humoured disdain for Shasta and humans in general, and his bracing lack of sympathy for Shasta's aches and pains: 'It can't be the falls. You didn't have more than a dozen or so.' As an experienced war-horse, Bree takes initial charge of the escape. Both he and Shasta want to go north and he's sure that Shasta comes of 'true northern stock'. Pairing up will improve both their chances: no one will try to catch him as a stray, and on his back Shasta can outpace any other horse in the county, Bree boasts. Announcing that he is the one who will direct the journey, Bree instructs the ignorant Shasta never to touch the reins – and on discovering Shasta has put on the Tarkaan's spurs he tells him briskly to take them off again. And they're away: Narnia and the North!

There is food in the Tarkaan's saddle bag, along with forty crescents, more money than Shasta has ever seen before. But he wonders aloud if they should use it; wouldn't it be stealing? This is one of a number of moments when Shasta seems more like a nice English schoolboy than a runaway urchin. Where could he possibly have picked up such a scruple? Does Lewis intend it to indicate his inner nobility (*the boy has fine instincts*)? It's odd, considering so much of this story is about class distinctions: both Bree and Shasta suffer anxiety about who they are, where they belong and whether they're good enough. (And at one important point in the narrative Shasta not only feels but actually *is* an imposter.)

This anxiety is well illustrated when Bree lies down to enjoy the best roll he will have for weeks. Shasta bursts out laughing at the comical sight he makes on his back, waving his legs in the air, and this apparently confident, officer-class warhorse is hit by terrible insecurity. Has he picked up bad habits from dumb, common horses? Would a true Narnian Talking Horse enjoy a good roll? Bree is an adorable snob.

Day by day Shasta's riding improves as he and Bree travel up the coast, until one night they hear another horse and rider accompanying them northwards along a broad sandy plain between the forest on their left and the sea on their right.

> 'Ssh!' said Bree, craning his neck around and twitching his ears ... ' ... *That's* not a farmer's riding. Not a farmer's horse either. ... I tell you what it is, Shasta. There's a Tarkaan under the edge of that wood. Not on his war horse — it's too light for that. On a fine blood mare, I should say.'[96]

---

[96] *HHB* 27

'Craning his neck around and twitching his ears'; Lewis never lets us forget that Bree is a *horse*.

The strange 'horseman' seems as eager to avoid them as they are to avoid him, when suddenly they are attacked by lions. The two horses are driven together in a mad gallop across the sands and into an arm of the sea, where are they forced to swim side by side and the rider is seen to be a 'small, slender person, mail-clad ... and riding magnificently'. As streaming with water the horses gain the further shore, the 'Tarkaan' and his horse try to ride on, but Bree physically blocks their way and challenges the mare: she's a Talking Horse of Narnia! He heard her speak!

> 'What's it got to do with you if she is?' said the strange rider fiercely, laying hand on sword-hilt. But the voice in which the words were spoken had already told Shasta something.
>
> 'Why, it's only a girl!' he exclaimed.
>
> 'And what business is it of yours if I am *only* a girl?' snapped the stranger. 'You're only a boy: a rude, common little boy — a slave probably, who's stolen his master's horse.'[97]

I was cheering her on; Aravis takes no prisoners. This 'only a girl' thing used to be everywhere, a universal gas we all breathed. In *Little Women*, in *What Katy Did* — in Enid Blyton's books about the Famous Five — everywhere — my friends and I encountered heroines who wished they were boys, and we didn't always understand this wasn't because boys were naturally superior, but because society privileged them with

---

[97] *HHB* 31

better opportunities. So it was great to meet competent, confident Aravis who rode a horse as I only wished I could, and wore a sword too. And when Shasta comes out with this classic 'only a girl' put-down, she annihilates him *de haut en bas*, with a stinging grain of truth. It's therefore the horses, not the children, who decide that from now on the four of them will go on together: a rebalancing of power reinforced by Bree's rebuke to Aravis when, laying his ears back slightly, he reminds her that if she's running away to Narnia, Hwin isn't *her* horse any more:

> 'One might just as well say *you're* her human.'
> The girl opened her mouth to speak and then stopped. Obviously she had not quite seen it in that light before.[98]

Privileged and rich, Aravis has to begin adjusting her attitude and sense of entitlement. Shasta, so poor he has never owned anything, feels inadequate and jealous around her. He reacts by becoming aggressive and sulky, and while the horses find much in common to talk about, even discovering they are distant cousins, the children remain awkward and uncomfortable. At last Bree suggests that Aravis should tell them her story.

Through Bree we at last hear something good about Calormene culture. He praises their high, elaborate style of story-telling — 'the grand, Calormene manner' is the sort of thing we expect of 'Eastern' tales (although this may be an artefact of the translations: in her edition of *The Thousand and One Nights*, Hanan Al-Shaykh praises the original's 'flat,

---

[98] *HHB* 33

simple style'). When Arsheesh talked like this we knew he was being insincere, but it seems Lewis approves it for formal storytelling.

Aravis begins by introducing herself and her genealogy (she claims descent from the god Tash). Her story is effectively another fairy tale: her cruel stepmother has persuaded her weak father to marry his daughter to the Vizier Ahoshta Tarkaan, a rich but ugly old man. In angry despair, Aravis rides her mare Hwin into the woods and prepares to kill herself, when the mare suddenly speaks: 'Oh my mistress, do not by any means destroy yourself, for if you live you may yet have good fortune but all the dead are dead alike.' (Hwin charmingly interrupts at this point with a muttered, 'I didn't say it half so well as that.')[99]

Hwin's description of the beauties of Narnia with its woods and castles makes a great impression on Aravis. She longs to go there, especially when Hwin adds that in that land there are no forced marriages. She hatches a plot:

> 'I put on my gayest clothes and sang and danced before my father and pretended to be delighted with the marriage which he had prepared for me. Also I said to him, "O my father and O the delight of my eyes, give me your licence and permission to go with one of my maidens alone for three days into the woods to do secret sacrifices to Zardeenah, Lady of the Night, as is proper and customary for damsels when they must bid farewell to the service of Zardeenah and prepare themselves for marriage."'[100]

---

[99] *HHB* 37
[100] *HHB* 38

This seems to be Lewis's conscious recall of a very dark Old Testament story (Judges 11:34-39) where, in another ancient fairy tale motif, the warrior Jephthah makes a bargain with God: victory over his enemies in exchange for a burnt offering of the first thing that greets him on his return home.

> And Jephthah came ... unto his house, and, behold, his daughter came out to meet him with timbrels and with dances; and she was his only child ... And he rent his clothes, and said, Alas, my daughter! thou hast brought me very low ... for I have opened my mouth unto the Lord and I cannot go back. And she said unto him, My father, if thou hast opened thy mouth unto the Lord, do to me according to that which hath proceeded out of thy mouth. ... And she said unto her father, Let this thing be done for me: let me go alone two months that I may up and down upon the mountain and bewail my virginity, I and my fellows. And he said, Go. And he sent her away for two months: and she went with her companions and bewailed her virginity upon the mountains. And it came to pass at the end of two months that she returned unto her father, who did with her according to his vow which he had vowed.

Aravis has considered suicide rather than accept a forced marriage. Now she does what we might wish Jephthah's unnamed daughter could have done. She tricks her father, obtains three days grace, drugs her maid, dresses in her brother's armour and races for Narnia on Hwin — covering her tracks further by sending her father a letter as if from her betrothed husband, claiming they have married already after a chance meeting in the woods. From the moment we meet her, Aravis displays competence, coolness and fortitude: she is, as Lewis later comments, proud and sometimes hard, but 'true as steel'. What she doesn't have is empathy: it's left to Shasta the underdog to wonder what might have happened to the maid Aravis drugged and left behind.

> 'Doubtless she was beaten for sleeping late,' said Aravis coolly. 'But she was a tool and spy of my stepmother's. I am very glad that they should beat her.'
>
> 'I say, that was hardly fair,' said Shasta.
>
> 'I did not do any of these things for the sake of pleasing *you*,' said Aravis.[101]

When I first read this book I can't say the fate of the maid upset me very much, and I appreciated tough, unsympathetic Aravis who does the necessary without wringing her hands. The adventure story is a genre which requires a brisk pace and little consideration of those who fall by the way or *get* in the way. But of course this isn't your average adventure story and Lewis has a moral agenda. He wants his child readers to notice the collateral damage. Aslan is watching and Aslan will repay – an eye for an eye, a tooth for a tooth, as he tells Aravis later:

> 'The scratches on your back, tear for tear, throb for throb, blood for blood, were equal to the stripes laid upon the back of your stepmother's slave because of the drugged sleep you cast upon her. You needed to know what it felt like.'[102]

[101] *HHB* 41
[102] *HHB* 158

'Tear for tear, throb for throb, blood for blood' is retributive Old Testament justice and honestly it's quite nasty. Does Aslan punish Aravis because her action got the slave-girl into trouble? Or because she wasn't sorry about it and didn't care? Clearly the latter. Aravis's punishment cannot help the slave-girl, who will never even hear of it. 'You needed to know what it felt like': this is about Aravis herself, to correct a flaw in her character and teach her to empathise. It seemed fair to me as a child. But now? Now I think this is penny-in-the-slot justice. You do something bad: something bad is done to you: end. Where's the good in it? Jesus said, 'With what measure ye mete it shall be measured to you again,' but it bothers me that Aslan lays no responsibility on Aravis to consider that slave-girl again, or to try and help her. He even discourages her from doing so, saying as he often does that it is 'not her story' to know.

Again: this is an adventure, and most adventure stories would never raise the issue of 'what happened to the slave girl?' in the first place – but having raised it, Lewis doesn't seem to me to deal with it well. So long as you're *sorry* there's no need to do anything more, just leave the rest to God? It is easy but dangerous to hand over justice to one's notion of the divine. Where was that justice for Jephthah's daughter? I don't always like Aslan very much, in this book.

Now comes the tricky journey through the city of Tashbaan. It's essential no one spots that Bree is a war-horse, or recognises Aravis who is known to many people there; Shasta has often felt left out hearing her and Bree chatting about mutual acquaintances in the capital. But now they must all work together. The best hope of getting straight through the city from southern to northern gates, is to look like a couple of slaves leading a pair of common horses. (Hwin's sensible suggestion.) If they get separated, Bree suggests meeting at the Tombs of the Ancient Kings on the far side of the city, a site avoided by the Calormenes who believe it is haunted by ghouls. This sparks some amusing one-upmanship: Aravis mentions she has heard that the Tombs are haunted. Bree declares that as a Narnian horse he doesn't believe these Calormene tales. Shasta claims untruthfully that he doesn't believe them either, and this spurs Aravis to announce that she herself doesn't care about 'any number of ghouls' – if they're indeed there. It's a nice little exchange which neatly introduces the reader to the Tombs' sinister reputation.

The horns sound to open the city gates and the guards let them through without stopping them, though it's a close thing. Bree can't help proudly arching his neck, prompting one of the guards to shout at Shasta that he'll catch it if his master discovers he's been using his war-horse as a pack animal. Shasta unwisely answers back and gets a clout for his pains that almost knocks him down. He only cries a little: he's used to it.

Making slow progress through the crowded streets where the only rule is that you have to get out of the path of anyone important, they meet a procession coming the other way. A party of Narnian lords are in Tashbaan on a state visit to discuss the possible marriage of Susan of Narnia to Prince Rabadash, eldest son of the Tisroc. In contrast to the Calormene lords and ladies who loll on litters carried by 'gigantic slaves', the Narnians are on foot:

> Their tunics were of fine, bright, hardy colours – woodland green, or gay yellow, or fresh blue. ...The swords at their sides were long and straight, not curved

> like the Calormene scimitars. And instead of being grave and mysterious like most Calormenes, they walked with a swing and ... chatted and laughed. One was whistling. You could see they were ready to be friends with anyone who was friendly and didn't give a fig for anyone who wasn't. Shasta thought he had never seen anything so lovely in his life.[103]

I was thrilled to be back with real Narnians at last, and Lewis makes them sound attractive indeed – a breath of fresh air. Now I can't help noticing how every word is loaded so that even the Narnians' dress choices appear 'better' than those of the Calormenes. It's absurd to suggest that no Calormene people dress in blue, yellow or green: but why in any case should those colours be preferred to red, purple or brown? It would be even sillier to say out loud that the 'straight' Narnian swords suggest directness and honesty while the 'curved' Calormene scimitars denote indirectness and treachery; but that's what this passage manages to imply.

Jostled to the front of the crowd, Shasta is spotted by the Narnians, who mistake him for young Prince Corin of Archenland (who will turn out to be his identical twin). Having accompanied the Narnian delegation to Tashbaan, Corin has been missing overnight, and believing they've found him, the Narnians snatch Shasta off the street and take him to their suite in a great palace where they scold him for a truant. Just as young Tom Canty in Mark Twain's *The Prince and the Pauper* (from which this adventure is borrowed) is mistaken for Henry VIII's son Prince Edward and assumed to have lost his memory from 'too much study', so Mr

---

[103] *HHB* 51

Tumnus (Mr Tumnus! Hooray!) suggests to Edmund and Susan that the young prince's confusion must be due to a touch of sunstroke. 'Look at him! He is dazed. He does not know where he is.'

Told to rest on a sofa and given iced sherbet to drink, Shasta overhears the Narnians' most private discussions. Queen Susan no longer wishes to marry Prince Rabadash. When he came to court her at Cair Paravel, he had seemed a splendid and courteous young knight, but here in his home they have now found him to be in King Edmund's words, 'a most proud, bloody, luxurious, cruel and self-pleasing tyrant'. (Prince Rabadash ends the book as a figure of fun, and his name is suspiciously close to that of the Wantonly Wicked Prince Rubdub in Noel Langley's children's book *The Land of Green Ginger* which is an Orientalist comedy – half Arabian Nights, half pantomime – published in 1937.) Susan wishes to leave Tashbaan at once, but Edmund tells her this may not be possible. In fact, they may be prevented.

Edmund guesses the Tisroc's designs on Narnia are less about forming an alliance and more about annexing this 'little land' on the edge of his 'great empire'. Narnia is a stone in the Tisroc's shoe. Rabadash may even have been sent to Cair Paravel for the very purpose of picking some quarrel with Narnia and its neighbour Archenland. He wants Queen Susan, however, and since he is unused to being made to wait, he has begun dropping veiled threats. If the Narnians try to leave before Susan consents to marry him, Edmund fears Rabadash will make her his wife by force. Or worse!

One of the Dwarfs objects that Narnia has a navy to match the Tisroc's, and is surely safe from attack by sea – while the Calormenes can hardly lead an army across the desert which separates their country from Archenland. But Sallowpad the Raven tells of a secret way to cross the desert: you must start from the Tombs of the Ancient Kings and ride north-west, keeping the double peak of Mount Pire straight ahead. After a day's riding you will come to a dry valley: if you go on down it you will find a river which you can follow into Archenland.

This is how Shasta learns of the desert route which he and his friends will take once reunited. Meanwhile the Narnians make an alternative plan to deceive Rabadash and escape by sea, and once Shasta's eaten a magnificent meal which includes 'a complicated dish of chicken-livers and rice and raisins and nuts' (wherever did Lewis come across pilaf in 1950s Britain?[104]) and Mr Tumnus has 'reminded' him of the wonderful life waiting for Prince Corin back home in Archenland, he begins to think he would like to go with them.

Though the Narnians do not intend it, the temptation now facing Shasta is the same as Edmund's in *The Lion*: to betray or abandon his friends in return for delicious (Eastern) food, luxury and status. And he pretty much falls for it. He doesn't give a thought to the real Prince Corin, abandoned in Tashbaan; he tells himself that he can't help it if Bree and Aravis have to wait for him at the Tombs not knowing what's happened to him. Since Aravis thinks she's too good for him, 'she can jolly well go alone' – and it will be so much easier to get to Narnia by sea ...

---

[104] The Trinidadian-British poet Vahni Capildeo has reminded me that '1950s Britain wasn't lacking in West Indian and South Asian people (including lots of my family in Oxford and London), or white Brits born or raised with a taste for food from "their" corners of the empire ... there was a curry house on Turl St in Oxford in my father's time (the 50s).'

Inexperienced and naïve, Shasta wants to be something better, but he doesn't know how. He's ready to think badly of Aravis not because she is a girl, but because her status, confidence and manners make him jealous and insecure. None of this is unsympathetic. We understand it and can make allowances while waiting for him to show his true worth. Right now though, his behaviour is not very admirable. He simply falls asleep, and if it were not for Corin's sudden return via a window, he would probably go with the flow and abandon his friends.

Corin sports a black eye and a missing tooth, having been in several fights sparked by 'a beastly joke about Queen Susan' (another black mark against the Calormene people). His arrival galvanises Shasta into action: no way can he stay here now! Nor is there any way the Narnians can confuse the bruised and battered Prince with Shasta, so they'll have to be told the truth. (The hauteur with which Corin responds to the suggestion that he might lie nicely distinguishes the two boys and their backgrounds.) In 'a frantic whisper' Shasta tells Corin all he knows about himself: that he's a Narnian or thinks he is, 'something northern anyway', but has lived in Calormen all his life and is escaping north across the desert with a Talking Horse. And now he's in a hurry to leave. Quick, which way? As Corin points out the best getaway route, the boys realise that they like each other and hope to meet again. Then Shasta drops from the window and runs.

Exiting the city by the northern gate he crosses the bridge over the river and heads for the desert and the Tombs, to find his friends aren't there. What if they've gone on without him? As the horns of Tashbaan sound to close the city gates, he knows with a sinking heart he must spend the night alone among the Tombs.

This is a memorably atmospheric chapter. The Tombs look at first like 'gigantic stone beehives' but later in the night are more scarily personified as huge people whose features are concealed under voluminous robes. Shasta now remembers the ghouls; I didn't know quite what a ghoul was, and I'm not sure I do yet, but it sounded much nastier than ghosts. Something touches his leg! He yells with fright and looks down because — and I could only agree —

> Anything would be better than being chased round and round the burial places of the Ancient Kings with something he dared not look at behind him.[105]

And it's a cat. Not a talking cat, not here in Calormen, but a big 'solemn' cat with eyes that seem to hint of secrets it will not disclose. Stalking ahead of Shasta it leads him to the desert side of the Tombs, where it keeps him company and watches over him during a terrifying night. At one point it even drives away a pack of jackals (although when Shasta remorsefully confesses to it that he once threw a stone at a 'mangy old stray', it gives him a quick sharp scratch). It is of course Aslan, although Shasta doesn't know this; in fact there's no evidence that he's ever even heard of Aslan, whose name to this point has barely been mentioned. By morning the cat has gone, and he endures a long anxious day waiting for his friends and wondering if they will ever turn up. Eventually, just before sunset, he sees Bree and Hwin being led towards the Tombs by a stranger who looks like a groom. Where's Aravis? Can it be a trap?

Aravis's adventures have rivalled Shasta's. As he is taken away by the Narnians she grabs the horses' halters and is

[105] *HHB* 72

spotted by her old friend Lasaraleen Tarkheena who is being carried past in a litter. As Lasaraleen cries out her name, cool-headed Aravis jumps into the litter and tersely tells her friend to shut up, take her somewhere private and bring the horses along. 'I'm running away.'

Lasaraleen, a bubbly airhead, can't understand why her friend doesn't want to marry the rich Vizier, but she agrees to help. The horses can simply be led out of the city by a groom. But Aravis's father is in Tashbaan, looking for her. How can she get through the gates unobserved? Then Lasaraleen remembers a little water-door opening on to the river from the bottom of the Tisroc's garden. It's 'only for palace people, of course', but (she simpers) 'we almost *are* palace people'. She is, she claims, on such friendly terms with the Tisroc and princes and ladies of the palace, that it should be no problem at all for the two of them to pop in any time after dark. Lasaraleen will then let Aravis out, and Aravis can cross the river in one of the pleasure-craft moored there.

With Aravis veiled and disguised as a slave-girl, the pair set off next evening through the labyrinthine palace – through the Hall of Black Marble, the Hall of Pillars and the Hall of Statues, down the colonnade, past the throne-room, out through a garden-courtyard and into the Old Palace where Lasaraleen loses her way in 'a maze of corridors lit only by occasional torches ...' Here once more is that imagery of a rambling old building, endless passages and a secret room: and this time the secret is a frightening one. Light blooms down a dark passage and two men appear around the corner, walking backwards with candles. They are lighting the way for the Tisroc. Seconds later a terrified Lasaraleen is dragging Aravis back the way they've come, looking for a hiding-place. In pitch dark, the girls open a door to a furnished room and squeeze into the space between a divan couch and the wall.

In the English fairy tale *Mr Fox*[106] a gallant young woman named Lady Mary explores the apparently empty castle of Mr Fox, the man to whom she is betrothed. She passes through a series of arches and doorways over which are carved the consecutive mottoes, *'Be Bold'* and *'Be bold, be bold, but not too bold'* until on a top floor she finds a doorway over which is written:

> *'Be bold, be bold, but not too bold*
> *Lest that thy heart's blood should run cold.'*

Behind this door is a room full of Mr Fox's murdered victims. Attempting to leave, Lady Mary sees him coming home at the head of a band of robbers, and hides behind a large cask in the great hall from where she witnesses his attempt to remove a ring from the hand of his latest victim and — when the ring won't budge — drawing his sword to slash the woman's hand off at the wrist. It springs into the air and falls beside Lady Mary, who snatches it up while he proceeds upstairs to the Bloody Chamber. Making her escape, she uses it next day as evidence to bring him to justice.

The tale is so old it was known to both Shakespeare and Spenser. The latter uses the tag *'Be bold'* in his long narrative poem *The Faerie Queene* when the female knight Britomart, who represents Chastity, enters the house of the enchanter Busyrane to rescue the lady Amoret. The House of Busyrane is full of many richly furnished rooms which appear empty — 'No wight appeared, but wasteful emptiness' —

---

[106] Jacobs, Joseph, *Mr Fox*, *English Fairy Tales*, 148 *et seq*

> And as she lookt about, she did behold,
> How over that same dore was likewise writ,
> *Be bold, be bold*, and everywhere *Be bold,*
> That much she mused, but could not construe it
> By any riddling skill or commune wit.
> At last she spyde at that room's upper end,
> Another yron dore, on which was writ
> *Be not too bold*; whereto though she did bend
> Her ernest mind, yet wist not what it might intend.[107]

At midnight the iron door opens to allow the masque of the false Cupid to appear, and next day Britomart goes through it herself to find Busyrane tormenting Amoret, whom she rescues. In both the fairy tale and the poem the undaunted heroine wins through and I think Lewis had the poem in his mind when he wrote about Lucy in the Magician's House in the *Voyage of the Dawn Treader*. Here, in *The Horse and His Boy*, the closer parallel is with *Mr Fox*. Crushed behind the divan, Lasaraleen and Aravis are in the same terrible position as Lady Mary behind the cask. The door opens, the torch-bearing slaves enter, and in come the Tisroc, Prince Rabadash and Aravis's betrothed husband, Ahoshta the Vizier, to hold a secret council. If the girls are discovered they will be put to death.

Rabadash plans to cross the desert with a small force of two hundred horsemen and surprise King Lune's castle of Anvard. From there he'll ride through the mountains and repeat the process at Cair Paravel, ready to seize Queen Susan as soon as her ship puts in. If the raid succeeds, the Tisroc will keep Anvard, the threshold to Narnia. If it fails, the Tisroc

---

[107] Spenser, *The Faerie Queene*, Book III, Canto XI, verse 54

can blame Rabadash's youth and passion, which — the Vizier points out, prostrate on the floor — may even incline Susan's heart towards him. Win-win, all round! The Tisroc grants Rabadash permission, and muses as the young man dashes out, that if his son succeeds, good! — but if he dies, well, he was becoming dangerously ambitious and can easily be replaced ... Dismissing the Vizier, the wicked Tisroc continues to sit on the divan for what seems an age before finally rising to leave, preceded by his slaves. At last the room is empty.

The girls extricate themselves, trembling. Aravis has to bully Lasaraleen to show her down to the water-gate, but here at last is the river, boats and freedom. (For a girl interested in nothing but clothes and parties, Lasaraleen has done rather well, I think.) Aravis crosses the river and rejoins Shasta and the horses at the Tombs.

Both children have made important discoveries. Aravis knows Rabadash's plans; Shasta knows the secret route across the desert. The race is on to reach Archenland ahead of Rabadash, and warn King Lune.

The desert crossing is a memorable ordeal, especially the bit where the hot sand burns Shasta's bare feet so he can no longer dismount. When at last they reach the valley and follow it down to water, they are so exhausted they fall asleep for hours. On waking late next morning, Hwin shyly suggests that tired or not, it would be wise for them go on, but Bree retorts crushingly that they need to eat and refresh themselves first: 'I think, Ma'am ... I know a little more about campaigns and forced marches and what a horse can stand than you do.'

Er ... sorry? Hwin *is* a horse! Stallionsplaining — who knew? Hwin says no more because she is a 'nervous and gentle person who was easily put down', so Bree gets his snack of lush grass, and hours more are wasted. I love this bit of social interaction, straight out of *#everydaysexism*, so well observed. For Hwin is right and Bree is wrong, and it's soon made very clear that his decision was a bad one. From the top of the first ridge of Archenland they see behind them the glittering dust-cloud of Rabadash's army, seeking for a place to cross the river.

The horses race for Anvard. Beyond each ridge is another. The horses are doing what they *think* is their utmost, when out of nowhere a lion comes streaking after them and Bree discovers that after all he has an extra gear. He whizzes past Hwin, galloping full pelt for a tall green hedge with an open gate which seems to have materialised out of nowhere and is the home of the Hermit of the Southern March. Behind, the lion is catching up on Hwin, and Shasta does the bravest, most unselfish thing he's ever done. As the lion rakes its claws down Aravis's shoulders, he jumps yelling from Bree's back to defy it, and to his amazement it turns and rushes off. Exhausted as he is, he then runs on at the Hermit's urging and succeeds in warning King Lune, whom he finds out hunting, of Rabadash's approaching force. Though deeply struck by Shasta's likeness to his son Corin, the King wastes no time but lends him a horse and rides for Anvard.

With the main characters separated again, the story splits into different branches. Aravis and the Horses remain with the Hermit: they meet and speak with Aslan but take no further part in the action, which they view at a distance through the Hermit's 'seeing pool'. Shasta (who has never learned to make an ordinary horse go) falls behind King Lune's party, gets lost in the mountains, encounters a mysterious Fellow Traveller (Aslan), arrives in Narnia, joins a relief force sent from Cair Paravel to lift the siege of Anvard, and after the victory is publicly recognised as Cor of Archenland — King Lune's lost-lost eldest son and heir, kidnapped as a child to prevent the fulfilment of a prophecy that he would save Archenland from deadly danger. (As usual in these tales, the action taken to defeat the prophecy is the very thing which causes it to come to pass.)

Aslan, it turns out, has masterminded nearly the entire plot of *The Horse and His Boy*. He explains it himself, pacing unseen at Shasta's side in the dark misty night of the mountain pass.

> I was the lion who forced you to join with Aravis. I was the cat who comforted you among the houses of the dead. I was the lion who drove the jackals from you while you slept. I was the lion who gave the Horses the new strength of fear for the last mile so that you should reach King Lune in time. And I was the lion you do not remember who pushed the boat in which you lay, a child near death, so that it came to shore ...[108]

Lewis means us to find this moving, satisfying, perhaps even reassuring. At nine years old I accepted it but it didn't move me, and now it seems almost manipulative. Aslan reconfigures Shasta's account of his misfortunes to show that all the seemingly 'bad' things that have happened to him have really been for the good. The entire series of events has worked to illustrate a set of propositions: *God ordains all things; God knows and judges all things; God takes care of the good and punishes the sinner; God is with us always.* It reminds me of those 'footprints in the sand' posters which can be bought in Christian bookshops: a charming parable in which God reassures us that 'when you thought you were walking alone, that is when I was carrying you.' Such parables undoubtedly

[108] *HHB* 129

comfort some people, and heaven knows we all need comfort. However, sincerity is required to make these things work. To me this feels strained, as if Lewis is trying too hard.

There's something uncomfortably controlling about Aslan's sequential incursions into the lives of Shasta, Aravis and Bree even though *it's all for their own good* and even though Bree certainly deserves to be taken down a peg or two. As a child I found the scene irresistibly comic in which Bree confidently asserts that Aslan is not a real lion – aimed presumably at those who say they believe in a God but deny that he became incarnate in the person of Jesus Christ – while Aslan creeps up behind him. To describe Aslan as a Lion, says Bree, is to use a metaphor which shouldn't be taken literally.

> 'Why!' (and here Bree began to laugh) 'If he was a lion he would have four paws, and a tail, and *Whiskers*!... Aie, ooh, hoo-hoo! Help!'
>
> For just as he said the word *Whiskers* one of Aslan's had actually tickled his ear.[109]

It is still funny. Just not as funny as it was.

The most joyful moment of this book ought to be the road-to-Damascus moment at the end of Chapter XI, when a golden light shines through the mist and Aslan at last reveals himself to Shasta, who falls at his feet, dumb with awe:

> The High King above all kings stooped towards him. Its mane, and some strange and solemn perfume that hung about its mane, was all around him. It touched his forehead with its tongue.[110]

[109] *HHB* 157
[110] *HHB* 131

This is a stately, High Church Aslan, far removed from the flesh and blood Lion who played so joyfully with Lucy and Susan in *The Lion, The Witch and the Wardrobe*. From what does Shasta's conversion spring? Compare it to Eustace's transformation into a dragon in *The Voyage of the Dawn Treader* and the numinous, terrifying dream in which Aslan peels away the crusted layers of dragon hide and restores his human shape. Remember how changed Eustace is, afterwards? What has happened to Shasta? In what way has *he* changed?

Even as he finds himself to be Prince Cor, eldest son of King Lune of Archenland, Shasta is the same anxious, well-meaning person – still worried what Aravis will think of him – still expressing himself in tongue-tied clichés like a prep-school boy:

> Father's an absolute brick. I'd be just as pleased – or very nearly – at finding he's my father even if he wasn't a king.[III]

Yes, perhaps his inarticulacy is a touching revelation of the fears and inadequacies that boys often conceal, but there are a few fleeting moments which show what Lewis *could* have done with Shasta. One comes early on when Bree presses the question of whether Shasta can eat grass. 'Ever tried?' he asks, and Shasta says, 'Yes, I have. I can't get it down at all.' Another is when the guard hits him at the gates of Tashbaan and he only cries a little because he's 'used to it'. And when he tries dismounting on the desert ride and screams with pain as his bare foot touches the burning sand ... A boy who tries to eat grass, who's used to blows, whose shoeless feet

---

[III] *HHB* 161

scorch in the hot sand: here is poverty made pitiable and tangible. It's just that most of the time Shasta doesn't sound like that boy.

Still, as a child, I felt the adventure had been wrapped up very satisfactorily. The story ends in slapdash humour. Prince Rabadash makes a fool of himself ('The bolt of Tash falls from above!' – 'Does it ever get caught on a hook half-way?') and is transformed by Aslan into a donkey, so he can do no more harm. Shasta is heir of Archenland, while Corin (bound for the Bullingdon Club if ever a boy was) is delighted to shed the responsibility. Bree casts off his anxiety and has a good roll. Cor and Aravis's eventual marriage, made so that they can go on quarrelling 'more conveniently', seemed to me a reasonable and un-sloppy basis for a relationship. They were clearly good friends. I closed the book and reached for the next.

What has surprised me on this re-reading is how didactic and prescriptive I found a book which in my memory was one of the least 'religious' of the Narnia stories. What I've truly enjoyed are just the things I enjoyed as a child: the easy, brilliant, vivid writing, the social comedy (this is often a very funny book) and the gallery of characters: gallant Aravis, gentle Hwin, and bossy, class-conscious Bree, horsiest of horses.

Prince Caspian

Prince Caspian: The Return to Narnia is its full title: fittingly, since in a number of ways the story is a reprise of that of *The Lion*. Once again Narnia is existentially threatened and the children are called to its aid; once again Lucy is disbelieved when she claims to have seen Aslan, who again appears only quite late in the book; again the girls get to ride on his back; there's a battle and a romp. All of this pleased me enormously when I was a child: it was just what I wanted, although Caspian's long back story tried my patience a little.

But you can never step in the same river twice and *Prince Caspian* is almost *about* that sad fact: about growing up and leaving things behind, and the changes wrought by time on people and places. Now I'm so much older it's the elegiac notes that speak to me: the irresistibly mournful music of Queen Susan's horn calling me back to a country where neither she nor I any longer really belong.

It begins so simply and well, with the four children sitting at the railway station waiting for the two trains which will separate them and take them away to school, always bad news in the Narnia stories. Lewis hadn't enjoyed his own schooldays. Then each child experiences a sudden unwelcome sensation. 'Lucy gave a sharp little cry, like someone who has been stung by a wasp.' A moment later Edmund too makes an exclamation. A surprised Peter turns on Susan and asks her to stop dragging him. Susan denies it; someone's been pulling *her* —

It's a horrible, shocking sensation. 'Everyone noticed that all the others' faces had gone very white.'

This brilliantly imagined magical summons is already very different from the easy passage through the wardrobe in *The Lion*. I don't know how Lewis managed to resist the temptation to have the children actually *hear* the far-off note of Queen Susan's magic horn, but he did, and they don't: and he was right. Tugged, jerked, dragged out of England, the children seize hands to keep together and are unceremoniously deposited in the middle of a thicket so dense they can hardly move for branches sticking into them. It's difficult and very uncomfortable, and it's going to keep on that way.

From Roland's to Boromir's there are many wondrous horns in literature, but Susan's seems derived from the horn of Oberon in the late medieval romance *Huon of Bordeaux*, a tale Lewis knew well. The knight Huon, journeying to Jerusalem, meets the fairy King Oberon in a magic wood: here we find both of Susan's gifts, the horn and her bow and arrows:

> [T]he dwarf of the fairies, King Oberon, came riding by ... He had a goodly bow in his hand, and his arrows after the same sort, and these had such a property that they could hit any beast in the world. Moreover, he had about his neck a rich horn, hung by two laces of gold

> ... and whosoever heard it, if he were a hundred days journey off, should come at the pleasure of him that blew it, far or near.[112]

Lewis is interested not in how it feels to blow such a horn, but what it's like to be *summoned* 'at the pleasure of him that blew it'. As Edmund later remarks, when a magician in the Arabian Nights calls up a Jinn, the Jinn has to come, and now they know what it feels like.

Struggling out of the trees, the Pevensies find themselves on a sea-shore which they greet with delight as a fine alternative to heading back to school on a train. They behave at first like the children they are, paddling and enjoying the unexpected treat, but before long they have eaten all their sandwiches and are thirsty. Exploring the shoreline they find they're on an island: here the narrative swerves briefly into shipwrecked-sailor mode, Lewis poking a little fun at 'Boys' Own' type adventures. Edmund suggests gathering gulls eggs – but there aren't any, nor do they have any means of cooking them. Susan says edgily that they shouldn't have eaten the sandwiches so soon. Tempers fray, till Edmund suggests they should explore the wood.

> 'Hermits and knight-errants and people like that always manage to live somehow if they're in a forest. They find roots and berries and things.'[113]

The children's responses have so far been either childish or derived from stories, but this reference to hermits and knight-errants heralds a change of tone and the discovery of

[112] Bourchier, John, Lord Berners, *Huon of Bordeaux*, 71-2
[113] *C* 13

the ruined castle, along with memories of the chivalric past which they once inhabited. Forget about paddling: they'll soon be engaged in a war.

Forcing their way through undergrowth into the wood, the children find an ancient apple orchard with an old wall and a gateway, and beyond the gateway a lawn of grass and daisies: 'a bright, secret, quiet space, and rather sad'. Susan makes the first discovery: she realises this isn't a garden, but the courtyard of an ancient castle. The others concur and Peter says he wishes they could know who lived in it, long, long ago. The place gives Lucy a strange feeling – as well it might, for the people who lived in the castle are they themselves, and this quiet ruin is the emotional heart of the book. The 'yellowish-golden' apples on the ancient trees come with memories of the Hesperides, the secret garden, Eden, the Golden Age – anywhere longed-for and lost. When the children do finally realise where they are, the realisation is laden with melancholy. This is Cair Paravel: but *their* Cair Paravel is gone for ever.

Exploring further through the ruins, the children enter what was the castle's great hall. Seeing a sort of terrace, Susan asks what it is, and Peter reminds her it's a dais where the king and lords would have sat. Has she forgotten how the four of them were once Kings and Queens?

> 'In our castle of Cair Paravel,' continued Susan in a dreamy and rather sing-song voice, 'at the mouth of the great river of Narnia. How could I forget?'[114]

It's such an ambiguous response. Susan may mean she hasn't and never could have forgotten – or it may mean she *had*

[114] PC 18

forgotten, and now wonders how. Why the word 'dreamy'; why 'singsong'? Have Susan's memories of Narnia begun to feel like dreams?

Alas, I never found my own way into Narnia. In a vivid dream though, I did once find myself in some other fantasy kingdom, with a band of companions trying to deflect a series of spells being shot, like filigree fireworks, from a grim castle across a wooded valley. All was going well until with a extraordinary sensation of *fading*, and hearing my startled companions exclaim, 'She's going – she's vanishing!' – I woke. I felt quite disturbed; I'd let them down. And I never got back. So here. It's as if Susan's presence in, her connection to Narnia, keeps fading in and out like a weak signal.

That connection is about to be temporarily strengthened. With night coming on, apples to eat, and well-water to quench their thirst, the children light a fire and make camp, still unaware of what this place really is. After a meal of raw apples, Susan goes to the well for another drink and comes back moved almost to tears, with something in her hand. She's found by the well a golden chess-knight with ruby eyes, and Lucy exclaims that it's identical to one of the chessmen they all used to play with, 'when we were Kings and Queens at Cair Paravel'.[115]

The chessman is significant. It is derived from a passage in the Icelandic tale *The Deluding of Gylfi* which tells how after the day of Ragnarok and the destruction of the Norse gods, the Aesir, a fresh green earth will rise from the sea. Baldur will return from death and the sons of the gods will sit in peace, talking together about hidden wisdom and remembering

[115] *PC* 20

the past: 'Then they will find there in the grass the golden chessmen the Aesir used to own ...'[116] In their new, changed world, the chessmen are the last scanty evidence of a race of vanished gods and heroes, and here in Narnia the same applies.

The emotional jolt of finding the little chess piece has called the past to vivid life for Susan. Delightful memories are now clear: she remembers games of chess with fauns, the mer-people singing in the sea, and her lovely horse ... And Peter suggests that impossible though it may seem given that only a year has passed since they left Narnia, they are standing in the ruins of Cair Paravel itself. This means there should be a door in the ivy-smothered wall behind them. Edmund probes with a stick, which strikes hollow-sounding wood. The boys and Lucy want to pull the ivy away, but Susan (who moments ago was dreaming of the past) strongly disagrees. She wouldn't feel safe spending the night beside an open door with a gaping dark hole behind it from which anything might emerge, 'besides,' she prosaically adds, 'the draught and the damp'.

Why does she switch so readily into negativity? Partly because she's not naturally a dreamy person: that's Lucy. Susan is the practical one who keeps the others real. But it's also to do with the dynamic of keeping four main characters 'alive' and distinguishable from one another. Stories are more dramatic when characters disagree, and the person who falls out with the others can't be Edmund; he took that role last time. Nor can it be Peter, who deviates hardly an inch from decent, fair-minded big brother and High King, and is consequently not very interesting. It can't be Lucy because

---

[116] The Deluding of Gylfi, *The Prose Edda*, 92

Lewis loves her and she's a shiningly 'good' character. That leaves Susan, and I feel that in many ways this is her book: she is certainly one of its more complex characters. Susan is gallant, a good swimmer and skilful archer, but she is also cautious and conventional. That is not necessarily a bad thing. She may be reluctant to change, or to believe, but she is also reluctant to hurt people's feelings, or to kill. If she doesn't always do the right thing, neither does she entirely fail, and when she points out the creepy, scary side of tearing down a rotten old door with no idea of what's behind it, she isn't being unreasonable. Needless to say, the others ignore her, but the job takes longer than they expect, and as they survey the black hole they've uncovered, none of them feel very comfortable.

Their exploration through the ruins has led them to the hidden room, and the revelation that awaits is 'the ancient treasure chamber of Cair Paravel' — important not for its value, but because it is treasure the children once owned, full of memories that confirm their place in this world. At Peter's suggestion, they take only the gifts they were given in *The Lion, The Witch and the Wardrobe*: Lucy's little diamond flask of healing cordial, Susan's bow and her ivory quiver full of arrows and Peter's sword and shield. All are still in their places. The only thing missing is Susan's horn, which she remembers was with her the day they hunted the White Stag. 'It must have got lost when we blundered back into that other place — England, I mean.'

'Blundered back into that other place' — just at this moment Susan is so fully engaged with Narnia that England has become an unreal dream-world whose name she can barely remember. Bending her bow she plucks the unperished string, and the evocative sound brings more memories

rushing back into the children's minds — memories 'of the old days', Lewis tells us, locating their experiences of just a year ago in a distant Narnian past. Peter draws his sword and holds it up, naming it: 'It is my sword Rhindon. With it I killed the Wolf.'

Now they know exactly who they are and where they are. As to *why* everything around them has changed so much, Edmund works it out the following morning: Narnian time doesn't flow at the same rate as time in our world, and the return of the four children is like that of Arthur, the Once and Future King who will wake when his land has need of him — or those less fortunate heroes who come back to find little trace of themselves in a world which has moved on.

There are many folktales and legends in which people step into fairy rings or disappear into a fairy kingdom for what seems a few hours or days, only to find on their return that a hundred or more years have passed, and no one now remembers them. Lewis would have been familiar with the twelfth-century story of King Herla, invited to a wedding by a goat-footed pygmy king who rules underground halls of unutterable splendour. After the celebrations the fairy king escorts Herla out of his kingdom:

> ... and then presented the king with a small blood-hound to carry, strictly enjoining him that on no account must any of his train dismount until that dog leapt from the arms of his bearer ... Within a short space Herla arrived once more at the light of the sun and at his kingdom, where he accosted an old shepherd and asked for news of his Queen, naming her. The shepherd gazed at him in astonishment and said: 'Sir, I can hardly understand your speech, for you are a Briton

and I a Saxon, but they say ... that long ago, there was a Queen of that name over the very ancient Britons, who was the wife of King Herla; and he, the story says, disappeared in company with a pigmy at this very cliff, and was never seen on earth again ...'[117]

Lewis has turned this around. England — the place they blundered back to, in Susan's words — becomes the unreal, fairy land. While they have spent a single year in England, hundreds or maybe a thousand Narnian years have sped by.

The book seldom again reaches the emotional depth of these passages in which a children's magical adventure unfolds into a poignant consideration of the mysteries of lost time. C. S. Lewis throws into the first thirty pages of *Prince Caspian* his own experience of *sehnsucht*, the stab of longing for something unattainable: his past. *Tell me where all past things are? Where beth they beforen us weren? Ou sont les neiges d'antan?* Children do ask profound questions about life, the universe and everything, and adults are frequently stumped. 'What would there be if there was nothing?' I asked my mother at about the same time I was reading these books. The Narnia stories were my introduction to all sorts of metaphysical thought-experiments. What if time ran at different speeds in different places? What if there were lots of different universes? What if a thing could be bigger on the inside than on the outside? It was exhilarating.

The children are still getting used to the idea that they've come 'back' to a future Narnia, and Lucy is exclaiming optimistically that people will be so excited to see them, when she is interrupted. A boat appears, rowed by armed

---

[117] Map, Walter, *De Nugis Curialium*, 13

men with a kind of bundle in the stern that jerks and kicks as if it's alive. Just as Peter realises this bundle is a trussed-up Dwarf who is about to be drowned, Susan's bow twangs. Her arrow strikes one of the soldiers on the helmet and he falls overboard. Though 'very pale', she's about to shoot again, but her decisive, unprompted action has done the job. The panicked soldiers (who believe the area to be haunted) flounder to the far shore and vanish into the trees, while Peter and Susan leap into the water to seize the boat and save the Dwarf — cheerful, capable Trumpkin who after a meal of fish and apples roasted in the embers, tells the children what has been happening in Narnia.

Now begins a fifty-page parenthesis, the history of Prince Caspian whose throne, like that of Hamlet's, has been usurped by the wicked uncle who murdered his father and under whose alien Telmarine rule the magic of Old Narnia has been suppressed. I am afraid I tapped my foot through much of this story when I was a child. I wanted to be with the Pevensies, not Caspian — who in this book was younger than me and seemed a bit of a baby. Bits of his back story I didn't get at all — names like 'Queen Prunaprismia' and jokes in dog-Latin aimed over my head, such as Caspian's grammar book written by one Pulverentulus Siccus. It felt rather too much like Thackeray's *The Rose and the Ring* — another version of Hamlet which now seems a lot funnier than it did when I tried to read it as a serious fairy tale aged eight or nine: full of puns, topical allusions and characters with names like Lady Gruffanuff and Captain Kutasov Hedzoff. Uneasily aware of jokes I didn't understand, I was never quite comfortable with *The Rose and the Ring*, and the court of King Miraz seemed similarly artificial. I see now that this is the perfect foil for the natural magic of Old Narnia. Back then, if I disliked a thing, I skipped it.

Since he and the Queen are childless, Miraz makes Caspian his heir and dismisses the old nurse for telling the boy stories of the old days when the woods were full of dryads, and four kings and queens reigned with the help of Aslan the great Lion. 'There's no such person as Aslan,' Miraz thunders as Caspian sobs – adding for good measure that lions don't exist and animals cannot talk. (I enjoyed the absurdity of this, given that the middle claim isn't true even in our world.) In place of his nurse, Caspian gets a tutor, Doctor Cornelius, who is small, bearded, fat, wise and kind.

Caspian learns from Cornelius more of the history of the current royal family than his Uncle Miraz would like. They came from Telmar beyond the Western Mountains (a previously unpeopled land of which we will never learn anything more) and invaded Narnia under Caspian I, 'the Conqueror': Cornelius hints that those he conquered were *not human*. Shortly after this he takes Caspian to the palace roof to see a rare conjunction of two planets. Wrapped against the cold, Caspian follows his tutor 'through many passages and up several staircases', out across the leads of the roof and up six floors into the dark spiral staircase of the castle's central tower.

And so we encounter another instance of that recurring motif of an exploration through an old house or castle, with a discovery – magical, marvellous or terrifying – at its end. Emerging into the open (yet still enclosed) space of the turreted tower roof, surrounded by a wide vista of night-time Narnia with two bright planets hanging in the southern sky, Caspian, like Hamlet on the battlements of Elsinore, is told something of the past and assumes a duty. The stories of

Old Narnia are true: this is not a land of men! It is Aslan's country: the home of 'Waking Trees', of naiads, fauns and centaurs, of dwarfs and giants and Talking Beasts, and the old god-like spirits of rivers. The Telmarine invaders killed, silenced, or drove them away, and tried to stamp out their very memory: a narrative of colonialism and suppression which seems surprisingly relevant.

Filled with regret for what his ancestors did, Caspian suddenly queries whether Cornelius himself is a Telmarine. He is — isn't he? Or at least, he's a Man? 'Am I?' Cornelius responds, flinging back his hood. And Caspian sees.

> Two thoughts came into his head at the same moment. One was a thought of terror — 'He's not a real man, not a man at all, he's a Dwarf, and he's brought me up here to kill me.' The other was sheer delight — 'There are real Dwarfs still, and I've seen one at last.'[118]

It's brilliantly honest — this involuntary thrill of fear as Caspian, brought up in a racist society even though he's imaginatively sympathetic, realises the Otherness of a person he has long known and trusted. *'Not a real man, not a man at all'* chimes with the warning Mr Beaver gave the children in *The Lion* to beware of things that look human but aren't. Cornelius means nothing but good, and has a sad history to relate of hate and prejudice. He himself is not a pure-blooded Dwarf. His ancestors were those Dwarfs who escaped the bloodshed by passing as humans, 'shaving their beards', wearing high shoes and mixing with the Telmarines. And he regretfully explains that because of this, any true Dwarfs left

[118] *PC* 49

in the world will probably despise him as a half-blood and a traitor.

In fact it seems as though the Telmarine regime has done even worse damage to Narnia's culture and traditions than that of the White Witch. Though her reign was despotic, it was specifically humans she wished to exclude from Narnia: fauns, dwarfs and Talking Beasts etc. not only survived, but if Tumnus and the Beavers are anything to go by, could live quite comfortably. The Telmarines are bent on eradicating Narnia's indigenous inhabitants, and the grotesque stratagems to which the Dwarfs are forced in order to pass and be treated as human, are a terrible indictment.

Soon after these revelations, Cornelius wakes Caspian to tell him his life is in danger. The Queen has borne a son and heir, and Miraz will seek to murder Caspian as he murdered his father — this last comes as shocking news to Caspian. Advising him to flee over the mountains to Archenland, Cornelius gives him Queen Susan's horn, a treasure to be blown only at greatest need.

As Caspian rides south alone through woods and over wild heaths, a storm rises and his horse bolts. Struck by a branch, he comes to his senses in the firelit cave of the dwarfs Nikabrik and Trumpkin, and Trufflehunter the Badger. It is no cosy awakening: the three are arguing whether to kill him (Nikabrik is in favour, the other two are against) and Caspian nearly screams when he realises the person giving him a hot drink is a non-human — is in fact a Badger. And the dwarfs seem wild and unsafe, 'ancient Dwarfs with not a drop of human blood in their veins.' It's very different from the warm welcome the Beavers gave to the Pevensies in *The Lion*. As Nikabrik remarks a few days later, if they can't trust Caspian enough to let him go, then killing him would actually be kinder than keeping him prisoner for life – the only other option. And Nikabrik doesn't trust easily.

Nikabrik is a Black Dwarf, which seems to mean not only that his hair and beard are black, but that he has a harder nature than the Red Dwarf Trumpkin. It's perhaps a pity that all Black Dwarfs seem to be dodgy customers, but because we know the history of oppression visited on his race, Nikabrik is by no means a totally unsympathetic character. We understand where he's coming from, though he hates very readily. 'A renegade Dwarf ... I hate 'em worse than Humans,' he says, apparently wedded to a racist theory of pure blood. He initially refers to Caspian as 'it', and later suggests killing Doctor Cornelius: 'A half-and-halfer! Shall I pass my sword through its throat?'

But I notice Trumpkin uses the same disparaging language, even as he attempts to silence Nikabrik: 'Be quiet ... the creature can't help its ancestry.' It's left to Caspian, maturing rapidly, to defend Cornelius in no uncertain terms: 'This is my greatest friend and the saviour of my life. And anyone who doesn't like his company may leave my army at once.'

The still-recent Second World War afforded plenty of examples of race-based hatred and ethnic cleansing, but I do wonder whether as an Irishman Lewis may also have had the recent history of his own country in mind: the struggle for Irish independence marked by the 1916 Easter Rising and its brutal suppression, the Irish War of Independence fought in 1919-21, and the even bloodier Irish Civil War of 1922-3. The three Old Narnians are carefully differentiated. Trufflehunter is a faithful believer who reverences Caspian as his true, divinely appointed King. Trumpkin is a cheerful sceptic who offers Caspian the practical service of a soldier.

Nikabrik is a passionate, narrowly focused rebel with no use for anything or anyone unless it will further the cause. He has in Yeats' words, 'a fanatic heart' and is prepared (barely) to tolerate Caspian for the sole purpose of destroying the Telmarine regime. Nikabrik is a study in miniature of the psychological damage caused by injustice. I always felt sorry for him, as Lewis clearly intends.

Once convinced of Caspian's credentials and good intentions, the three allow him to stay and introduce him to the hidden people of Old Narnia: fauns, dwarfs and Talking Beasts (including Reepicheep!) but no tree or water spirits: the land itself remains unwoken. At a council of war held at Dancing Lawn, Doctor Cornelius himself brings news that Miraz's troops are searching for Caspian. He advises a retreat to the great woods and the shelter of Aslan's How, ancient site of the Stone Table — which has changed considerably since the days of the White Witch. It is now a round green hill with a single, low doorway and stone-lined tunnels on which are graven 'strange characters and snaky patterns'.

Aslan's How is unmistakeably modelled on the magnificent Neolithic passage grave of Newgrange, Brú na Bóinne, in Ireland's County Meath. I don't know if Lewis ever visited Newgrange; he might have known of it from photos, but from the early 1900s when the entrance was cleared, it became possible to walk down the stone-lined passage to the central chamber and view its elaborately carved spirals and chevrons. The altered structure of the Stone Table not only suggests the great span of elapsed time since the events of *The Lion*, it situates the story in an Irish landscape and supports my proposal that Nikabrik's hatred for the Telmarines owes something to the Irish sectarian divisions of which Lewis, an Ulsterman, cannot possibly have been unaware.

The How is less a refuge than a trap. The fighting goes badly, and when a last-ditch stratagem ends in disaster, Caspian and his close advisors gather in the heart of the How to discuss their last chance: Queen Susan's horn. All agree it should be used, but as they cannot be sure at which significant spot help may arrive, they send Pattertwig the Squirrel to Lantern Waste, and Trumpkin to the site of Cair Paravel.

Trumpkin's story ends as he describes how he blundered into a check-point and was taken prisoner. At last the children know how they were brought here, and why. First though, since Trumpkin accepts they're the four ancient kings and queens but dismisses them as mere kids, they arrange a quick contest in which to prove themselves.

Of course they do brilliantly; as a child myself I liked this bit very much. Edmund quickly disarms Trumpkin in a fencing match. Susan bests him at archery even though she's 'so tender-hearted that she almost hated to beat someone who had been beaten already'. When Lucy finally heals a wound on Trumpkin's shoulder with a drop of her cordial, the Dwarf is fully convinced of their worth as allies, and they set out at once for Aslan's How, which Edmund reckons they should reach by next morning if they row up the coast. It is hard, hot work. Most of the party fall fast asleep that night. But Lucy remains awake.

Now comes a half-visionary experience. She lies thrilling to the once-familiar sight of the bright Narnian stars. As the moon rises she gets up to walk among the trees, remembering with longing the days when they were alive and talked to her. She speaks to them, conjuring them to remember her, remember the past and wake. It's a powerful, emotionally charged invocation, though all they do is stir and rustle. Lucy feels 'as if she had spoken to the trees a split second too soon or a split second too late, or used all the right words except one, or put in one word that was just wrong.'[119]

I love that. Lewis is good at pinning down subtleties of feeling.

Next morning is grey and miserable: there's nothing to eat but apples, and no one is quite sure which way to go. The children's lived experience of Narnia on this visit is mainly of hunger and discomfort: no shelter, no marmalade rolls, no trays of hot tea. Little wonder they get snappy. 'I thought all along we should have gone by the river,' says Susan, with her tendency to say *I told you so*. Then a wild bear charges from the bushes and knocks Lucy down. Trumpkin has to shoot it; Susan hesitates too long, afraid it might have been a Talking Bear. While the boys and Trumpkin skin and butcher the carcass and make up parcels of meat, this encounter triggers an odd exchange between the girls. Lucy tells Susan of a horrible thought she has had:

'Wouldn't it be dreadful if some day, in our own world, at home, men started going wild inside, like the animals here, and still looked like men, so that you'd never know which were which?'[120]

Susan sensibly tells her sister there's enough going on at the moment without finding more to be worrying about. It is

[119] *PC* 105/6
[120] *PC* 109

quite a thought, though. It makes you stop. The Narnia books are at least as much about ideas as events and here we're back with Mr Beaver again, thinking about 'things that look human but aren't'. In *The Princess and Curdie*, George MacDonald's sequel to *The Princess and the Goblin*, there is a passage which may have been in Lewis's mind. Curdie bathes his hands in the old princess's fire of roses and gains the power to tell 'when a man is growing into a beast' by feeling the beast's hoof or paw within the human hand. The old princess tells him:

> '[It] is always what they do, whether in their minds or their bodies, that makes men go down to be less than men, that is, beasts ... They do not know it, of course; for a beast does not know that he is a beast, and the nearer a man gets to being a beast the less he knows it. ... But there are not a few who feel something repulsive in the hand of a man who is growing a beast.'[121]

Lucy's 'horrible idea' is triggered by Susan's worry about whether the bear was a rational creature — and forms part of Lewis's ongoing consideration of what happens to the humanity of those who do terrible things.

Susan's scruples about the bear and her dislike of killing do her credit, as does her practical dismissal of Lucy's fears: who wants their little sister worrying about such disturbing things? As the day goes on though, she grows impatient and grumpy. The river, when they come to it, runs in a deep gorge they can't cross. Susan complains she knew they'd get lost, and as they decide to try going downstream, Lucy suddenly cries with a shining face that she's seen Aslan!

---

[121] MacDonald, George, *The Princess and Curdie*, 67

The others haven't, though, and they are sceptical. Lucy gets snappy when Susan asks, not where Aslan *was,* but where Lucy *thought* he was. And unfortunately for her, this visionary Aslan whom nobody else has seen wants them to head in the opposite direction from the one they've chosen. Only Edmund supports her, so she is voted down. With Susan driving them 'to get *on* and finish it and get out of these beastly woods' they come in sight of the Bridge of Beruna — only to be driven back by a flight of Telmarine arrows. It has been a wasted journey. They have to retrace their steps.

In camp that night Lucy hears someone calling her, and gets up to see the trees moving, wading through the earth in a sort of sleeping dance — a gradual awakening that never quite happens. Joining the dance she weaves between them to find Aslan waiting for her in a moonlit glade. Filled with joy Lucy flings herself on him, hugging as much of him as she can reach and burying her face his mane.

Here at last is the Aslan of *The Lion*: tactile, physical, bracing, loving. He sets Lucy a task she should already have performed: she must wake the others and insist that this time they follow him. If they won't, she is to follow him alone. Lucy shakes her brothers and sister awake and gives them this ultimatum: but still they cannot see Aslan. It's a test not so much of faith as of simple belief. Susan reacts with the brisk anger of an adult needlessly disturbed: in her view Lucy is simply being naughty. Edmund points out that Lucy was right before. Trumpkin says he will fall in with whatever the others decide, but adds scathingly that he has 'no use for magic lions which are talking lions but don't talk, and friendly lions though they don't do us any good, and whopping big lions though nobody can see them.'[122] As Peter rather grudgingly agrees to do what Lucy wants, Susan becomes even more difficult. If Lucy can throw her weight about and threaten to go off alone, why shouldn't she, Susan, threaten to stay right here? In an implied rebuke, Trumpkin reminds her of her rank. 'Obey the High King, your Majesty,' he says, 'and let's be off.'[123]

Her behaviour is hardly a match for Edmund's betrayal in *The Lion*, but this is Susan's lowest point and I actually love it: so natural, so recognisable, so irritating – seesawing between a developing maturity and a childishness which as the eldest sister perhaps she's never allowed herself. Is it because she's always been the sensible, responsible one that she's suddenly so self-indulgent? She keeps right on making a fuss as they all follow Lucy (following Aslan) down the gorge, across the river and up the other side. One by one, as they do so, they begin to see Aslan for themselves. When Susan does, she admits it at once and apologises to Lucy. Deep down inside, she confesses, she really did believe all along that Aslan was there.

> 'Or I could have, if I'd let myself. But I just wanted to get out of the woods and – and – oh, I don't know. And whatever am I to say to him?'
>
> 'Perhaps you won't need to say much,' suggested Lucy.[124]

It is a very good apology, full of self-knowledge. Perhaps she *doesn't* need to say much. Aslan tells her she has listened

---

[122] *PC* 131
[123] Ibid
[124] *PC* 134

to fears — this I find puzzling, and not something the text supports — and breathes on her. 'Are you brave again?' he asks. 'A little, Aslan,' says Susan. Perhaps she finds him puzzling too.

All are greeted and forgiven, although Aslan teases Trumpkin by pouncing on him and shaking him. Philip Pullman might judge this sadistic, but I thought it was very funny when I was nine: after all, Trumpkin's said some quite rude things about lions, and however alarming it may be for the Dwarf, the children can see perfectly well that Aslan likes him. It's not a very Christ-like thing to do, but Aslan's a lion and this might well suit a lion's sense of humour.

With the How in plain sight, Aslan sends Trumpkin and the boys into the mound to deal with what they will find there. Then — as he did hundreds of years before beside the broken Stone Table — he roars. We're given a wonderful glimpse of the river god and naiads rising from the waters to listen. In Miraz's camp the soldiers shiver, while far off in the northern wilds, giants peer from their castle gates. Last of all, the trees finally wake, rushing to greet Aslan in their human shapes. Amid grapes and vines, Bacchus and his Maenads appear and a wild romp begins which lasts till sunrise.

Under Aslan's How, Trumpkin and the boys track through dark tunnels where they ponder the age of the carved marks on the walls in the strange knowledge, says Edmund, that he and Peter are even older. Approaching the central chamber, they hear voices raised in angry argument. Nikabrik has lost all faith in the Horn. No help has arrived, and since desperate times call for desperate remedies he has brought two 'friends' into the Council. One seems to be an old woman who claims she knows a few spells and is good at hating. The other, who sounds to be a man, memorably boasts in 'a dull grey voice':

'Where I bite, I hold till I die ... I can lie a hundred nights on the ice and not freeze. I can drink a river of blood and not burst. Show me your enemies.'[125]

The pair are really a Hag and a Wer-Wolf, who plan to raise the White Witch from the dead and set her on the Telmarines. Caspian objects, Nikabrik shrieks at him, and a fight erupts. The boys and Trumpkin rush to help, the light is knocked over, and it's all 'swords, teeth, claws, fists and boots for about sixty seconds.' Edmund strikes a light and they see their enemies lying dead. Peter comments that the Wer-Wolf must have been changing from man to wolf just as he was killed. Caspian gazes at Nikabrik with sadness, recognising that the dwarf had been soured by 'long suffering and hating. If we had won quickly he might have become a good Dwarf in the days of peace ...'[126] It is a fair and poignant valediction.

Peter now sets about righting Caspian's fortunes. Since the Narnian army isn't strong enough to meet Miraz in pitched battle, he challenges Miraz to single combat, and recalling to mind the style he had used in Narnia's golden age, he dictates to Cornelius a splendid piece of mock-Elizabethan prose, charging Miraz with two counts of treachery,

> *'... in withholding the dominion of Narnia from the said Caspian and in the most abominable,* − don't forget to spell it with an H, Doctor − *bloody and unnatural murder of your kindly lord and brother, Caspian, Ninth of that name ...'*[127]

[125] *PC* 146
[126] *PC* 152
[127] *PC* 156

I guessed as a child that 'abhominable' was an old-fashioned spelling. It is: but more than that, Peter insists on the word 'abominable' being spelled with an H because the archaic form derives from Latin *ab + homin*: 'not human'. His deeds, Peter implies, make Miraz no better than the Wer-Wolf. He may look like a man but he is a lawless beast inside.

Carrying green branches in token of a parley, Edmund delivers the challenge with marshalls Giant Wimbleweather and Glenstorm the Centaur. Miraz has no reason to accept it, but two lords envious of his power, Glozelle and Sopespian, make sure he does. I'm not sure where Sopespian's name comes from (perhaps there's a suggestion of sophistry?), but the name Glozelle is derived from the Middle English verb 'to gloze' which means to deceitfully flatter, or put a false complexion on things. The pair deliberately infuriate Miraz by suggesting he is no match for either Edmund or Peter, and that cowardice is excusable in a man of his age. Flinging the insult back at Glozelle, Miraz storms out to accept Peter's challenge.

The set-piece combat is a close-run thing. The lists are remarkable for being surrounded not only by the two armies but by hundreds of the beautiful towering forms of dryads and hamadryads and silvans woken by Aslan, though as Trumpkin says, their presence will do nothing to assist Peter if Miraz proves the stronger swordsman. This is almost the case: in fierce combat Peter is hard pressed, receiving some near-crippling blows until Miraz trips and falls. Peter steps nobly back to let him rise, but the two traitor lords leap into the lists crying that he has stabbed Miraz. In fact Glozelle stabs his king, while Sopespian rushes at Peter. At this treachery both armies now pour into the field and battle is joined. The Giant swings his club, the Centaurs charge,

Reepicheep and his mice leap about stabbing at Telmarine feet. As the Trees plunge into the fray, roaring like woods in a gale, the Telmarines flee towards the Bridge of Beruna, hoping to barricade themselves in the town. But the bridge is gone! In total disarray, they surrender.

The bridge is gone because of what Aslan, Bacchus and the Maenads have been doing. Early that morning, in a reprise of their ride across Narnia in *The Lion*, the girls are invited by Aslan to jump on his back, and with the Maenads tumbling alongside they race down to the river and the bridge. Here the dripping, bearded head of the river god rises from the ripples and greets Aslan as 'Lord'. He is a god with a small 'g', one of the elemental nature spirits described by the Renaissance philosopher Paracelsus. As such, he is Aslan's subject and creature, not his rival: which is how we should view the entire Bacchanal. 'Loose my chains,' the river-god begs. At Aslan's command, Bacchus and his wild girls splash into the river and ivy smothers the piers of the bridge, splitting stone from stone. Lucy and Susan cheer as it collapses into the water, and they all wade and dance across the re-made ford and into the town — where people flee from them.

Lewis introduces these wild revellers into Narnia (Susan and Lucy have already agreed they wouldn't feel safe if they'd met them without Aslan) because the story requires the Telmarine regime not merely to be defeated, but for all visible signs of it to be torn down and for the natural magic of Narnia to be set free. It's bound to be a bit scary. The worship of Bacchus or Dionysos involved ecstatic frenzy and tapped into the darkness of human nature, the id rather than the ego: in Greek legend the Maenads tear Orpheus to pieces. Aslan is in charge here, directing the verdant energy of Bacchus and his troop to good outcomes: but the means are destructive, and for me there's an uncomfortable mismatch between what we're meant to see as release and restoration, and what actually happens. (What after all is wrong with a nice stone bridge? And how is it worse for the river god than the Beavers' dam?)

In *The Lion*, Aslan's joyful gallop with Lucy and Susan through the springtime Narnian woods was sheer delight, culminating in the return to life and freedom of the Witch's stone prisoners. The exuberant romp with Bacchus and the wild girls in *Prince Caspian*, which seems so closely to resemble it, turns out on examination to include a dark streak of vengeance. The first house in town is a girls' school. Yes, the girls are dressed in tight, uncomfortable uniforms and are being badly taught (Lewis *never* has anything good to say about schools) but there's an edge of cruelty in the way Aslan frightens them and their teacher. As he roars, ivy invades the classroom, and only one child stands her ground as the teacher Miss Prizzle screams and runs – 'and with her fled her class, who were mostly dumpy, prim little girls with fat legs. Gwendolen hesitated.'

By disassociation we are led to assume that in contrast to the fat legged, dumpy little girls, Gwendolen is slender and pretty – and *therefore* good, brave, open-minded? Guilty of fat legs or not, Gwendolen joins Aslan's wild troupe. This passage has not stood the test of time very well, and neither has its companion piece a page later, in which Aslan terrifies a classroom of nasty little boys who jump out of the window and turn into piglets, as Circe transformed Ulysses's crew. We are meant to understand that the boys deserve this because they have been tormenting their tired young teacher whom Aslan welcomes and addresses as 'Dear Heart' – but the general air of 'serves 'em right' leaves a bad taste.

I'm forced to admit that I enjoyed it immensely when I was nine. I was sure that if I'd been in that classroom, I'd have been Gwendolen, and I didn't bother to wonder whether my own legs would have passed muster. And I thought the mean, nasty boys deserved everything they got. Who wants schools in Narnia, who needs bridges? If you can't cross a river in spate, too bad! A bacchanal is about tearing down structures, solid or social, in an explosion of emotional energy. If Aslan's really in charge here, he's definitely not being a tame lion ... Still, there's a nice moment when he restores Caspian's faithful old nurse to health and brings her, accompanied by much merriment, singing and dancing, to meet Caspian at the place where Miraz's army have surrendered.

Peter presents Caspian to Aslan, who confirms him as King of Narnia, Lord of Cair Paravel and Emperor of the Lone Islands. They are then interrupted by a sad little procession of Talking Mice, carrying their heroic leader Reepicheep on a litter, terribly wounded, with a crushed paw and 'where his tail had been, a bandaged stump.' Though Lucy is able to heal him as she healed Edmund after the battle with the White Witch, it's a reminder that the Narnia books continue to be fairly graphic about wounds and physical damage. It takes many drops from her diamond bottle before the Mouse is able to spring to his feet, twirl his whiskers and bow. Just as he's greeting Aslan, however, he makes the terrible discovery that his tail is still missing! Lucy's cordial could heal, but not re-grow it.

Aslan views Reepicheep's dismay as a vanity, and refuses to restore the lopped-off tail until he sees the other mice preparing to cut off their tails too, in solidarity with their brave leader. At this, remembering the kindness of the mice who nibbled away the cords that bound him on the Stone Table (he might have remembered too that his own mane grew back), Aslan relents. Reepicheep gets a new tail, knighthoods and offices are bestowed, a bonfire is lit, a feast is prepared and celebrations go on late into the night.

From now on, Narnia will belong to all its creatures, not just the humans. Any Telmarine who chooses to stay may do so, but those who don't — significantly, 'most of the older men' — are given a choice to leave. In a woodland glade Aslan has set up a wooden frame, two uprights and lintel, like a doorway leading nowhere; this, he tells them, is the way back to their country of origin in another world: the Pevensies' world, our world. Like Fletcher Christian's mutineers on the *Bounty*, their ancestors were pirates driven to a tropical island where (in another brief glimpse of the unpleasant ways colonisers feel at liberty to behave) they 'killed the natives and took the native women as wives'. Then they quarrelled amongst themselves until some who escaped into the mountains found a crack or 'chasm' leading from that world to Narnia. (Why it's there remains mysterious, and Aslan seems to suggest there are others.) The island they left is now unpopulated. Will they go back?

The first volunteer walks between the doorposts and vanishes. His apparent annihilation terrifies the other Telmarines. 'If you want us to believe in it,' says one, 'why doesn't one of *you* go?'

At this, Peter suddenly turns to Edmund. 'Our time's up,' he says, and as Edmund asks bewilderedly what he can mean, Susan takes charge and tells her younger brother and sister to come into the trees and change their Narnian clothes for their school uniforms. Not only must the children set an example to the Telmarines by going through the Door to their own world, but Susan and Peter have been talking with Aslan, who has told them they will not be coming back to Narnia. They are growing too old.

Too old for Narnia! This was a crushing blow; I was almost as dismayed as Lucy and Edmund. 'Can you bear it?' Lucy asks, but Peter thinks he can. 'You'll understand when it comes to your last time.' Susan doesn't comment further herself, but her grown-up manner seems for the first time to be absolutely right. And she presents her horn to Caspian — for, though Lewis unfortunately makes it sound little more than a polite gesture, it is actually hers to give. Queen Susan's horn began this adventure, and now that she is leaving Narnia never to return she seems composed, as if she knows what she's doing.

Ignoring the Telmarines who jeer at their school clothes, the children say goodbye to their friends and — 'wonderfully and terribly' — to Aslan. As they pass in line through the Door they briefly see three places at once: the 'glaring green and blue of an island in the Pacific' where the Telmarines will go, the Narnian glade they are leaving, and 'the grey, gravelly surface' of the railway platform, and the seat where they find themselves sitting as though they had never left.

It might reasonably be asked just exactly what it was that Aslan brought the four Pevensies into Narnia to do, this time? What is their actual, narrative function, and how have they affected anything? Exciting though it is, Peter's challenge to Miraz is ultimately a failure that ends in the very wholesale battle he had hoped to avoid. It is rather the intervention of the Awakened Trees, so reminiscent of the march of the Ents in *The Lord of the Rings*, that saves the day for the native Narnians, and one assumes Aslan could have roused the trees whenever he wished. Susan and Lucy simply go along for the ride.

Or do they? As Peter says at one point, 'We don't know when [Aslan] will act. In his time, no doubt, not ours. In the meantime, he would like us to do what we can on our own.'

And isn't that the whole function of the Church?

I would still say that the long backstory in the middle of the book is structurally awkward and takes us away from the Pevensies for too long. For all that, this is a rich story with characters more developed and nuanced than in *The Lion* and with some unforgettable moments: Susan's discovery of the chessman in the ruins of Cair Paravel, Lucy *almost* waking the trees as she dances through the moonlit wood, Caspian's flash of mingled terror and joy at discovering Cornelius is a Dwarf ...

And of course, the first appearance of one of Narnia's greatest characters, the chivalrous and martial Reepicheep.

The Voyage of the Dawn Treader

I have two very different personal memories relating to this book. One is from childhood, vividly happy against a background of family drama. The other is from a time when I was a young adult working in London, and it still makes me cringe.

The childhood one first: late one night I woke to hear my parents criss-crossing the landing and my eight year-old brother crying in the next bedroom. Calling out, I was told to be good, my brother was poorly, go back to sleep. Next morning I found he'd been rushed to hospital during the night. At a children's party the previous week, the little boys had played at fitting the spiky sticks from cocktail sausages into drinking straws, then puffing them across the room like darts from a blow-pipe. Instead of blowing, however, my little brother inhaled; the cocktail stick flew down his throat and somehow he swallowed it. He hadn't wanted to explain this in detail to my mother, as he thought she'd be cross. It went right down inside and perforated his intestine, and since the wooden stick didn't show up on X-rays, the surgeon had to perform a major operation to find it. I've never felt comfortable around cocktail sticks since.

My brother remained in hospital for some time. Visiting rules in those days were strict and I wasn't allowed to see him, so I didn't realise what an awful time he was having, but I *did* notice he was (quite deservedly) being deluged with treats, toys and other goodies from friends and relations. To keep me quiet, my parents bought me the book I'd been longing for, the only Narnia book I hadn't yet read, *The Voyage of the Dawn Treader*. While they visited my brother I curled up in an armchair – I can still feel its bristly upholstery on my bare legs – and was swept away into an open-air world drenched in light – the light of sunrise over the sea, the quiet sunlit passages of the Magician's House, sunbeams slanting through the green waters of the undersea world, birds flying out of the rising sun to the table of the Three Sleepers, the almost painful light of the Silver Sea. Like Lucy as she watches the crimson sun setting behind the ship and dreams of the unknown Eastern lands ahead, I felt I was 'almost too happy to speak'.[128]

Now for the second memory. I'm in my early twenties, chatting to a colleague, Richard. For some reason we are talking about the Narnia books, which he has never read but on my recommendation is willing to try. Which ones are the best? 'Oh,' I say, 'my favourites are *The Silver Chair* and *The Voyage of the Dawn Treader*. I can even quote the beginning of that one.' And I do: '"There was a boy called Eustace Clarence Scrubb, and he almost deserved it."' Richard starts to smile and I continue from memory: '"He didn't call his father and mother 'Father' and 'Mother', but Harold and Alberta.

---

[128] *VDT* 27

They were vegetarians, non-smokers and teetotallers, and wore a special kind of underclothes."' Richard's smile vanishes. He says stiffly, flushing, 'I call my parents by their first names, as it happens, and I'm a vegetarian too.'

And so I learned, not before time, at least to *try* and think before I speak. (Richard, if you ever read this, I'm sorry!) Why hadn't I noticed? Could Lewis truly have believed that a dislike of tobacco, alcohol and meat made a person into some kind of prissy, unimaginative bore? I fear he could. Sigh.

The Voyage of the Dawn Treader doesn't become the book I fell in love with until the story and the ship get beyond the Lone Islands. There are rather too many unexamined value judgements going on before then. I don't know if I need to pick them all apart, but how about this, on only the second page of the story, where we learn why Edmund and Lucy are staying with their cousin Eustace at all. Peter, it seems, is being coached for an exam by the old Professor. The children's parents are going to America and taking Susan with them:

> Grown-ups thought her the pretty one of the family and she was no good at school work (though otherwise very old for her age) and Mother said she 'would get far more out of a trip to America than the youngsters.'[129]

'Pretty', 'no good at school work' and 'very old for her age' – a euphemism for sexual precocity – this, not *The Last Battle*, is the book in which Lewis dismisses Susan, and he never gives her another chance. Susan's trip to America, though

[129] *VDT* 8

sanctioned by her mother, is viewed by Lewis as a dangerous frivolity, and what she will 'get out of it' is — to use an old term of religious disapproval — *worldliness*. Why a liking for lipstick and nylons should be more *worldly* than a taste for tobacco and beer I don't know, but this is farewell to the Susan of old — Susan the archer and swimmer, the practical, sensible one, the girl who didn't enjoy beating Trumpkin because he been beaten already, the person who at the end of *Prince Caspian* appears to have found a fitting and proper maturity. It's all very silly.

Back to Eustace, who has overheard Lucy and Edmund talking about a picture hanging in Lucy's room, of what looks very much like a Narnian ship. On a visit to his cousins the previous year he had caught them talking together about Narnia, and now enjoys making fun of what he assumes to be silly childish make-belief — for Lewis comments that 'he was far too stupid to make anything up himself'.

Given that the next thing Eustace does is make up a limerick, I don't know that it's fair to call him stupid, but he certainly is very irritating. He nags Lucy about the picture and why she likes it, and she tells him it's because it looks real, as if the ship is moving, as if the waves are really going up and down — and the next moment, they are. A wind blows into the room and 'a great, cold, salt splash' breaks out of the frame and soaks them. Eustace rushes to break the picture, Edmund and Lucy spring to drag him back. Next thing all three are teetering on the frame and are swept into the sea. Another effortlessly brilliant transfer into Narnia has been accomplished.

They are rescued by Caspian, three years older than when we saw him last, who dives from the ship with a rope and manages to get them all hauled dripping on board. Lucy and Edmund greet him with delight, but the shocked and frightened Eustace rushes to the ship's side, as if expecting to see the picture frame suspended above the sea — a wonderfully surreal image which Lewis conjures up only to immediately dismiss: nothing like that is visible in the Narnian sky; and isn't Eustace silly? This deftly does away with any question in the reader's mind about what happens to the portal: after all, Lucy could still see the wardrobe behind her once she'd entered Narnia, but this time the children will not be going back by the way they came. Given the incredible thing which has just happened, though, Eustace can hardly be blamed for looking — nor that, seeing nothing but sea and sky, the poor boy is promptly sick.

Gauche and ungracious, he begins as he means to go on. It's very funny and a little unfair: he spits out his delicious mouthful of hot spiced wine and demands 'Plumptree's Vitaminized Nerve Food', which sounds comically horrible. Next, he makes the mistake of insulting Reepicheep the Mouse, made to sound here as magnificent and dangerous as Sir Walter Raleigh:

> A thin band of gold passed around its head under one ear and over the other and in this was stuck a long crimson feather ... Its left paw rested on the hilt of a sword very nearly as long as its tail.[130]

Wailing that he hates mice and performing animals, Eustace almost provokes an immediate duel, but Caspian hurries them all below to find dry clothing — and gives up his cabin to Lucy for the duration of the voyage, an utterly desirable

---

[130] *VDT* 16

room with three stern-windows overlooking the ship's wake, a silver lamp hanging from the ceiling, a gold image of Aslan, and bright, panelled walls painted with all kinds of wonderful beasts and 'crimson dragons and vines'. I wanted it badly. No wonder Lucy feels she is in for a lovely time.

Introducing his captain Lord Drinian, Caspian explains the purpose of the voyage. All is currently well in Narnia, so leaving the dwarf Trumpkin as his regent, he has set out to fulfil an oath sworn at his coronation to sail east for a year and a day in search of the seven lords, friends of his father, whom his uncle Miraz sent to explore 'the unknown Eastern Seas beyond the Lone Islands' and who never returned. 'But,' he adds, 'Reepicheep here has an even higher hope.'

Reepicheep's hope is to find Aslan's country itself, at the eastern end of the world — something as ungraspable and holy as the Grail — and fulfil the mysterious words spoken by a Dryad over his cradle, which have haunted him all his life:

> *'Where sky and water meet,*
> *Where the waves grow sweet,*
> *Doubt not, Reepicheep,*
> *To find all you seek,*
> *There is the utter East.'*[131]

The *Dawn Treader*, a beauty from her gilded dragonhead to her curling tail, is already four hundred leagues out from Narnia, having passed Galma, Terebinthia and the Seven Isles (places on the Narnian map I would have loved to have known more about). The Lone Islands lie ahead, after which they will literally be in uncharted waters. Caspian offers to show them over the ship and begins by taking Lucy and Edmund to the

[129] *VDT* 21

cabin under the poop, almost below the waterline, where Eustace is lying, green with seasickness. Lucy cures him with a drop of her cordial, which Caspian has brought with him, but the ungrateful Eustace despises the little ship and makes a bad start worse by grabbing Reepicheep's tail and swinging him around by it as a 'joke'. He has picked on the wrong Mouse. Even upside down, Reepicheep manages to draw his sword. He sticks Eustace in the hand with it, bounces to the deck, rights himself and — brandishing the skewer-like rapier at Eustace's stomach level — demands satisfaction. In response the alarmed Eustace merely splutters and blusters, so Reepicheep deals him several stinging blows with the side of the sword.

There are two ways of looking at this: the chivalric way and the schoolboy way. From Reepicheep's point of view, Eustace has insulted him and honour must be restored by fighting a duel. Eustace doesn't understand this: he has acted like a nasty schoolboy, bullying someone smaller than himself — or what may be worse, tormenting an animal. I was quite happy to see Eustace 'catching it' for his bad behaviour, but Lewis compounds his odd relationship with schools by commenting that the sensation of being beaten is new to Eustace since he goes to a school without corporal punishment. The inescapable inference is that more beatings would have done Eustace good. (There really seems no way for schools to do anything right in the Narnia series.) Anyway, Eustace is forced to apologise — and sulks.

First landfall for the children is the three Lone Islands, Avra, Felimath and Doorn, which Edmund and Lucy remember from the days of Peter the High King. (I lovingly copied Pauline Baynes' map of these islands and touched them in with red, blue and yellow poster-paint.)

THE VOYAGE OF THE DAWN TREADER

The ship steers for the port of Newhaven on Doorn, but Caspian orders a boat to land him, the two Pevensies, the Mouse and Eustace (who longs to get off the 'blasted boat') on lonely Felimath, where they can stretch their legs and be picked up on the other side. Once out of sight of the ship, they are unluckily overpowered by a party of slavers and marched to a village on the shore. While the others are taken to the slaver's ship to be sold in Newhaven next morning, Caspian is bought by a local Lord who has seen in his face a resemblance to his father, King Caspian IX of Narnia. Seizing the chance, Caspian declares he *is* the King of Narnia, and proves it:

> 'I know within six guesses who you are. You are one of those seven lords of Narnia whom my Uncle Miraz sent to sea and whom I have come to look for — Argoz, Bern, Octesian, Restimar, Mavramorn — or — or — I have forgotten the others ...'[132]

It is a standing joke that Caspian can never remember all of the names. Lord Bern, for it is he, is convinced and kneels to kiss the King's hand. As the Dawn Treader comes rounding the point, Caspian and Bern board her, and knowing they have but a small force, send a series of signals to imaginary ships so that the islands' corrupt ruler, Governor Gumpas, will suppose Caspian to have a large fleet at his command. Next morning Bern, Caspian and Drinian arrive in Newhaven with a small troop of fifty men and depose Gumpas. (The moment when Bern and Drinian overturn Gumpas's table in 'a cascade of letters, dossiers, ink-pots, sealing-wax and

---

[132] *VDT* 40

documents,' has a money-changers-in-the-Temple vibe.) Making Bern the Duke of the Lone Islands, Caspian bans the slave trade and rescues his friends from the slave market. All have been sold except Eustace (whom nobody wanted to buy), but no one has yet been taken away. As Caspian sets them free, two Calormene merchants approach him, hoping to regain the money they have paid. Since *The Voyage of the Dawn Treader* was written earlier than *The Horse and His Boy*, this is Lewis's first description of people from that land.

> The Calormen have dark faces and long beards. They wear flowing robes and orange-coloured turbans, and they are a wise, wealthy, courteous, cruel and ancient people.[133]

'Wise, wealthy, courteous and ancient' is all very well until we reach that word 'cruel': in its company all other adjectives are contaminated. Their polite, elaborate compliments to Caspian are implicitly critiqued as insincere. Slave-owning people with dark faces, beards and turbans: as a thumbnail sketch of Calormen culture it is a discouraging one.

Eustace of course is as ungrateful for his rescue as he is for everything else. On his release he marches up to Caspian and accuses him of having been enjoying himself while the rest of them were in durance vile. 'I suppose you haven't even found out about the British Consul,' he adds absurdly. 'Of course not.'

Yes, Eustace is spoiled, bad-tempered, self-centred and sneaky. This is staple fare for a children's book. Some of Roald Dahl's characters are far nastier, but

[133] *VDT* 51

Dahl's baddies remain baddies and usually meet a sticky end. Eustace has the capacity to learn and change. His bad attitude is blamed on his upbringing, his liberal school, and the fact that having read nothing but books of information with 'pictures of grain elevators or of fat foreign children doing exercises in model schools' (why, Lewis, *why?*) his imagination has been starved. He doesn't have the resources of the Pevensies in *Prince Caspian,* when finding themselves stranded on the island they turn for solutions to stories they've read. Eustace will change, but meanwhile his wonderful diaries, full of self-deception, self-justification and complaints are the comical high point of the book, as funny as Sue Townsend's Adrian Mole on whom Eustace was surely an influence.

> *6th September*
> A horrible day. Woke up in the night *knowing* I was feverish and *must* have a drink of water. Any doctor would have said so. Heaven knows I'm the last person to try to get any unfair advantage but I never *dreamed* this water-rationing would be meant to apply to a sick man. In fact I would have woken the others up and asked for some only I thought it would be selfish to wake them. ... I always try to consider others whether they are nice to me or not ...[134]

After days of terrible storm followed by even more terrible days of becalmed heat and thirst, the battered Dawn Treader drops anchor in a narrow, cliff-encircled bay on a strange island. Here, Eustace's transformation begins. Shirking

---

[134] *VDT* 59

the hard work of setting the ship to rights, he slips off into the interior and gets lost in a fog. Descending into a deep, rocky ravine, he hears a noise behind him and turns to see crawling out of a cave something he has literally never imagined (having not read the right books).

It is of course a dragon, but it seems old and weary. It drags itself down over the stones to drink from the pool at the bottom of the valley, but before it can do so, it lets out a great 'clanging cry' – convulses, twitches, and finally rolls over and lies still with one claw thrust in the air.

> A little dark blood gushed from its wide-opened mouth. The smoke from its nostrils turned black for a moment and then floated away. No more came.[135]

I said this book was full of light and so it is, but there's a lot of darkness too. As a description of death, this is about as grotesque and physical as books for young children get. Lewis doesn't flinch from the twitches, the convulsions, the gush of 'dark blood'. All the dragons I'd ever read about were strong and splendid, requiring at least a Saint George to quell them. This weary, repulsive creature dies of natural causes before it can even get a drink of water, which makes its lonely end more pitiable. All that treasure – and all it wanted at the end was a sip of water! This may become Eustace's own sordid fate as, gloating over the dragon's hoard, he falls asleep with a gold and diamond bracelet pushed up over his elbow.

If Eustace had been familiar with some of the books C. S. Lewis had read as a boy, he might have come across the story of Fafnir from Völsunga Saga, who kills his own

---

[135] *DT* 69

father to possess a treasure which includes the cursed ring Andvaranaut. Hoarding the treasure in the wilds and 'allowing no one to enjoy it but himself', he changes into a dragon. And another story which lurks in the background is the Danish fairy tale *Prince Lindworm*[136]. A queen gives birth to twin boys, one human and the other a Lindworm — the type of wingless, poisonous Northern serpent which we will meet in *The Silver Chair*. When the twins are grown, Prince Lindworm asserts his right as the eldest to be given a bride before his younger brother: 'A bride for me before a bride for you!' he cries: the only trouble is that he eats them all. Eventually a shepherd girl deals with him. Dressed in 'ten snow-white shifts' and equipped with a tub of lye, a tub of milk and an armful of whips, she faces the Lindworm in the bridal chamber. As soon as the door is shut, the Lindworm orders her to 'shed a shift', and she commands him to 'slough a skin'.

> Then he began to moan and wriggle: and in a few minutes a long snake-skin lay upon the floor beside him. The girl drew off her first shift, and spread it on top of the skin.
>
> The Lindworm said to her again, 'Fair maiden, shed a shift.'
>
> The shepherd's daughter answered him, 'Prince Lindworm, slough a skin.' ... Then with groans and moans he cast off the second skin, and she covered it with her second shift ...
>
> And so this went on until nine Lindworm skins were

[136] Often mistakenly claimed to be one of Asbjørnsen and Moe's Norwegian tales, in fact 'Kong Lindorm' is from Axel Olrik's *Danske Sagn og Aeventyr fra Folkemunde*, 1913.

> lying on the floor, each of them covered with a snow-white shift. And there was nothing left of the Lindworm but a huge thick mass, most horrible to see. And the girl seized the whips, dipped them in the lye and whipped him as hard as ever she could. Next, she bathed him all over in the fresh milk. Lastly she dragged him on to the bed and put her arms around him ...[137]

Next day, there's the girl 'all fresh and rosy, and beside her lay no Lindworm, but the handsomest Prince that any one could wish to see.' I feel sure C. S. Lewis knew this story, for the shedding or sloughing of multiple reptilian skins, the naked 'mass' that results, the scarification and the healing bath are all replicated in Eustace's eventual restoration.

For now though, Eustace wakes to a pain in his left arm: the bracelet feels too tight. When he moves his right arm, a dragon's claw moves into view. Two thin streams of smoke ascend in front of his eyes: they vanish when he holds his breath. He edges leftwards; a dragon's claw moves there, too. Eustace panics and bolts – on all fours. He has become a dragon, and the stolen bracelet which he had pushed up his arm is now far too small for him.

> The bracelet ... had sunk deeply into his scaly flesh and there was a throbbing bulge on either side of it.[138]

Every child knows that panicked moment when a sweater sticks as you pull it over your head, or a ring won't come off your finger and your mother tries to ease it over your knuckle with water and soap. That 'throbbing bulge' sounds

[137] Nielsen, Kay, *East of the Sun and West of the Moon*, 61/2
[138] *VDT* 71

horrible; Lewis makes us very aware of the physical cost of this transformation. Eustace tears at the ring 'with his dragon's teeth' but he can't get it off.

If you are callous and greedy like a dragon, you'll become one (at least inside): you are the sum of your acts. It's the obverse of Socrates' 'Be what you wish to seem.' ('All in Plato, it's all in Plato ...') Despite the pain, Eustace's first reaction is relief: now he is a dragon, there is 'nothing to be afraid of any more' – an interesting glimpse into the reasons for his bad behaviour. A dragon can do terrible things: he can 'get even' with Caspian and Edmund ... but now he has the power, he doesn't want to use it. He wants to be human again, and have friends he can share things with. Just as Edmund, in the power of the White Witch, longed to be back with his brother and sisters, Eustace begins to question his own behaviour. Lonely and horrified, he bursts into tears and then, realising his only option is to return to his friends – and that they *are* his friends – he fortifies himself with a drink of water, and then eats 'nearly all the dead dragon'.

No one in the 1950s said 'Ewww, gross!' but the sentiment was the same. Children love moments like these, and I will bet Lewis loved this idea when it struck him. He adds that he knows it sounds shocking, but it's natural really, since although Eustace's *mind* is still his own, 'his tastes and his digestion were dragonish'. And dragons, it seems, are cannibals. It certainly made me blink, and it still does, but it feels truthful – and again I notice how very aware Lewis is of *bodies*: their pleasures and pains, the opportunities and limitations of different forms, and the ways in which they affect the minds which inhabit them.

The ship's company are much alarmed by the sight of

a dragon landing on the shore between them and the ship. They draw swords and approach it together, but it backs off and seems to understand what they say. Seeing the bracelet sunk in its flesh, Lucy tries unsuccessfully to cure it with her cordial, but Caspian recognises it as Lord Octesian's arm ring. They have found the second of their seven lords, for as Edmund says, 'it's a safe bet that Octesian got no further.' Unless – Lucy suggests, the dragon *is* Octesian, enchanted? Or maybe someone else enchanted? Could it be ... Eustace?

Unable to speak, Eustace tries to write his story in the sand, but with his massive dragon claws and muscles it's hopeless: indecipherable as a spilled Scrabble board. But he is far nicer and much more use as a dragon than he has ever yet been as a human: he can light fires with a puff of his breath, fly all over the island and provision the ship with carcasses of wild goats he has killed, even uproot a pine tree to replace the ship's mast. As Reepicheep becomes his chief comforter, telling him many a story of the turning of Fortune's Wheel, Eustace grows ever more ashamed of his previous behaviour.

It takes Aslan to strip off the horny layers of dragon hide which symbolise the carapace of sin – or if you prefer, of anti-social behaviour which Eustace has constructed around himself. In dream or actuality Eustace is visited by a great lion which leads him up a mountain he's never seen before. At the top is a garden and in the middle of the garden a circular marble well containing a spring of clear water. This is the well at the world's end – and we know, though Eustace doesn't, that he is on Aslan's holy mountain. He longs to bathe in the well and ease the pain in his arm, but the lion tells him he must undress first, which Eustace realises must mean shedding his dragon skin. He scratches it off, but underneath each scaly layer he finds another one. He cannot do it himself. The lion will have to help him, and although Eustace is very afraid, he knows it must be done. It hurts horribly when the lion plunges its talons so deep into his chest it feels as if it's going to reach his heart, and begins wrenching the skin off; but there's a satisfaction in it too.

> 'The only thing that made me able to bear it was just the pleasure of feeling the stuff peel off. You know – if you've ever picked the scab off a sore place. It hurts like billy-oh, but it *is* such fun to see it coming away.'[139]

It's a brilliant metaphor any child can recognise. Once his skin is off, the soft and naked Eustace is seized and tossed into the well by Aslan. Swimming and splashing, he turns into a boy again and finds himself back on the beach, dressed in new clothes.

The sheer cost of this process – the failure of Eustace's attempts to help himself, the necessity of surrender to Aslan, the ripping away of the thick, dark, knobbly dragon hide, the renewing waters, the fresh clothes – this isn't a story 'about' repentance and baptism: this is the *experience* of which repentance and baptism are the symbols. Not for a second did I connect it with anything 'churchy' when I was nine, but what it showed me, what I would always afterwards have an image for although I might not be able to express it, was how deep within yourself you might have to go in order to change. Eustace has undergone a much deeper conversion than Shasta's. 'I was hating everything,' he apologises, telling

[139] *VDT* 86

Edmund his story. 'I'm afraid I've been pretty beastly', and Edmund comforts him by sharing his own experience: 'You were only an ass, but I was a traitor.'

From now on, Lewis tells us, Eustace begins to live a different life. He has to work at it; there are days when he has lapses, but he tries, and with this, the focus on Eustace ends. *The Voyage of the Dawn Treader* isn't his story alone, and this becomes clear in the next chapter, 'Two Narrow Escapes'.

So much *happens* in this book! I'd forgotten the sea-serpent which almost crushes the ship to matchwood and goes sniffing along its own body looking for wreckage with an expression of 'idiotic satisfaction' on its face. A purely physical danger, it's a lively and exciting contrast to the spiritual sickness embodied in the dragon, and it's nice to see Eustace breaking Caspian's second-best sword as he hacks energetically at the monster's coils. But a graver peril awaits them at the next island, where they find a deep little mountain lake almost encircled by cliffs. The water is crystal clear, and at the bottom they can see what appears to be the solid gold statue of a man lying on his face on the stones, with his arms stretched out above his head.

What seems a statue is really a horror: the body of another of the seven lords they have come to seek. This water turns everything it touches to gold: only by chance do they escape the same fate themselves. And there's a worse danger.

> 'The King who owned this island,' said Caspian slowly, and his face flushed as he spoke, 'would soon be the richest of all the Kings of the world. I claim this land forever as a Narnian possession. It shall be called Goldwater Island. And I bind all of you to secrecy. No

one must know of this. Not even Drinian – on pain of death, do you hear?'[140]

'On pain of death'?! Eustace is not the only person vulnerable to greed. Caspian is a King, and what do Kings do but acquire lands and power? In this passage Caspian reveals a high-handed, bullying side to his character. He might go either way – a just ruler, or a cruel despot.

There will be no more sea-serpents. When Caspian threatens his friends for the sake of wealth and power, we see the story turn towards intangible, internal adventures. Each of the main characters (except Edmund whose trial came in the first book) is put to the test. Like the knights on the Grail Quest, Caspian and even Lucy falter along the way, though Aslan intervenes each time to avert real disaster. Only Reepicheep, Narnia's Galahad, will succeed. For now, though, as Caspian and Edmund start to quarrel and Lucy starts to scold, Aslan passes warningly along the hillside and they gaze at one in another in confusion, as if waking from sleep. Reepicheep advises leaving the island at once; the place is cursed and he should like to name it 'Deathwater'. They all agree this is a fitting name, and unable to remember quite what has happened they return to the ship knowing only that another of the lost lords is accounted for.

When I was a child, the island-hopping voyage of Caspian and his friends to the end of the world seemed to me completely original, but I know now that Lewis was borrowing from the very old Irish voyage tales known as *immrama*, in each of which a hero or saint – Bran, Maeldune, Brendan – sets out for some kind of Otherworld, stopping

---

[140] *VDT* 100

at a number of fantastic or miraculous islands along the way. Written down in the Christian era, they hark back to older pre-Christian Celtic voyage tales, themselves possibly influenced by the classical tales of the Odyssey and Argonautika.

Saint Brendan for example puts out into the Atlantic Ocean in a hide boat or curragh, with twelve companions. Searching for the Land of the Blessed he spends years wandering the sea from island to wondrous island, such as the island of the Comely Hound which leads them to a hall and a table spread with food, the Island of Sheep, 'every sheep the size of an ox', or an island called The Paradise of Birds on which some of the angels who fell with Lucifer live together as small birds, rejoicing and singing psalms. Like the *immrama*, *The Voyage of the Dawn Treader* is the tale of a spiritual quest.

After Goldwater/Deathwater Island, the next landfall is the Island of the Voices or the Island of the Dufflepuds. The adventure is Lucy's, and it affords comic if slightly sinister relief after the strain of the last few encounters.

Having sailed towards the rising sun many days in succession the ship's company spy a low-lying island and drop anchor in a wide bay. Beyond the beach the island appears cultivated, with smooth lawns and an avenue of trees leading to a large house, but no one is about. Stopping to take a stone out of her shoe while the others walk on, Lucy overhears a number of invisible, thumping creatures discussing how they will wait in ambush on the shore to catch the travellers as they return to the ship.

The isle is full of noises: Lucy runs to alert her friends, who have arrived in the courtyard of the house to see smoke rising from a chimney and a pump-handle working apparently by itself. How spooky this seemed the first time I read it! – a spookiness accentuated by the afternoon stillness and manicured order surrounding them. It seems spooky to Caspian and the others, too. An invisible foe lying in wait on the beach to prevent them from leaving makes alarming news – especially as Eustace points out that if it comes to a fight, their friends on the ship will assume they are merely swinging their swords about in a burst of high spirits.

The invisible people, who seem to proceed everywhere in enormous leaps like grasshoppers, explain that they are the enchanted and 'uglified' servants of a powerful and equally invisible magician whose spells only 'a little girl' can undo. They need Lucy to enter the Magician's House, find his magic book and remove the 'invisibleness'. If she won't comply, the owners of the invisible voices will cut all their throats. Lucy agrees to the task, supported by Reepicheep: 'If the Queen's heart moves her to risk the magician, I will not speak against it.'

Why a magician? The only other magician in the Narnia series is Uncle Andrew (although Caspian's tutor Doctor Cornelius admits to knowing a little magic) and in general they seem to have no place in Narnia. And why can only 'a little girl' undo the spell? I think it's because in the chapter that follows, Lewis has in mind Book III, Canto XI of Spenser's *The Faerie Queene*, in which the gallant virgin knight Britomart enters the house of the evil magician Busyrane. She can pass the 'flaming fire ymixt with smouldry smoke' which guards the porch because she is armed in her chastity, and she then roams room after room of the richly furnished house, seeking the imprisoned lady Amoret and becoming more and more amazed that there's no sign of anyone: no footsteps, nothing but 'wastefull emptinesse/And solemn stillness'. As Lewis wrote:

> [O]ne of the noticeable things about Busyrane's house is its desertion. You go through room after empty room, all in silence, and the whole place ignores you: nothing ever happens until midnight.[141]

Only Britomart the virgin can successfully enter the House of Busyrane, and only the innocent little girl Lucy can undo the spell in the Magician's House. This Magician isn't evil, however, so instead of his house being dark and full of night, Lucy sets off upstairs on a sunny summer morning to find the secret room and the revelation. It's just as quiet and empty, though, and just as full of suspense. At the top of the stairs she stands and listens. There's not a sound to be heard. Not a fly buzzing or a curtain stirring – nothing but her own anxious heartbeats. And to reach her goal of the last doorway on the left, she has to walk past other closed doors, behind any of which the magician may be hiding.

> It would have been nicer if there had not been strange signs painted in scarlet on the doors – twisty, complicated things which obviously had a meaning and it mightn't be a very nice meaning either.[142]

It's so rich and cosy and creepy – the silence, the masks, the strange Bearded Glass which gives Lucy a fright. The corridor seems to stretch for ever, but at last she arrives in the Magician's study, one of those rooms filled from

[141] Lewis, C. S., *Spenser's Images of Life*, 39
[142] *VDT* 114

top to bottom with shelves of books of all shapes and sizes which we've met before in *The Lion* and formed part not only of Lewis's childhood but his entire life. Lucy has no need to look through them all, though. The Magic Book is unmistakeable, a huge volume clasped in lead, resting on a lectern in the middle of the room.

Even in this bookish haven, Lewis creates an atmosphere of unease. Those lead clasps hint that the Book may be dangerous to open (shielding against radioactivity). Lucy's fingers tingle as she touches it: there is power inside. And her position is vulnerable: she can turn the pages only if she stands with her back to the open door: it won't shut, and anything might come creeping silently through ...

So in spite of the fact that the Book is so beautiful, we are half-prepared for something to go wrong. I loved the spells – of *course* Lucy wanted to try one, and Pauline Baynes' gorgeous illustration made them even more tempting (which is the point). She draws an illuminated manuscript scattered with tiny birds and bees, flowers and magic signs, a slithering dragon and a running stag: 'Cure for warts: wash in a silver basin by moonlight.' Page after enchanted page, Lucy comes across spells such as 'how to remember things forgotten, how to forget things you wanted to forget' (that one sounds dangerous), 'how to tell whether anyone was telling the truth' (so does that); till at last she finds a page that's 'a blaze of pictures' with the words: *'An infallible spell to make beautiful her that uttereth it beyond the lot of mortals.'*

Now the pictures in the Book show Lucy herself – first as her present self – next with 'a rather terrible expression on her face', chanting the spell – then changed by dazzling beauty. Like Galadriel tempted by the Ring ('All shall love me, and despair!'), Lucy is tempted to speak words which, the pictures show, will transform her into another Helen, and the cause of wars to lay Narnia and its neighbour countries waste. Her desire contains a strong dash of sibling rivalry: the magical Book shows her back in England, where Susan, considered the beauty of the family, has returned from America.

> The Susan in the picture looked exactly like the real Susan, only plainer and with a nasty expression. And Susan was jealous of the dazzling beauty of Lucy, but that didn't matter a bit because no one cared anything about Susan now.[143]

We saw in *The Lion* that Edmund was jealous of Peter, but we have never been told before that Lucy is jealous of Susan. The effect is to unfairly demonise Susan even while we know it is nothing but Lucy's fantasy. (And the heartbreaking line 'no one cared anything about Susan now' seems prophetic, though I doubt Lewis intended it so.)

Lucy's prickly feeling of not being safe is justified: the Magician's Book puts her to the test like Caspian on Goldwater, and like Caspian she fails. Giving in to temptation she declares that she *will* say the spell, even though she's seen what it will do and knows that she shouldn't. 'I don't care,' she adds defiantly. 'I will.'

Once again Aslan has to intervene: his painted golden face appears on the page, snarling with bared teeth. Lucy turns the page in fright, but instead of heeding the warning, she feels she has missed out and deserves to try again. Finding a lesser spell that lets you know what your friends think of

[143] *VDT* 119

you (noooo!) she gabbles it off – only to be terribly hurt as the spell reveals a schoolfriend being catty about her.

Lucy has succumbed to vanity, to jealousy and then to curiosity, but the spell on the next page for 'refreshment of the spirit', with its Gospel hints of 'a cup and a sword and a green hill' seems to cleanse her. I think Lewis may be trying to convey the ambiguous nature of magic (aka science): not necessarily good, not necessarily bad either, but something to be careful with. It depends what you do with it: Coriakin is not a Black Magician.

Finally she finds the one spell she's looking for – the only one she has any right to say – the one which will disenchant the Voices and render them visible. As soon as she's read it aloud – this must be at noon, the opposite of Britomart's midnight – she hears the heavy pad of footfalls behind her and turning to face whatever it is, sees Aslan himself and joyfully runs to greet him. He is in a tender but chiding mood and ticks her off for eavesdropping on her friends. Spying is spying, he points out, whether by magic or not. Listeners never hear good of themselves, but in any case what Lucy has seen is the weak side of a friend who genuinely loves her: 'She was afraid of the older girl and said what she does not mean.'[144]

To me as a nine year-old schoolgirl this made a lot of sense. Girls of that age are always breaking off friendships and forming cliques and choosing scapegoats and being hurtful to one another. As a victim, it's easy to feel it must be your own fault. Yet here it was, happening to Lucy who is so nice she surely doesn't deserve it. I'd never heard the term 'peer pressure' (if it had yet been invented) but here it was: one girl afraid of what the other might think or say.

[144] *DT* 123

Alas, now she's overheard her friend's betrayal, Lucy doesn't think she'll ever be able to forget it, and Aslan offers no consolation. She has brought it on herself.

The Voyage of the Dawn Treader is a light-filled, summery book and Aslan darts in and out of it like a swallow, each touch sure. It's very possible Lewis knew of a passage by William Temple, (Archbishop of Canterbury from 1942 until his death in 1944) in which Temple examines the well-known verses in St John's Gospel, 14:1-4:

> 1 Let not your heart be troubled: ye believe in God, believe also in me.
> 2 In my Father's house are many mansions: if it were not so, I would have told you. I go to prepare a place for you.
> 3 And if I go and prepare a place for you, I will come again and receive you myself; that where I am, there ye may be also.
> 4 And whither I go, ye know, and the way ye know.

Temple's reading of this passage hinges on the meaning of the word 'mansion' in verse 2, usually translated as 'rooms' in modern versions. He explains that in the original Greek the word means 'resting places':

> The resting places (μοναί) are wayside caravanserais — shelters at stages along the road where travellers may rest on their journey. It was the custom in the East ... for travellers to send a dragoman [interpreter or guide] forward to make preparation for the next of these resting-places along the road, so that when they came they might find in it comfort as well as shelter.

> Here the Lord presents Himself as our spiritual dragoman, who treads the way of faith before us. ... We have a long journey of many days ere our pilgrimage is accomplished, but there are, by God's mercy, *many resting places*. [145]

This understanding changes the metaphor from a static image — a house of many rooms in which Christ waits for us — to the active one of a journey in stages, with Christ as the leader and guide who goes on ahead to arrange shelter and then, as Temple says, returns 'to encourage us and lead us to the resting place prepared.' It illuminates Aslan's role in *The Voyage of the Dawn Treader*: the voyagers traverse the ocean island by island, while Aslan makes encouraging or warning appearances along the way. And it seems to me that it's possible to view the ocean through which the Dawn Treader sails as yet another 'in-between place' like the Wood Between the Worlds, and the passage under the slates in *The Magician's Nephew*, with each landfall on each island an entrance into an individual room or world.

Before he vanishes again — to visit Cair Paravel by sunset and bring Caspian's regent Trumpkin news of their voyage — Aslan introduces Lucy to the now visible Magician. Coriakin, the benign Prospero of this island, looks very like a Druid in his white robe and chaplet of oak leaves. We learn later that he was once a star, whose time in the sky was cut short by some undisclosed fault: as penance, Aslan has sent him to govern a race of foolish little dwarfs. The Duffers are so silly that they do things like planting boiled potatoes to save cooking

---

[145] Temple, William, *Readings in St John's Gospel*, 226: I owe this reference to a conversation with my friend and neighbour Geoffrey Maughan who is an Anglican priest.

them later, but the Magician's task is gradually to teach them wisdom. Rather randomly (even good Magicians aren't entirely reliable) he has turned them into one-legged Monopods, each with a huge single foot which, in a stroke of brilliance, Reepicheep teaches them to use as canoes. This pleases them greatly, and so does their new name of Monopods, which they mispronounce till it ends up as Dufflepuds. I enjoyed this chapter, but a little of the Dufflepuds goes a long way and I wasn't sorry when the Magician magically mends the Dawn Treader's splintered stern (snapped off by the sea serpent), and sends the voyagers on their way.

Next comes the terrible Dark Island, more strong meat for my nine year-old self, who like most children knew plenty about the kind of dreams that 'make you afraid of going to sleep again'. Lewis possibly got the idea of the darkness from a 'dark mist' in *The Voyage of Brendan*:

> They took their ship and sailed for forty days eastward. And ... there came a great shower of hail and then a dark mist came about them, and they were in it for a long time. Then their Helper came to them and said, 'Let you be glad now and hearten yourselves for you are come to the Land of Promise'. Then they came out of the dark mist and they saw to the east the loveliest country that anyone could see.[146]

Caspian takes the ship into this darkness — wonderfully represented by Pauline Baynes as an inky, cross-hatched cloud — at the urging of Reepicheep, who remarks that their honour is at stake. ('Honour be blowed,' the sailors mutter:

[146] Gregory, Lady Augusta, The Voyage of Brendan, *A Book of Saints and Wonders*, 113

The Voyage of the Dawn Treader

Reepicheep can be hard to live up to.) With lamps lit, they row slowly into the darkness until they hear a terrible cry and the sound of someone swimming, and pick from the water a man like a deranged Ancient Mariner with eyes so wide 'he seemed to have no eyelids at all' — a vividly gruesome detail which always made me shiver.

Hysterical with fear he urges the company to turn the ship around at once and flee, for this is the Island where Dreams come true — and when some of the sailors misunderstand, he stamps his foot at such folly: this is an accursed place 'where dreams — dreams, do you understand — come to life, come real. Not daydreams: dreams.' As soon as they grasp his meaning, the humans on the ship panic, haunted by memories of nightmares at which Lewis hints in surreal, disturbing images: the blades of gigantic scissors clashing, *things* crawling up the ship's sides, the sound of beating gongs ...

I understood that the Dark Island isn't entirely real: the ship never comes to land. All the terror and madness and horror happens inside the minds of the crew, who have to escape from *themselves*, the darkness of their own minds. There's terrible tension as they try to row out; it seems to be taking much longer than rowing in ... Will they ever see daylight again? Can a person escape the black night of despair?

> The stranger, who had been lying in a huddled heap on the deck, sat up and burst into a horrible screaming laugh. 'Never get out!' he yelled. '... What a fool I was to have thought they would let me go as easily as that. No no, we shall never get out.'[147]

---

[147] *DT* 142

By Aslan's help they do. Is it too easy? I think not. The albatross (of course an albatross, to redeem this poor Ancient Mariner) which circles the ship crying in a 'strong, sweet voice' to lead them back to the light is Aslan — or Christ or hope or what you will: the emotion is true. Help from some quarter is needed: few drag themselves out of depression unaided. The re-entry into sunlight surprises them all: they almost expect the darkness to cling to the ship's paintwork. Tears of joy roll down the cheeks of the lost mariner. Brokenly he thanks them for saving him from unspeakable anguish and tells them his name: Lord Rhoop, one of the seven Telmarine lords whom Caspian set out to find.

Even more light follows this darkness at the ship's next landfall. About sunset one evening they arrive at an island of low hills and anchor in a shallow bay. Going ashore, Caspian and his friends find an unroofed hall of stone pillars, where a magnificent feast is spread on a long table surrounded by stone chairs. (We're not told if the table is also made of stone. I suspect it is, but as it's covered in a rich crimson cloth, there is no way to confuse it with the Stone Table.) At the far end, so entangled in their long beards they look like a sinister haystack, the last three lost Narnian lords lie in an enchanted sleep.

Many countries have legends of 'sleeping knights', woven around heroes like Bran, Arthur and Charlemagne who slumber with their men in hidden caves beneath mountains, ready to wake and ride forth at some future time when their land is in danger. One such tale is told of the Holy Roman Emperor Frederick Barbarossa (1122–1190). With six knights he sleeps at the head of a stone table in a cavern under the Kyffhäuser mountain in Thuringia, Germany. He has been there so long, his great red beard has grown right through the stone, and this is probably the source for the tangled beards of the three Narnian lords. But when Caspian tries to rouse them and they mutter in their sleep — 'Out oars for Narnia' and 'Get to the east while you've a chance — lands behind the sun' and 'Mustard, please' — Lewis is echoing the two sleepers in the Enchanted Ground of John Bunyan's *The Pilgrim's Progress*. The Enchanted Ground is one of the very last temptations placed by the Enemy along the way to Beulah Land and the Celestial City. Here, Heedless and Too-Bold lie in enchanted slumber, forever dreaming of deeds they will never accomplish.

> The Guide did shake them, and do what he could to disturb them. Then said one of them, *I will pay you when I take my Mony*. At which the Guide shook his head. *I will fight so long as I can hold my Sword in my Hand*, said the other. At that, one of the Children laughed.[148]

Unwilling to touch the food which they fear has caused the three lords' slumber, Caspian and his company wait uneasily around the Table till dawn, while strange stars burn in the eastern sky. As the night wanes, a door opens in a low hill beyond the pillars and a lovely girl comes out carrying a light. She is Ramandu's daughter, and she tells them the three Narnian lords fell into their long sleep when they quarrelled, and one of them snatched up the Stone Knife which lies on the table — the knife which killed Aslan and was brought here 'to be kept in honour while the world lasts'. This did seem to me as a child an odd thing to honour —

---

[148] Bunyan, John, The Second Part of the Pilgrim's Progess: *Grace Abounding and The Pilgrim's Progress*, 408

surely, I thought, the White Witch's Stone Knife was evil? — but of course it's the equivalent of a crucifix.

For this is Aslan's Table which by implication means that it is an altar; the rich cloth which covers it is an altar-cloth and the food on it is consecrated. No wonder the sacrilegiously quarrelling lords were struck with sleep. This particular Enchanted Ground is holy: this liminal island marks the beginning of the end of the world. But Caspian and his company can eat and drink without fear, the lady tells them, and Reepicheep first braves the challenge and drinks to her.

From here on, the story is all wonder and grace. We meet silver-haired Ramandu, once a star, and witness great white birds flocking to the Table from the rising sun. Every morning they feed from the Table, clearing away the food which is miraculously replaced at sunset, and bring Ramandu a fire-berry from the valleys of the Sun; little by little each berry diminishes his age. (We may remember here that Lucy's cordial is made from the juice of the fire-flowers that grow in the mountains of the sun: it's rather lovely to get these glimpses into the heavens.) When Ramandu is as young as a day-old child he will rise again from the eastern rim of the world, and 'once more tread the great dance' in the spacious Narnian firmament.

Ramandu tells Caspian the only way to break the three lords' enchantment is to sail as close as they can to the World's End and come back having left at least one of the company behind to continue into the uttermost east, never to return — and this is Reepicheep's heart's desire.

I've said that Reepicheep is Narnia's Galahad. Well, Galahad's father Lancelot is the Round Table's best *earthly* knight; his passions and faults prevent him from achieving the Grail but make him human and relatable. Galahad himself is inhumanly virtuous: he performs miracles and dies a holy and prayed-for death after receiving the sacrament from the hands of Joseph of Arimathea himself, surrounded by angels:

> Then he began to tremble right hard when the deadly [ie: mortal] flesh began to behold the spiritual things. Then he held up his hands towards heaven and said, 'Lord, I thank Thee, for now I see that that hath been my desire many a day. Now, blessed Lord, would that I might no longer live, if it might please Thee, Lord.'[149]

T. H. White has some slightly unfair fun with Galahad in *The Once and Future King* when Sir Lionel retells an incident from *Le Morte d'Arthur*[150] in which Galahad saves Sir Perceval's life by beating off twenty men-at-arms — and then rides away without speaking to him.

> 'You know,' said Lionel, pausing, 'it may be all very well to be holy and invincible, and I don't hold it against Galahad for being a virgin, but don't you think that people might be a little human? I don't want to be catty, but that young man makes my hair go the wrong way. Why couldn't he say Good-morning or something, instead of rescuing a fellow and then riding off with that white nose of his in the air?'[151]

---

[149] Malory, Sir Thomas, *Le Morte d'Arthur*, Book XVII, Ch 22, 370
[150] Ibid, Book XIV, Ch. 4, 279
[151] White, T. H., *The Once and Future King*, 449

Reepicheep desires the same union with the divine as Galahad and he sets a high, almost too high example to Caspian and his company. He is utterly single-minded. When Caspian's crew mutinies on Ramandu's Island, longing to turn for home, Reepicheep announces in a ringing voice that his own intention is to sail east in the Dawn Treader until she can go no further. At that point, he will paddle his coracle east; when the coracle sinks he will swim east, and when he can no longer swim, then if he hasn't reached Aslan's country or hurtled over the waterfall at the world's edge, he intends to sink with his nose pointing to the sunrise.

It's almost frightening. Perfection *is* inhuman. This was made plain when only Reepicheep was unmoved by the terror of the Dark Island. 'There are some things no man can face,' Caspian exclaims as he orders the retreat. 'It is, then, my good fortune not to be a man,' Reepicheep replies stiffly. He remains lovable though, and we can tolerate his disapproval because he's an animal and doesn't understand or share our fears. Nothing stands between him and the best. He is less than us, and greater.

Caspian deals with the sailors' mutiny by making a favour out of allowing them to remain with the ship. Only the best will be chosen! In a speech that owes something to King Harry's at Agincourt,[152] he exclaims that all who come with him shall hand down 'the title of Dawn Treader to his descendants,' and be made rich for life. The mutiny is quelled. Movingly, the Lord Rhoop chooses to heal his broken mind by joining the dreamless sleep of the other lords until Caspian's return. As the ship's company departs, Caspian leaves Ramandu's daughter with the meaningful promise to have speech with

---

[152] *Henry V*, Act 4, Sc 2: 'We few, we happy few, we band of brothers,' etc.

her when he returns. She will become his queen and Rilian's mother; it's a pity she never gets a name.

As the Dawn Treader sails into the Last Sea, the strength of the light and the clarity of the sea affects everyone on board: they sleep less, eat less, talk less. The water is as clear as glass; as Lucy leans over the ship's rail, she can see right down to the bottom.

In the Irish *immram The Voyage of Maeldune*, the hero and his companions sail into 'The Very Clear Sea':

> They went on after that till they came to a sea that was like glass, and so clear it was that the gravel and the sand of the sea could be seen through it, and they saw no beasts or monsters at all among the rocks, but only the clean gravel and the grey sand. And through a great part of the day they were going over that sea, and it is very grand it was and beautiful.[153]

Lewis populates his sea with mer-people. I can't tell you how much I loved and still love the beautiful passage where Lucy recognises a road, fathoms down, tracing its way between forests of seaweed and gradually rising to a submerged peak on which stands a castle of the sea people. Then she sees the people themselves, mounted on large sea-horses, out hunting fish.

> There were men and women both. All wore coronets of some kind and many had chains of pearls. They wore no other clothes. Their bodies were the colour of old ivory, their hair dark purple.[154]

---

[153] Gregory, Lady Augusta, The Voyage of Maeldune, *A Book of Saints and Wonders*, 65
[154] *VDT* 170

Purple hair and ivory bodies? These people rock! Looking up at the ship, the Sea King shakes his spear in challenge, and with a sudden splash, Reepicheep leaps overboard to meet him. The Dawn Treader puts hastily about, but by the time they haul him back on board, the drenched and dripping Mouse is no longer interested in the Sea People. He chirps that the water is sweet — 'Sweet, sweet!' and repeats the old prophecy sung over his cradle:

> *'Where the waves grow sweet,*
> *Doubt not, Reepicheep,*
> *There is the utter East.'*

A bucket is lowered and comes up filled with water that shines like glass. Caspian tries it and looks up with a changed face. It is 'drinkable light', they decide as they taste it — spiritual food, strong and sweet enough to make them gasp. It strengthens their eyes so that they can look into the rising sun and even distinguish the feathers of the white birds flying from it.

Aslan's country is very close now and its luminous aura fills every page. Any child reading will come away (unaware) with a better understanding of what the word 'holiness' is meant to convey. Not the prissy holiness parodied by T. H. White, but the terrifying, heart-stoppingly beautiful encounter with the thing we call divine, the thing that made Galahad's mortal body tremble. 'Take off your shoes,' God says to Moses out of the burning bush. 'This is holy ground.'

But the ship glides on and there comes the moment when Lucy sees in shallow water below her a lonely little herd-girl of the Sea People, and their eyes meet in sudden, transitory communion: 'Neither could speak to the other

The Voyage of the Dawn Treader

and in a moment the Sea Girl had dropped astern. ... There does not seem to be much chance of their meeting again in that world or any other. But if ever they do they will rush together with their hands held out.'[155]

I don't know why this should be so immensely touching, but it is.

Ahead of the ship now appears a whiteness on the sea which turns out to be fields of blossoming waterlilies. The current which has been sweeping them along bears them deep into this Lily Lake or Silver Sea, until the open sea behind becomes a blue line and vanishes, and they are surrounded by leagues of lilies like leagues of ice.

The Lily Lake reminds me of a story by Rudyard Kipling, *The Brushwood Boy*, in which a boy and girl meet in a mutual dream-land for adventures that always begin at a brushwood pile on a beach, by a road that climbs to a ridge crowned with a lamp-post which may well have inspired the Narnian one in Lantern Waste. In one of his many dreams the boy climbs into a clockwork steamer which bears him away 'with surpassing swiftness over an absolutely level sea' to a lily lock at the world's end. On the way, it stops beside:

> ... a lily carved in stone, which, most naturally, floated on the water. Seeing the lily was labelled 'Hong Kong,' Georgie said, 'Of course. This is precisely what I expected Hong Kong would be like. How magnificent!' Thousands of miles further on it halted at yet another stone lily, labelled 'Java'; and ... he knew now that he was at the world's end. But the little boat ran on and on

[155] *VDT* 177

till it stopped in a deep fresh-water lock, the sides of which were carven marble ... Lily pads lay on the water and reeds arched above.[156]

Kipling's haunting story tells how Georgie finds his soulmate in the real world. The parallels are interesting, but Lewis's tale is quite different in style and affect.

The water under the Dawn Treader becomes so shallow that the ship can go no further. Feeling the world's end call to him, Caspian decides he will take the ship's boat and go on with Reepicheep; he orders Drinian to return to Narnia without him. Told in no uncertain terms by Edmund and the others that to do this would be to fail in his duty as a King, he storms off below to emerge later, chastened and tearful. Aslan has spoken to him – the gold image in the cabin came to life – and told him that Lucy and Edmund and Reepicheep and Eustace are to go on, but Caspian is to turn back at once. In an attempt to comfort him, Lucy reminds him that Ramandu's daughter is waiting: but it is a sorrowful parting.

So with the Dawn Treader flying all her flags in their honour, and with Reepicheep's coracle on board, the three children and the Mouse push off in the ship's boat and the steady current takes them further east.

Near the beginning of this book, Lucy asks Reepicheep if he thinks that Aslan's country would really be the kind of place you could physically *sail* to? The answer is a qualified *yes, but not for everyone*. Close to the end of the Irish *immram The Voyage of Brendan*, the saint and his companions reach the very boundary of the Blessed Land. Landing in a 'clear and lightsome' country full of fruit trees, they travel inland for forty days.

---

[156] Kipling, Rudyard, The Brushwood Boy, *The Day's Work*, 352-3

Then they came to a river that they could not cross but they could see beyond it the country that had no bounds to its beauty. Then there came to them a young man ... and took [Brendan] by the hand and said to him, 'Here is the country you have been in search of, but it is our Lord's will you should go back again and make no delay ... And this river you see here is the mering,'[157] he said, 'that divides the worlds, for no man may come to the other side of it while he is in life; [and when he dies] it is then there will be leave to see this country towards the world's end.'[158]

When Reepicheep and the children catch a glimpse of Narnia's own Blessed Land, over the crest of the great wave at the world's edge, Lewis recounts it in the same flat, awed manner of the *immrama:* the voice of one reporting or recording genuine wonders. To the east beyond the sun they see a range of mountains so tall that they can't see any sky. These mountains are beyond the world — behind even the rising sun, and instead of being covered in snow they are green and fertile, 'full of forests and waterfalls': the immortal mountains of Aslan's country. A breeze blows from the east,

> ... tossing the top of the wave into foamy shapes and ruffling the smooth water all round them. ... It brought a smell and a sound, a musical sound. Edmund and Eustace would never talk about it afterwards. Lucy could

---

[157] 'the mering': from the context this word must mean 'boundary' but I do not know the derivation.

[158] Gregory, Lady Augusta, The Voyage of Brendan, *A Book of Saints and Wonders*, 113

only say, 'It would break your heart.' 'Why,' said I, 'was it so sad?' 'Sad!! No,' said Lucy. [159]

It still almost breaks *my* heart when, alive with joy, Reepicheep hurls his sword into the Silver Sea like Arthur at the brink of Avalon, and sets off alone in the coracle, swooping up the glassy breast of the wave to vanish forever over the crest. In the spirit of St Brendan who returns to Ireland to die with his whole mind set on the heaven he has already seen, Reepicheep sails over the edge of the world in his coracle:

> ... and since that moment no one can truly claim to have seen Reepicheep the Mouse. But my belief is that he came safe to Aslan's country and is alive there to this day.[160]

The Voyage of the Dawn Treader is at an end. It is time for Caspian to turn back, even though he has longed to go on. His last tantrum over, he accepts his duty and destiny. He will marry Ramandu's daughter and return to rule well and wisely over Narnia.

The three children come to their own final landfall. Walking parallel to the wave, they wade hand in hand through ever shallower water to a green strand where the blue sky literally comes down to touch the earth, and a snow-white Lamb offers them a meal of roast fishes. The Lamb of course is Aslan, and he tells Edmund and Lucy it is their last time here. They have come very close to the boundary of his country, but from now on they must seek

[159] *VDT* 184
[160] *VDT* 185

it from their own world. Then with 'a rending of the blue wall' and 'a terrible white light', Aslan tears open a door in the sky, and they are back in Aunt Alberta's suburban Cambridge home. But we shall meet Eustace again — and Caspian — in the next book.

THE SILVER CHAIR

The Silver Chair was the very first Narnia book I ever read. My mother gave it to me for Christmas when I was eight years old, along with about six other books, most of them probably by Enid Blyton. All I ever asked for was books: but I didn't like the look of this one.

The picture on the cover (it was the Puffin paperback edition) showed a gloomy-looking cavern filled with a lot of grotesque little gnomes, and it put me right off. I had no idea what the story might be about, but it looked downright sinister. The gnomes reminded me of Gollum in *The Hobbit*, a book which had given me the creeps – and worse still, of *The Hobyahs*, a truly ghastly fairy tale inexplicably included in my school reading book, in which the nasty little goblin Hobyahs cut all four legs off a faithful dog.

So naturally I put off reading this new horror. I read my Enid Blytons and (I seem to remember) Elizabeth Goudge's *The Little White Horse*. Then with nothing else left, and as I was the sort of child who reads the back of cornflake packets if there's nothing better, I reluctantly opened *The Silver Chair*. And it started quite manageably after all: 'It was a dull autumn day and Jill Pole was crying behind the gym.'

It sounded like a school story, but almost immediately the narrator went on to say it wasn't a school story; and then Eustace Scrubb, whoever he was, came along to tell Jill there's this chance of escaping the bullies of Experiment House by using magic to get into another world — but just as they're trying some kind of incantation, the bullies find them and they have to run. 'If only the door was open again!' pants Scrubb — as Eustace is known in this book — and Jill nods, for apparently the school grounds are surrounded by a high stone wall, with a door that opens on to moorland, and though the door is kept locked, it's rumoured that it has occasionally been found to open ...

It does open, but not on to dull English moorland. Jill and Scrubb find themselves in bright sunshine and clear air on a high mountain — and Jill shows off at the edge of the cliff, and Scrubb grabs her — and they struggle — and he falls — and suddenly a great lion rushes to the cliff-edge and blows him to Narnia 'as steadily as a vacuum cleaner sucks in'.

Since I'd never met Aslan before, I was as taken aback as Jill. Neither did this lion seem particularly friendly. When (after crying her eyes out) Jill tries to drink from a stream he is guarding, he refuses to give any assurance that he won't eat her; in fact he informs her with unhelpful indifference that he has 'swallowed up girls and boys, women and men, kings and emperors, cities and realms'. Which is disconcerting to say the least.

Jill dares to drink, however, and when the Lion questions her about what has happened to the Boy, she tells him the truth: Eustace fell because she was showing off at the cliff edge. The Lion approves of this honest answer, and tells her that Eustace is safe, but that their task will be more difficult because of what she has done.

Task?

'Far from here in the land of Narnia there lives an aged king who is sad because he has no prince of his blood to be king after him. He has no heir because his only son was stolen from him many years ago, and no one in Narnia knows where that prince went or whether he is still alive. But he is.'[161]

Jill and Scrubb's job is to find the lost prince and bring him back to his father's house. And the Lion gives her four signs. First, as soon as Eustace arrives in Narnia he will meet an old friend whom he must greet at once. Second, the two children must journey north out of Narnia to the ruined city of the giants. Third, in this ruined city they will find a writing which they must obey. Fourth, and most important, when (or if) they find him they will recognise the lost prince because he will be the first person in their travels who asks them to do something in the Lion's own name — in the name of Aslan.

So there I was in this adventure full of old castles and dying kings, snowy moors and talking owls — and Puddleglum the Marshwiggle, the best pessimist since Eeyore, and the beautiful belle-dame-sans-merci-type Green Witch — with time running out to save Prince Rilian from that terrible engine of sorcery, the Silver Chair itself. I was hooked. This colourful, colloquial, exciting, fast-moving fairy tale was the best story I'd ever read.

As Aslan leads Jill back to the cliff edge to blow her too to Narnia, he tells her to remember the signs he's given her

---

[161] *SC* 25

— to repeat them over and over. He warns her it will not be easy to keep them clear in her mind once she has dropped down from the pure air of the mountain into the thicker air of Narnia, and he adds that the signs will not look as she may expect. She must get them by heart and not be deceived by appearances.

Aslan is powerful and good in this book, but remote: he appears in person only at the very beginning and the very end and his role is mainly that of absent lawgiver rather than saviour, comforter and friend. As he finishes speaking, Jill is already hundreds of yards out into the air, speeding on his breath west over the sea to Narnia, retracing (had she or I known it) Eustace's voyage in the Dawn Treader. It takes the best part of a day before she comes gliding down to Cair Paravel where a brightly-dressed crowd is watching a frail old king standing on the gangplank of a great ship, ready to board.

Seeing Scrubb, Jill grabs him and demands to be told if he's seen anyone he knows; but of course Scrubb isn't pleased with her. He hasn't recognised anyone, and he accurately if rather misleadingly tells her he's never been in Narnia before. The ship departs to sounds of sobbing from the crowd, and the children are greeted by Glimfeather, a Talking Owl who has spotted them both flying in. As Jill explains they've been sent by Aslan to find the lost prince, Glimfeather mentions the king's name: Caspian the Tenth. This is a dreadful shock to Scrubb, who realises that seventy years have passed since his first visit, and the young man who was his comrade-in-arms when they fought the Sea Serpent is now a white-haired old man. It would have been easier, he exclaims, to have come back and found Caspian dead.

Also, as Jill unsympathetically points out: 'We've muffed the first Sign.'

If the King's Regent, Trumpkin, learns of their quest he will forbid it: too many lives have been lost trying to find the prince, so Glimfeather smuggles the children out of Cair Paravel to a parliament of owls in an old tower, where they hear the story of how Prince Rilian disappeared. Ten years earlier, he went a-Maying with his mother the Queen – Ramandu's daughter, still unnamed – in the north of Narnia, but while the Queen rested by a natural fountain she was stung to death by a huge, green, poisonous serpent. The grieving Rilian searched the northern marches to find and destroy the serpent – only to disappear for ever after he met a mysterious lady dressed in green.

Each Narnia book has its own flavour. There's the Snow Queen winter world of *The Lion*, the mystical Celtic voyage-tale of the *Dawn Treader*, the E. Nesbit style of *The Magician's Nephew*, the Arabian Nights adventure of *The Horse and His Boy*. With its quest element, and snowy winter journey over rough northern countryside, I now see parallels between *The Silver Chair* and the medieval English poem *Gawain and the Green Knight*, while the supernatural Lady of the Green Kirtle seems derived from the beautiful but dangerous fairy queens of ballads like *Tam Lin* and *Thomas the Rhymer*. (In fact, there's a powerful, magical woman called the 'Dame of the Fine Green Kirtle' in a Scots fairy tale which Lewis may well have known: '*The Fair Gruagach, Son of the King of Eirinn*'[162]) This particular Green Lady's power to transform herself into a serpent also recalls two other Scottish ballads, *Alison Gross* and *The Laily Worm and the Machrel*. In the first, an ugly witch courts a young man and turns him into a 'worm' when he refuses her. Like the green serpent that stung Rilian's mother, this

---

[162] Campbell, J. F., *Popular Tales of the West Highlands* Vol 2, 156

creature is a lindworm, the poisonous northern dragon which has a serpentine body, no fire and no wings. The witch Alison Gross blows on 'a grass-green horn' and takes out a silver wand:

> And she's turned her three times round and round,
> She's muttered sic words, that my strength it failed,
> And I fell down senseless on the ground.
>
> She's turn'd me into an ugly worm,
> And gar'd[163] me toddle about the tree ...[164]

In *The Laily Worm and the Machrel* [165] the narrator complains:

> I was but seven year auld
> When my mither she did die
> My father married the ae warst woman
> The warld did ever see.
>
> For she has made me the laily worm
> That lies at the fit o' the tree
> An' my sister Masery she's made
> The machrel of the sea.[166]

The Green Lady of *The Silver Chair* is both the worm that stung Rilian's mother to death, and the woman who replaces her as his mother-figure, captor, and bride-to-be.

The owls now take the children as far north as the

---

[163] *gar'd*: made
[164] *The Oxford Book of Ballads*, 55, 56
[165] *Laily worm*: loathsome serpent; *machrel*: mackerel
[166] *The Oxford Book of Ballads* 59, 60

Marshwiggles' territory, which they must cross to reach Ettinsmoor and the north. Dropped off in the dark at Puddleglum's wigwam-like hut, the children meet the Marshwiggle properly next morning. Long familiarity makes it easy to forget what a wonderful creation he is: steadfast, pessimistic and indefatigable, with a gloomy yet dry humour all his own.

> 'We've got to start by finding a ruined city of the giants,' said Jill. 'Aslan said so.'
> 'Got to start by *finding* it, have we?' answered Puddleglum. 'Not allowed to start by *looking* for it, I suppose?'[167]

Puddleglum is the wise adult of the group; he often calls the children to sense when they bicker, but the three form a close, interdependent bond.

The travellers now cross Ettinsmoor. An Ettin or Etain is the northern giant (the word is derived from Norse *jötunn*) and they meet some very uncouth examples of the breed as they run the gauntlet of a whole row of them hurling rocks. After ten days' travel over bare moorland they come to the edge of a deep ravine, spanned by a massive arched bridge of stones as big as the ones at Stonehenge, many of which have dropped out and left gaps. Looking down from the top of the arch, they view an ancient road on the other side, and riding towards them on it, two normal-sized people.

Puddleglum is rightly on his guard, but the two strangers seem reassuringly human – and noble. One is a

[167] *SC* 61

knight in black armour on a black steed, who never speaks. The other, drawn by Pauline Baynes like someone out of the *Très Riches Heures du Duc de Berry*, is a lady richly dressed in green velvet with dagged sleeves, riding a 'scrumptious' white horse.

Green is the warning colour of the fairy world, and has been considered unlucky right down into modern times (you should never wear green at a wedding). The Green Lady is very different from the White Witch: where Jadis is harsh, autocratic and frightening, the Green Lady conforms outwardly at least to the courtly courtesies of the Middle Ages. She employs charm, ultra-femininity, logic-chopping and outright deceit, as well as spells and violence, to get her way.

> 'Good day, t-r-r-avellers,' she cried out in a voice as sweet as the sweetest bird's song, trilling her R's delightfully. 'Some of you are young pilgrims to walk this rough waste.'[168]

I don't think, when I first read this book, that I immediately connected this lady with the serpent-woman, and neither do the travellers, even though Jill spotted the link when she heard Rilian's story. I'm not sure why it shouldn't be obvious: the lovely white horse may have something to do with it. Only good people ride snowy white horses, don't they? The Lady denies knowledge of any ruined giant city, but offers some delightfully tempting (and sinisterly ambiguous) advice: they should visit the gentle giants of Harfang, where their 'merry hosts' will supply warm and comfortable lodgings,

---

[168] *SC* 72

and where all kinds of delicious food — hot, *cooked* food! — will be set on the tables four times a day. The children are thrilled, but will these gentle giants admit them?

> 'Only tell them,' answered the Lady, 'that She of the Green Kirtle salutes them by you, and has sent them two fair Southern children for the Autumn Feast.'[169]

As the Knight and Lady pass on over the bridge, the children almost fall out with Puddleglum over whether to trust them. Puddleglum finally agrees to visit Harfang as long as the children promise to say nothing about Narnia or their quest, but the Lady's description of the luxuries of Harfang has made them snappy and discontented, and Jill stops bothering to repeat the signs.

A great thing about this book is the vivid discomfort of the winter journey. The travellers' struggle through the harsh snowy landscape is as testing as Gawain's winter quest for the Green Chapel:

> Nere slayn wyth þe slete he sleped in his yrnes
> Mo nyʒtez þan innoghe in naked rokkez,
> Þer as claterande fro the crest the colde borne rennez
> And henged heʒe ouer his hede in hard iisse-ikkles.[170]

Or in translation:

> Near slain by the sleet he slept in his armour
> more nights than enough in the naked rocks

---

[169] *SC* 73
[170] Tolkien, J. R. R., Gordon, EV, ed, *Sir Gawain and the Green Knight*, lines 729-732

> where clattering from the crest the cold burn ran
> and hung high over his head in hard icicles.

Like Gawain, the children and Puddleglum find shelter, comfort and courtesy in a castle in the wilds, and like him they discover this apparent refuge to be full of perilous deception. Intent on reaching the shelter of Harfang, they scramble ignorantly through the very ruined city they've come to find. It's snowing so hard they catch no more than glimpses of great stone blocks which they're too busy dealing with as obstacles to recognise as masonry. The way to the castle is barred by a set of four-foot high ledges covered in thick snow. Long-legged Puddleglum can clamber up, but he has to help the children. Wet, freezing, blinded by the weather and longing for shelter, they quite fail to see that they are climbing a giant stairway to a tableland, or that the strange, maze-like trenches they encounter there, half filled with snow, form the words of the third sign. From the top they can see the lights of Harfang, but they still have to climb down many ledges on the other side before struggling up a final slope to the gateway of the giants' castle.

Faced with its vastness, the children are suddenly daunted and in spite of his strong objection to coming here at all, Puddleglum takes the lead. Telling them to show no signs of fear, he shouts for a porter, and slaps the snow from his hat in a show of insouciance.

Hearing that the travellers have been sent to them by the Lady of the Green Kirtle 'for the Autumn Feast', the giant King and Queen give them a warm welcome, though Jill *is* startled by the King licking his lips with a very large, red tongue. But oh, the joy of that fireside bath the giant Nurse prepares for her!

> If you can swim — as Jill could — a giant bath is a lovely thing. And giant towels, though a bit rough and coarse, are lovely too, because there are acres of them. In fact you don't need to dry at all, you just roll about on them in front of the fire and enjoy yourself.[171]

All my life I've I wanted to try one.

At the dead of midnight though, Jill has a dream. One of the giant nursery toys, a wooden horse, comes to life and rolls towards her across the room. In the shape-shifting way of dreams it becomes Aslan himself, who takes her in his jaws and carries her to the window. There in the moonlight, she sees 'written in great letters across the world or the sky' the words: UNDER ME.

In the morning it's obvious. The ruined city of the giants lies right there beneath the window. The broken terrain they struggled across the previous night is a maze of high walls and vast pillars, while across a plateau-like pavement run those same words: UNDER ME — which they later learn formed part of a longer inscription, the epitaph of a dead king along the lines of Ozymandias: *'Look on my works, ye mighty, and despair.'* For the three travellers, however, the message is clear: they must search beneath the ruined city. But have they missed the opportunity?

Of the four signs given to Jill by Aslan, the travellers have 'muffed' the first three, but the pace is so brisk and the writing so strong there's no room for the reader to become impatient. Besides, as a child I felt I'd have done the very same things; I could sympathise, I still can. They've been so horribly wet and tired and cold. No wonder they fall for a bit of warmth and comfort.

[171] *SC* 93

Whose fault is it then? Is missing the signs a sin thing? Is the fault, like Eve's, Jill's alone, another strike against Lewis to place beside the problem of Susan and the fact that Narnia's most spectacular villains are female? (Though frankly if you're going to be a villain, you may as well be a charismatic one. Who'd be Uncle Andrew, or Shift the Ape?)

While there is an obvious parallel between Jill receiving the signs on Aslan's mountain, and Moses receiving the Ten Commandments on Mount Sinai, I do not believe we're meant to think of it while we're reading. To do so would destroy the story: it would be as reductive as the Freudian claim that a king in a fairy tale is 'really' a father, or a garden is 'really' a woman's body. In an essay on John Bunyan, Lewis complained of people who treat allegories as if they were riddles to be solved or codes to be cracked, adding that to do so 'leads you out of the book'. The purpose of allegory, he suggests, is to add richness to what may seem a dry, abstract concept, and so to deepen our understanding:

> We ought not to be thinking 'this green valley where the shepherd boy is singing, represents humility'; we ought to be discovering, as we read, that humility is like that green valley.[172]

In other words the story is king, and if you read the Narnia books trying to pick out isolated religious references and pull some moral message out of them, then whether you are an approving Christian or a disapproving atheist, you are doing what Lewis never intended and did not want.

---

[172] Lewis, C. S., *The Vision of John Bunyan*, Selected Literary Essays, 149

Besides, rather than *being* blamed for forgetting, Jill blames herself, which is an important difference. The others immediately accept collective responsibility and they all move on: they're a team. Unlike *The Horse and His Boy*, if there's a punishment in this book it's not a penalty imposed by Aslan but follows as a simple consequence of their decisions — as when at dinner with the giants they discover in horror they have been eating a Talking Stag.

And once again Lewis chooses a girl as his viewpoint character. We see Narnia through Jill's eyes, and she has courage, obstinacy and what is now called 'attitude'. Jill and Eustace indulge in similar amounts of bad-tempered bickering, and their relationship — friendship with a touch of rivalry — feels realistic. The two are equals. If Jill is afraid of tight spaces, Eustace is afraid of heights. Jill doesn't fight the serpent, but she can tack up big, nervous horses and ride them without fear. It's Jill who fools the giants by putting on a comedy act of Shirley Temple-type cuteness, and Jill who discovers an important entry in the Harfang cookery book.

> MAN: this elegant little biped has long been valued as a delicacy. It forms a traditional part of the Autumn Feast and is served between the fish and the joint. Each Man — [173]

This, after she has noticed two clean pie-dishes set out on the kitchen table, just the right size for her and Scrubb to lie down in. A recipe for Marshwiggles follows; the mixture of suspense and black comedy is masterful.

[173] 107

Next comes the frantic escape from Harfang. With the giants' hunting dogs at their heels they squeeze into a dark crack beneath the lowest of the giant steps, and — inadvertently following the signs at last — tumble down a long black slope into the Underland. As they lie at the bottom, bruised, bloody and half-buried in scree, they know there's no chance of climbing back. The darkness is complete and it's warm, too: Puddleglum thinks they may have descended nearly a mile. No one can think of anything to say. They almost give up, but after a very long while a cold grey-blue light floods the cave and they are captured by the gnomes with their dirge-like chant: 'Many fall down, and few return to the sunlit lands'.

The gnomes were not as creepy as I'd feared, perhaps because though various in shape — some only a foot high, others taller than men, with 'pointed noses, long soft noses like trunks, and great blobby noses' — they all look terribly sad. A fabulous underworld journey follows, *through caverns measureless to man, down to a sunless sea* — through endless caves of flabby trees and lizard-like creatures curled asleep in the moss — past the great sleeping giant Time, who will awake at the end of the world — down to the dark water, the pale beaches and the silent underground city with its wan lamps: 'as quiet, and nearly as dark, as the inside of an ant-hill'.

The Silver Chair is full of passages, doorways and openings: the door in the wall through which the children pass out of England, the confusing, maze-like trenches of the ruined city, the half-open door of the Harfang scullery which beckons them to escape, the tunnels and caves of Underland, the streets, squares, steps of the underground city, the 'many staircases' and murky rooms of the Green Lady's Dark Castle, where once again we climb an extra stair to a hidden chamber and a revelation: the lamplit, firelit room, 'richly tapestried' with 'red wine and cut glass sparkling on the table', in which the Black Knight dwells.

> A young man with fair hair rose to meet them. He was handsome, and looked both bold and kind, though there was something about his face that didn't seem quite right.[174]

Any adult will guess at once who he is. When I was eight I thought this *could* be Prince Rilian, but Lewis did an excellent job of misdirecting me. The Knight is very friendly, but foolish, shallow and disappointing. He doesn't recognise the name 'Rilian', he's never heard of Narnia and he seems to worship the Green Lady, whom by this time I *knew* to be wicked. And for an hour each night he turns into a snake? Maybe the very creature which bit the Queen?

Perhaps I wasn't quite deceived, but I wasn't sure either: the Knight is *so* irritating, especially the way he patronises Jill. The Green Lady, he explains, is dedicated to freeing him from the enchantment that binds him, by making him king of an Overworld land which she plans to invade. When Scrubb makes the obvious though understated objection that it's 'a bit hard luck on *them*', the Knight is faintly troubled, before bursting into laughter at the absurdity of it all: surely these folk will soon get over themselves and enjoy the joke of being conquered! When Jill exclaims hotly that it's not at all funny and he will be 'a

[174] *SC* 123

wicked tyrant', the Knight not only continues laughing but actually pats her on the head, with the words, 'Is our little maid a deep politician?'

Like Bree's condescension to Hwin, this is straight out of #everydaysexism, although Jill's next sally, 'Where I come from ... we don't think much of men who are bossed about by their wives,' hasn't quite arrived at 21st century feminism either. Still, she's not as far off as the Knight.

> 'Shalt think otherwise when thou hast a man of thine own, I warrant you,' said the Knight, apparently thinking this very funny.[175]

Lewis puts these sexist tropes in the Knight's mouth to make him seem as fatuous and annoying as possible, and it's a long way from that passage in *Prince Caspian* about little girls with fat legs. The reason for the difference is that Jill is the viewpoint character and Lewis is making the effort to see things through *her* eyes and mind, which goes to show what he can do when he tries. For the early 1950s it's quite impressive.

By the end of supper all three of them have had enough of the Knight and his chatter, and judge him in their own different ways. Grown-up Puddleglum considers him a 'young fool', and wonders what the witch's real motives may be. Schoolboy Eustace thinks the Knight 'a sap' and a 'baby' for being besotted with the Green Lady. And Jill, who's been treated as if her views are of no account, thinks him a 'conceited, selfish pig'. This is indeed how he seems; but we sense something else is going on.

---

[175] *SC* 128

It's this uncertainty about the Knight's character that makes the next passage so gripping. The Knight is roped to his Silver Chair and — here is the dreadful bit — *himself* begs the children and Puddleglum, for their own safety, not under any circumstances to release him. They all agree, promising one another that whatever he says or does — '*whatever* he says' — they'll stay firm. He has told them he will turn into a deadly serpent if they release him, and they believe it. They won't let him go, as for one brief hour, the witch's enchantment lifts.

> 'Quick! I am sane now. Every night I am sane. If only I could get out of this enchanted chair, it would last. But every night they bind me, and so my chance is gone. But you are not enemies. I am not *your* prisoner. Quick! Cut these cords.'[176]

It takes two and a half agonising pages before the children and Puddleglum change their minds and cut the cords, and all the while the Knight pleads, begs, threatens, shrieks, and finally adjures them in the name of Aslan — 'by the great Lion, by Aslan himself'! — the last of the four signs. They know at once what they must do. They've messed up the first three and this is the last chance — but what will happen next? The Knight will kill them all, like as not, says gloomy but staunch Puddleglum, adding, 'But that doesn't let us off following the sign.'

> They all stood looking at once another with bright eyes. It was a sickening moment. 'All right!' said Jill suddenly. 'Let's get it over. Goodbye, everyone ...!' They all shook

[176] *SC* 131

hands. The Knight was screaming by now; there was foam on his cheeks.[177]

It's a wonderful effect: the rescue of the Prince is a moment not of triumph, but of suspense and terror: 'Let's get it over.' Reading this now, I find myself remembering that Lewis fought in the trenches. I think of soldiers listening to the cries of wounded comrades out in No Man's Land, nerving themselves to a rescue which might result in their own deaths. Is it too fanciful to think the Silver Chair itself might be a metaphor for the terrible barbed wire in which so many men lay entangled? As a fairy tale motif, I know of nothing like it except perhaps the Siege Perilous in Malory's *Le Morte D'Arthur* – the seat devised by Merlin for Galahad, fatal for anyone else who sits in it. The Silver Chair is even more sinister. Look again at the passage where the liberated Rilian turns on the Chair with his sword and hacks it to pieces:

> The silver gave way before its edge like string, and in a few moments a few twisted fragments, shining on the floor, were all that was left. But as the chair broke, there came from it a bright flash, a sound like small thunder, and (for one moment) a loathsome smell.[178]

The Chair turns to wire-like 'string', its twisted metal fragments resemble shrapnel, it breaks with a flash, a crash like thunder and a loathsome smell – like gas? Lewis never wrote about his time in the trenches in any detail, but if his war experience did inform the image of the Silver Chair, it certainly lent it shadow and depth.

[177] *SC* 134
[178] *SC* 135

Turning to his rescuers, the Knight exclaims in amazed recognition at the sight of Puddleglum, hailing him as 'a real, live, honest Narnian Marsh-wiggle' and naming himself as Rilian, son of Caspian and Prince of Narnia. While the children and Puddleglum are explaining how they have been sent by Aslan expressly to find him, the Witch returns.

The Silver Chair is an exceedingly rich book. It had more going on in it than any story I'd ever read. It gave me so much to think about, or perhaps more accurately to soak up and grow on, like a plant that's been given a really nourishing fertiliser. It was Lewis who introduced me, at age eight and up, to the spacious idea that there might be other worlds, other universes besides ours, and in this book he introduced me, little as I realised it at the time, to the Platonic parable of the cave. As much as Christianity, Plato is one of C. S. Lewis's touchstones: he even gets a mention in *The Last Battle*: 'It's all in Plato – all in Plato,' says the Professor, Digory. 'Bless me, what *do* they teach them in these schools?'

As is well known (although not by children), Plato in *The Republic* compares humanity's perception of the world to that of prisoners chained in a cave, whose only knowledge of anything beyond is gained from shadows flung on the cave wall from the real world outside. Only the philosopher sees the truth behind appearances. That is what lies behind *this* passage in which the Green Lady, the Witch, tries to persuade the children and the Prince that there is no such place as Narnia. Strumming softly on her lute and throwing incense on the fire, she asks them what the word 'sun' means? Can they tell her? The Prince tries. With icy politeness, enhanced by formal-sounding archaic verb endings like 'giveth', 'hangeth', he indicates the lamp which lights the room and hangs from the roof, and explains that the sun (which he knows she has seen) is like a greater and brighter lamp which lights the entire world and hangs in the sky.

> 'Hangeth from what, my lord?' asked the Witch, and then, while they were all still thinking how to answer her, she added, with another of her soft, silvery laughs, 'You see? When you try to think out clearly what this *sun* must be, you cannot tell me. You can only tell me that it is like the lamp. Your *sun* is a dream; and there is nothing in that dream that was not copied from the lamp. The lamp is the real thing; the *sun* is but a tale, a children's story.'[179]

Her argument is a neat reversal of Plato's parable. The Green Lady wants the children and the Prince to believe the copies are the only reality. She wishes to keep them, mentally as well as literally, in the underground cave. She wants to imprison their minds, as the dwarfs at the end of *The Last Battle* are prisoners of their own scepticism, refusing to emerge from the rank stable of their own senses.

Fundamentalists of various types prefer, in my experience, to remain in the cave. Some live within the restrictions of a literal understanding of the Bible, refusing to consider metaphorical or historical interpretations. Others feel that telling fairy stories to children is tantamount to telling them lies. Yet others insist on or even enforce rigid adherence to particular political or social models. All reflexively shun the suggestion that there may be other ways of reading, explaining, experiencing or governing the world.

What is reality? Lewis demands of his child readers. Is

[179] *SC* 141

it no more than the evidence of our immediate senses, the things we can touch and taste and see? Then what about the imagination? What about poetry and religion and philosophy?

The moment when the Witch almost convinces the children and Puddleglum that her underground kingdom is *all there is* made a deep impression on me as a child: rightly, since it's the heart of the book. I especially loved the moment when practical, common-sense Puddleglum saves the day not by any subtle argument, but by stamping the witch's fire out with his big, webbed foot. It hurts him! But it substitutes 'the smell of burnt Marshwiggle' for the heavy sweet smell of the Witch's magical incense, and he follows his brave deed with a passionate credo. Suppose, he says, the upper world and all the things in it — sun, moon and stars, trees and grass and Aslan the Lion — really *are* only make-belief, and exist only in their dreams?

> 'Suppose this black pit of a kingdom of yours *is* the only world. Well it strikes me as a pretty poor one. And that's a funny thing, when you come to think of it. We're just babies playing a game, if you're right. But four babies playing a game can make a play world which licks your real world hollow. That's why I'm going to stick with the play-world. I'm on Aslan's side even if there isn't any Aslan to lead it. I'm going to live as like a Narnian as I can even if there isn't any Narnia.'[180]

This trumpet-call for the power and value of the imagination still makes me want to cheer. Puddleglum's credo isn't quite Christian, for traditional Christianity hangs upon upon the

---

[180] *C* 145

verity of the New Testament: 'If Christ was not raised, then our gospel is null and void, and so is your faith', says Saint Paul (1 Corinthians, 15:14). In fact Puddleglum speaks as a Platonist. *Even if* it's all make-belief, he says, it's important. If in this imperfect world you can even imagine goodness, it is because beyond material reality the perfect Good truly exists. Be the thing you wish to seem: choose the best in yourself and not the worst. It's not a bad message to come across, when you're still only eight.

Lewis hints at how impoverished the witch's world-view is by giving us a glimpse of the brilliant land of Bism far down in the depths of the earth, described to the travellers by Golg the gnome. Top-dwellers, it seems, have never seen *real* jewels — only dead ones. In Bism they are 'alive and growing' (like the silver, gold and diamond trees of the fairy tale)— and not only that but edible and nourishing: rubies you can pick and eat like grapes, cups brimming with diamond juice. Once again we're with Plato, penetrating layers of reality from the lesser to the greater, from the shadow to the form.

So there are worlds in Narnia that even the Narnians don't know about! What *is* real? Our world? Fiction? Narnia? Aslan's country? All of them? With such questions hanging in the Narnian air, no wonder that along with many other children I was possessed by a passionate half-belief that Narnia was real — *had* to be real. A friend and I invented a code word for it, 'The Garden' — so we could talk about it secretly in public and people wouldn't know. (I'm not sure we ever did, but it was fun to think we might.) Children take what they need from the books they read and ignore the other stuff. What I drew from the Narnia books has stayed with me for life: the colour, richness and beauty, the breadth, depth and glory of the world.

In the face of Puddleglum's defiance, the Witch transforms into a 'writhing green pillar' of flaming-eyed serpent, which flings several swift coils around Rilian and tries to crack his chest. This hair-raising passage owes a lot to Edmund Spenser's allegorical poem *The Faerie Queene*, when the Red-Cross Knight is attacked by Error in the form of a serpent-woman or lamia. 'Error' seems an excellent fit for the Witch's rejected world-view.

> With kindling rage her selfe she gathered round,
> And all at once her beastly body raizd
> With doubled forces high above the ground:
> Tho wrapping up her wreathed sterne around;
> Lept fierce upon his shield, and her huge traine
> All suddenly about his body wound,
> That hand or foot to stirre he strove in vaine ...
>
> His Lady sad to see his sore constraint
> Cride out, Now now Sir knight, show what ye bee,
> Add faith unto your force and be not faint,
> Strangle her, else she sure will strangle thee.'
> That when he heard, in great perplexitie,
> His gall did grate for grief and high disdaine,
> And knitting all his force got one hand free,
> Wherewith he gript her gorge ...[181]

Rilian does much the same, catching the serpent's neck in his left hand, holding its flickering tongue away from him and trying to choke it, while drawing back his sword in his right hand to give it the strongest blow he can deliver. Eustace and

---

[181] Spenser, Edmund, *The Faerie Queene*, Book I, Canto I, verses 18, 19

Puddleglum join in, and all chop together at the serpent till it loosens its hold and they can hack off its head. As usual with Lewis, this is a graphically described physical process: 'The horrible thing went on coiling and moving like a bit of wire long after it had died; and the floor, as you may imagine, was a nasty mess.'[182]

The death of the Witch breaks all her chains of enchantment, and her underground realm begins to collapse. The dark waters are rising, a red glow like a volcano is reflected on the cavern roof, and the gnomes appear to be in some kind of panicked revolt. The four friends head for the stables to tack up Coalblack and Snowflake. Frightened by the noises around them, the horses snort and stamp, but Jill goes fearlessly in between them and within minutes she and Rilian have them saddled and bridled. (Keen on ponies as I was, I could imagine myself in Jill's place, just as brave and competent.) Off they go, Jill riding Snowflake with Puddleglum behind her, and the Prince on Coalblack with Eustace behind. Fearing danger from the hordes of gnomes, they capture one — Golg — and discover they're on the same side. The gnomes too, were enchanted by the Witch. Now they are celebrating their freedom and preparing to re-enter their own deep kingdom, which Golg describes with such fervour that Rilian and Eustace are momentarily tempted to visit, Eustace even invoking Reepicheep whose honour could never refuse an such adventure.

But Jill, who hates tight underground places, refuses point blank to go to Bism and Puddleglum sensibly objects that if Rilian wants to see his father, he had better get moving. Rilian and Eustace turn reluctantly from the

[182] *SC* 146

glowing edge of Bism and the travellers make their way out of Underland through the tunnel the gnomes had excavated for the Green Lady to invade Overland. It opens into the classic heart of Narnia, where fauns and dryads dance in the snow on a cold moonlit night. Everything is now delightful, and the Narnians welcome their long-lost Prince with shouts of joy.

In an unheard-of gesture two Centaurs carry the travellers to Cair Paravel in time to meet King Caspian's ship as it comes slowly up river from the sea. (Aslan has called him back.) It berths. Then a delay; something is wrong. The old king and his son are reunited, but the king is lying on a bed, 'very pale and still'. He lifts a hand in blessing on his son — and falls back, dead.

The full impact of this did not strike me until I had read *The Voyage of the Dawn Treader,* and then I understood. Caspian was dead! Caspian, the brave and handsome boy who was always so nice to Lucy (who equalled me). It had all gone wrong, all turned sad. The Prince kneels at his father's bedside and weeps. All in the crowd doff their caps, and the great Lion banner above the castle is lowered to half-mast.

> And after that, slowly, mercilessly, with wailing strings and disconsolate blowing of horns, the music began again: this time, a tune to break your heart.[183]

The resurrection scene which follows, as Aslan blows away 'the ship and the dead King and the castle and the snow and the winter sky' and brings the children back to his holy mountain doesn't alter the poignancy of Caspian's death. Yes,

---

[183] *SC* 186

his raising-up is wonderful, a happy twist, but even on my first reading it was all still terribly sad. I felt keenly for Rilian. He only *just* got to see his father, after ten years of being enchanted! And after his mother had died too! Poor Rilian, left alone to grieve: *he* doesn't get to see King Caspian coming back to youth and strength. Aslan weeps, too.

Caspian's resurrection still moves me and I find the Christian imagery immensely powerful. We see the cost: blood and pain given with love, as Aslan restores Caspian:

> Eustace set his teeth and drove the thorn into the Lion's pad. And there came out a great drop of blood, redder than all redness you ever have seen or imagined. And it splashed into the stream over the dead body of the King.[184]

I prefer that to a magic wand. And you don't have to be a believer to understand it. If Christianity is a myth, and it is certainly no less, it is one that speaks as truly and strongly as any other.

Of course from my adult, liberal point of view it's a little disconcerting that the final action of Jill, Eustace and Caspian in this book is to inflict, with Aslan's co-operative approval, corporal punishment on the bullies of Experiment House. I have to tell you, though, that as a child I thought this bit was great.

I too had been bullied at school, as lots of children are, and to me it was unthinkable that after all they'd been through, Jill and Eustace would return to square one, cowering miserably in the shrubbery. I would have found

---

[184] *SC* 187

it equally unsatisfactory if Lewis merely had them quell the bullies by force of new-found confidence. ('Just stand up to them,' adults liked to bleat, 'then they'll back down!') I wouldn't have believed it anyway. No thanks, I wanted revenge and I was pleased to be given it. And here my adult and childhood selves part company, and the eight year-old me gives her older counterpart a sceptical and pitying glance.

THE LAST BATTLE

Of all the Narnia books, *The Last Battle* was the one I liked least. I read it perhaps only two or three times compared with countless re-readings of the others, because I found it disturbing. It's a book in which *absolutely everything goes wrong*, at least until the very end, and whether the ending truly succeeds in putting things right is open to question. Then too, this is the book in which we are told Susan is 'no longer a friend of Narnia'. Susan wasn't my favourite character but I still liked her, and she was one of the four kings and queens of Narnia's Golden Age. 'Once a king or queen in Narnia, always a king or queen' – what happened to that? In the other stories Lewis was clear-eyed about his characters' faults – jealousies, vanities and quarrels – but until the ominous paragraph near the beginning of the *Voyage of the Dawn Treader* where Susan is taken to America because she is the pretty one, 'very old for her age', he remained on their side, loyal to them. Something had changed.

> In the last days of Narnia, far up to the west beyond Lantern Waste, there lived an Ape.[185]

[185] *LB* 7

'In the last days of Narnia...' The bell tolls from the very beginning. And in the first sentence of the first page, instead of meeting one of the human children who are our avatars in Narnia, and a sort of guarantee that Aslan has sent them and all will be well, we meet Shift the Ape.

An Ape isn't the sort of Talking Beast you might expect to find in the northern kingdom of Narnia (the elephants and giraffes of *The Magician's Nephew* seem long ago to have wandered off). So why is he here? For one thing, though decades of nature programmes by David Attenborough have taught us differently, Lewis was writing within a literary and social tradition which regarded apes as caricatures of human beings, and a cunning ape makes a good villain. I still believe that's part of the reason, but I have found another. It seems not to have been widely noticed that a large piece of the plot of *The Last Battle* is lifted more or less *in toto* from a poem by — yet again — Edmund Spenser.

Prosopopoia, or Mother Hubberd's Tale is a vivid political satire written in 1578-1579, when the 46 year-old Elizabeth I was being courted by the much younger Duc d'Alençon, brother to the French King Henri III. The French match was regarded with suspicion by many of Elizabeth's councillors, but William Cecil, Lord Burghley, supported it, and Alençon's envoy Jean de Simier was a favourite of Elizabeth's, who gave him the pet name 'her monkey' or 'her ape'.

Spenser's poem tells the tale of an Ape (probably Simier) and a Fox (probably Burghley) who take on various guises to deceive and rob people. Exiled from court, they flee to a forest where they find the Lion, King of Beasts, asleep under a tree, having taken off his skin to be cooler. With the encouragement of his mentor the Fox, the Ape steals the lionskin, dresses in it and masquerades as King, despoiling the land. Worse! – he invites monstrous foreign troops into the country to support him, just as Shift invites the Calormenes – and Tash:

> He did appoint a warlike equipage
> Of forrein beasts, not in the forest bred ...
> For tyrannie is with strange aid supported,
> Then unto him all monstrous beasts resorted
> Bred of two kindes, as Griffons, Minotaures
> Crocodiles, Dragons, Beavers and Centaures:
> With those himself he strengthened mightelie
> That feare he need no force of enemie.
> Then gan he rule and tyrannize at will.[186]

(The Beavers in this list are a little odd, but they'd been extinct in England and Wales since the 12th century, so perhaps they seemed exotic.) The Ape's evil reign continues until Jove, noticing what is going on, deposes him and sets the land to rights. There's no question that much of this is a close match for what happens in *The Last Battle*, and Lewis knew the poem well, spending a whole page on it in his encyclopaedic *English Literature in the Sixteenth Century*, which he was writing at almost the same time.[187] How his heart must have leaped when he saw the possibilities! The main difference of course is that

---

[186] Spenser, Mother Hubberd's Tale, *Spenser's Poetical Works*, 506, lines 1118-1127
[187] Lewis sent the manuscript to the publisher, OUP, in May 1952; he was correcting proofs in July 1953; it was published in 1954. *The Last Battle* was completed in March 1953 and published in May 1955.

in *The Last Battle* it's the donkey, Puzzle, whom the Ape persuades to don the lionskin. This can be sourced to Aesop's fable *The Ass in the Lionskin*[188] where a donkey dressed in a lionskin has fun frightening people – until he gives himself away by braying. Fusing this fable with Spenser's poem provides a neat solution to the problems each tale poses: a donkey could not put a lionskin on, and an ape in a lionskin wouldn't really fool anyone.

Shift is greedy and ambitious. He wants exotic, difficult-to-get foods like oranges and bananas. His very name suggests someone unstable and sly. And his friendship with Puzzle, whose name and species suggest simplicity and patience, is a case study in manipulative abuse. The two animals are friends in name, but somehow Shift gives the orders and Puzzle does the work, and if he ever tries to put his own views forward, Shift squashes them:

> 'Now Puzzle, I know what needs to be done better than you. You know you're not clever, Puzzle.' And Puzzle would always say, 'No Shift, it's quite true. I'm *not* clever.'[189]

There's a lesson here about the dangers of accepting another person's low valuation of yourself. And I completely understood how Shift manages to make poor Puzzle jump into Cauldron Pool to retrieve the yellow lion-skin floating below the waterfall. Like most children I'd known at least one Shift: the person who says, 'I won't be your friend any more unless you do.'

---

[188] Aesop's Fables, 43 (My thanks to Michael Ward for reminding me of this.)
[189] Ibid

Shift made me deeply uncomfortable, as Lewis intends. And that lion-skin looked bad luck from the start — a horrible, slimy, cold, deathly thing. Once Shift has tied it to Puzzle's back there's no way the donkey can get it off by himself. He isn't blameless, though. Like the Ass in the fable, he could give the game away any time simply by braying, but he doesn't. He's used to doing what Shift says, and Shift has convinced him of his own incapacity. The scene is set for an immense deception.

We move on. Tirian, ominously introduced as 'the last of the Kings of Narnia', is sitting outside the door of his hunting lodge near the eastern end of Lantern Waste.

> There was no one else with him that spring morning except his dearest friend, Jewel the Unicorn. They loved each other like brothers and each had saved the other's life in the wars.[190]

The peaceful moment is of short duration. They are discussing the wonderful rumour that Aslan, unseen for generations, has been glimpsed in Lantern Waste — when Roonwit the Centaur gallops up to warn that disastrous conjunctions in the heavens presage some great evil descending upon Narnia. While Tirian is still trying to absorb this, a distressed Dryad rushes from the woods, crying for aid. Forty trees of her brother and sister nymphs have been felled in Lantern Waste. The King springs to his feet, demanding to know who is responsible, but too late. She gasps in pain, shuddering under a succession of invisible blows, and falls over.

[190] *LB* 17

> For a second they both saw her lying dead on the grass and then she vanished. ... Her tree, miles away, had been cut down.[191]

The death of the Dryad, so vivid, so tragic and so *tree-ish*, injects a huge spike of adrenaline into the story and it's unforgettable. I was a hundred percent behind Tirian who refuses to delay for even a fraction of a second and issues impetuous, unwise orders. Sending Roonwit galloping to Cair Paravel for help, he and Jewel set out alone to discover a party of foreigners – Calormenes – not only hacking down trees, but flogging Talking Horses whom they have harnessed to pull logs. Swept away by shock and anger, Jewel and Tirian kill the unarmed Calormene carters and rescue the Horses.

Let us step back for a moment, for there are a number of difficulties in this chapter which I never spotted when I was a child. I was so thrilled to meet a Narnian Unicorn, and so caught up in the excitement of what happened next, that it's taken me until now to pay attention to Lewis's carefully worded claim that Tirian and Jewel are alone. They're *not* alone. There are servants within the lodge, for when Roonwit arrives, Tirian calls a pageboy to bring his guest a bowl of wine: kings are *never* unattended. But the pageboy remains anonymous because in the approaching emergency Lewis needs Tirian and Jewel to be almost powerless and far from help.

Roonwit is dismissed for the same reason – though it's a terrible decision. Lantern Waste is in the top North-West corner of the Narnian map, about as far from Cair Paravel as

[191] *LB* 21

you can possibly get and remain within the country. In *Prince Caspian* it takes a half-day's march just to get from Aslan's How to the fords of Beruna. It will surely take Roonwit at least two days to reach Cair Paravel, and more than double that before reinforcements can arrive. Lewis tells us that Tirian and Jewel have both saved each other's lives in the wars: what wars? Tirian doesn't seem to have learned anything from them. This chapter is called 'The Rashness of the King'; rashness hardly begins to cover it.

And the presence of a Calormene force, thirty strong, in this remote corner of Narnia poses more problems. We learn much later that they came disguised as merchants, but it's hard to believe Tirian wouldn't have been made aware of them as they travelled through. To get here by land they must have crossed the desert and passed through Archenland. If they came by sea, they would have had to sail right past Cair Paravel and up the Great River. Landing further north, they would need to cross or loop around Marshwiggle territory. Narnia is full of Talking Birds and Animals, fauns, dwarfs and dryads, all of them with eyes in their heads. How can the enemy possibly have got to Lantern Waste and begun all this destruction undetected and unreported? And what is their strategic purpose? It's true that Narnia is not an internally consistent secondary world like Middle-Earth; it's almost (not quite) a fairy tale country: perhaps one can forgive a little fog around the edges. But Lewis was an excellent craftsman. This isn't mere sloppiness. Most of it is calculated sleight-of-hand, as we shall see.

So far Tirian has acted with an almost complete lack of common sense and he now compounds it, for as he and Jewel flee from the Calormene soldiers he has a crisis of conscience and turns back. To take unarmed men by surprise and kill them without a challenge is an offence to the rules of chivalry, and in his own esteem this deed makes him and Jewel no better than murderers. It might be argued that as King he has no right to place his personal honour above the safety of his people, and that this is an act of dangerous self-indulgence. The chivalric impulse however, once lightly touched upon, gives way to a more important consideration: one of the Horses has said that all this waste and misery was happening by Aslan's orders. 'Sire,' says Jewel, 'how *could* Aslan be commanding such dreadful things?'

This is the core question of the book, vitally important, with implications for nearly everything else that happens. As a believer, what do you do when your God appears to be commanding something that is wrong? How do you react? Some simply say that if God wants something, it must be right. Joseph Smith, founder of the Mormons, put that view with startling frankness: 'God said thou shalt not kill – at another time he said thou shalt utterly destroy. Whatever God requires is right ... even things which may be considered abominable to all those who do not understand the order of heaven.' Though very shaken, Tirian and Jewel do not think like that.

The problem Tirian has come face-to-face with is the impenetrability of the divine. Aslan's ways are beyond his understanding: he cannot speak about them. All he can hold to is the knowledge that he himself has done something morally wrong. He will give himself up to the Calormenes and ask to be brought before Aslan to receive justice. Jewel tells him this act will cost him his life. Tirian responds that he doesn't care if it does.

'That would be nothing, nothing at all. Would it not be better to be dead than to have this horrible fear that Aslan has come and is not like the Aslan we have believed in and longed for? It is as if the sun rose one day and were a black sun.'

'I know,' said Jewel. 'Or as if you drank water and it were *dry* water.'[192]

The Last Battle is a book about belief. Shift tells Puzzle to pretend to be Aslan, and when Puzzle wants to know what will happen if the real Aslan turns up, Shift replies, 'He never *does* turn up, you know. Not nowadays.'

Not nowadays. If there is a God, why does he not still intervene in humanity's affairs? If the personal encounters of the Old and New Testaments really happened, why do they not still occur? Why *is* it that Aslan never turns up in Narnia any more? Within the sub-creation that is Narnia, readers cannot doubt that Aslan exists. So why has he changed his behaviour?

Lewis poses these questions quite deliberately. In parallel with our world, no Narnian of this generation has ever met Aslan in the flesh. They hold beliefs about him — that he is the source of all that is good and generous and nurturing. But that aphorism 'not a *tame* lion' which we first met in *The Lion, The Witch and the Wardrobe* suggests there is something frightening about him, too. A lion is terrible as well as beautiful, and all concepts of the divine acknowledge a degree of terror. Lewis places Tirian, knowingly I am sure, in the situation of Job in the Bible, so I hope you will come with me on a small biblical excursion.

[192] *LB* 29

The Book of Job is a parable which investigates two questions: why do bad things happen to good people, and — given that they do — how do we retain a faith in God? Job is a good and pious man, blessed with a large family and great riches. The story begins like a folk tale: one day in the court of heaven, Satan insinuates that of *course* Job honours God — since God has given him everything he wants! 'But stretch out your hand and touch all that he has, and he will curse you to your face.' To prove Satan wrong, God puts Job to the test. He allows Satan to strip Job of his possessions, then to kill his family, and finally to cover Job himself with boils. (Back in Narnia, Aslan allows Shift to sell Narnia to its enemies with all the suffering and anguish that entails, and to bring King Tirian low.) Will Job still honour God after all this misery? Job hangs in there, more or less. He curses the day he was born, but refrains from cursing God. 'Though he slay me, yet will I trust in him: *but I will maintain my own ways before him.*' (My italics.)

Job declares his trust in God, but he is not prepared not to ask questions. By insisting, 'I will maintain my own ways before him,' he puts *God* to the test. 'Let me speak, and answer thou me,' he demands. 'Make me to know my transgression and my sin. Wherefore hidest thou thy face and holdest me for thine enemy?'

What have I done to deserve this? Why do the innocent suffer? The parable now transcends its folkloric frame: the answer is not going to be, 'Satan and I had a bet.' Job flings anguished questions into the void of the Divine and the Divine answers not with comfort, not with reasons or explanations, but with page after page of its own magnificent questions: *Where were you when I laid the foundations of the earth? Tell me who laid the measures on it? Who laid the cornerstone, when all the morning stars sang together, and all the sons of God shouted for joy? Have you descended to the springs of the sea? Can you draw up Leviathan with a hook?*

The Book of Job wrestles with the problem of suffering, which it does *not* explain as the result of Original Sin, or justice wreaked upon sinners by an angry Deity, or as in some way character-forming or good for you or all your own fault — or any of that. It acknowledges straight up that evil is evil, pain is pain. God confronts Job with the beauty and terror of a universe of which suffering is an integral part and says, effectively, *It is what is is. I am what I am. This is the only answer.* In the end, Job accepts it. You can read this how you like, because the genius of the book is to leave the question open after all. But Job says:

> I have spoken of great things which I have not understood,
> things too wonderful for me to know.
> I knew of thee then only by report,
> but now I have seen thee with my own eyes.
> Therefore I melt away,
> I repent in dust and ashes. [193]

Job has grappled with unanswerable questions but his integrity remains. He hasn't acquiesced. He's not been made to agree that he deserved any of this, or that the bad things that happened to him were some kind of disguised good. Evil is still evil. And God wasn't angry with him for asking. He even tried to reply.

Anyway here's poor Tirian trying to square the circle and make sense of this suddenly cruel and angry Aslan.

---

[193] Job 42, 2-7, New English Bible

Like Job, his first position is trust, not blind trust but provisional trust. He will put Aslan to the test and see what he will do. He is not prepared to believe in black suns and dry water.

What happens next is a charade (including some unfortunate racial stereotyping to which I will return). Tirian and Jewel give themselves up and are brought before Shift the Ape, who with the help of his Calormene allies is now lording it over a large community of miserable and bewildered Talking Beasts. 'Aslan', aka Puzzle the donkey, has been hidden away in a thatched stable outside which Shift sits in bullying state, significantly dressed in a scarlet jacket, jewelled slippers and a paper crown: in medieval illustrations, the Antichrist is often depicted wearing royal or papal regalia to signify his worldly power. I suspect the Ulsterman in Lewis of taking a sideways swipe at papal power when one of the animals asks why they aren't allowed to see Aslan properly and talk to him directly, and Shift replies:

> 'I'm the only one Aslan is ever going to speak to. He can't be bothered talking to a lot of stupid animals. He'll tell me what you've got to do, and I'll tell the lot of you.[194]

Under the new regime, the Talking Beasts are to be shipped out of Narnia to become slaves of the Tisroc, while Narnia itself is to be modernised in the sort of way Lewis deplores, with ' ... roads and big cities and schools and offices and whips and muzzles and saddles and cages and kennels and prisons ...'

[194] *LB* 33

Never mind the false equivalences (how many of these things are really bad?); Lewis is on a roll and knows his audience of children will shudder. As indeed I did, for Narnia is a wonderful, impossible dream where everyone is happy if only they are left alone, and nobody needs schools or offices or prisons – institutions so foreign to Narnia you might wonder how Shift has even heard of them. Now a little Lamb speaks up to ask what Aslan can have in common with Tash – a god with the head of a vulture who demands human sacrifices? And Shift responds that Tash and Aslan are identical. The Narnians and the Calormenes have been using different names for the same thing. 'Tash and Aslan are only different names for you know Who ... Tash is Aslan. Aslan is Tash.'[195]

No Narnian has ever thought like this, but Shift does, and so does Rishda Tarkaan the Calormene leader who says, '*Aslan* means neither more nor less than *Tash*,' and the atheistical Cat, Ginger, who suggests, 'Aslan means *no more* than Tash'. For these three, Aslan and Tash have equivalence because for them neither name has meaning, and in their mouths the concepts of interfaith tolerance and respect turn to cynical platitude.

As for 'you know Who' – what does Shift even mean? Though the Chronicles of Narnia a few times refer to Aslan's father, the great Emperor-beyond-the Sea, there's never really been the concept of a god in Narnia: as befits a land of animals, Aslan's presence is too physical for that. 'You know Who' is a banal euphemism, a nudge and a wink at a God so notional and irrelevant as to have dwindled to the level of popular superstition. When Shift says 'you know

[195] *LB* 35

Who', he sounds just as he did when he talked about roads and offices and prisons. Lewis is cracking Narnia open and a cold wind from our own world is blowing through.

Tirian is dragged off and tied to a tree. As night falls a number of small Talking Beasts arrive to comfort him. They daren't release him for fear Aslan should be angry, but they wipe his bleeding face and bring him food and drink. After that, the wood is dark and lonely. From his tree, Tirian witnesses the bonfire being lit outside the stable, and the pantomime of the false Aslan, a yellow, four-legged waddling thing, being shown to the crowd of frightened animals. The fire is put out. Alone again, Tirian begins thinking self-pityingly of the Narnian kings of long ago who were helped by mysterious children from beyond the world, right back to the times of the White Witch, a thousand years ago. 'That sort of thing doesn't happen now,' he thinks, echoing Shift. But then he remembers how Aslan himself had appeared in that story, and in other stories too, coming to Narnia's aid with children from another world whenever things seemed desperate. If only that could happen again! And he cries out, 'Aslan, Aslan, Aslan! Come and help us now.'

Till this moment Tirian has thought and spoken *of* Aslan, but never directly *to* him. This returns us to the question of suffering, why it exists and whether it has a purpose. Considering this in *The Problem of Pain*, Lewis wrote: 'God whispers to us in our pleasures, speaks to our conscience, but shouts in our pains: it is His megaphone to rouse a deaf world.'[196] While things were

---

[196] Lewis, C. S., *The Problem of Pain*, 81

easy, maybe Aslan was not much more than a beautiful legend to Tirian. Now in extremity, he attempts an active relationship; for in Lewis's view you need to petition God before he will come to your aid. There's a moment in *The Magician's Nephew* when Digory and Polly realise that although Fledge can eat grass, they themselves have nothing for supper. Digory grumbles that someone should have arranged this for them, and Fledge responds that doubtless Aslan would have done so — if they'd asked him. Yes, of course he would have known about it anyway: 'But I've a sort of idea he likes to be asked.'

This may sound pointless or even petty, but on the run-up to the Lord's Prayer in the Sermon on the Mount, Jesus advises people to keep their prayers simple, since 'your Father knows what your needs are before you ask him' (Matthew 6:8), but nevertheless includes a petition for daily bread — perhaps as a daily reminder of God's bounty, analogous to not taking your parents for granted? Tirian tries again, begging Aslan to let his voice 'carry beyond the world':

> 'Children! Children! Friends of Narnia! Quick. Come to me. Across the worlds I call to you; I, Tirian, King of Narnia, Lord of Cair Paravel, and Emperor of the Lone Islands!'[197]

With this stirring cry he is swept into a waking dream, appearing ghost-like before seven people of different ages whom we recognise as Polly and Digory, Peter, Edmund and Lucy, and Jill and Eustace — 'the seven friends of Narnia'.

---

[197] *LB* 45

(Where, I fleetingly wondered, was Susan?) Peter rises, adjuring Tirian to speak, if he is from Narnia; but Tirian is unable. As the vision melts and vanishes he finds himself back in the wood, still tied to the tree as day is dawning. It's a terrible moment – till with a bump and then another bump, two children appear from nowhere. Jill and Eustace have arrived!

It was with huge relief I greeted their appearance. I was hardly forty pages into the book, but so many awful things had happened it seemed a lifetime. Now at last things would begin to get better! Jill and Eustace would rescue Tirian just as they had rescued Rilian in *The Silver Chair*. Never mind that the book was called *The Last Battle*: at nine years old I had never heard of Armageddon. And never mind that Tirian kept being called 'the last king of Narnia'. I'd been with Jill and Eustace in dark places before and it had always been all right. It was good to hear their nice, ordinary voices as they cut Tirian free.

> 'I say,' said the girl. 'It was you, wasn't it, who appeared to us that night when we were all at supper? Nearly a week ago.'
>
> 'A week, fair maid?' said Tirian. 'My dream led me into your world scarce ten minutes hence.'
>
> 'It's the usual muddle about times, Pole,' said the Boy.[198]

'The usual muddle', that's what it was! The usual muddle which would now be sorted out, so all I had to do was sit back and enjoy the story. How wrong could I be?

---

[198] *LB* 47

The Last Battle

As Tirian leads the children towards one of his own watchtowers, we learn how they came here. Just wanting to get there doesn't take you to Narnia (as well I knew!) so Peter and Edmund had travelled to London to dig up the green and yellow magical rings which brought Polly and Digory to Narnia long ago. While on the train to meet Peter and Edmund and collect the rings, Eustace and Jill have been flung into Narnia naturally. As Eustace innocently explains: 'Aslan did it all for us in his own way without any Rings.' (We will find out about the train crash later.) In the meantime the three comrades arrive at the watchtower. It has no garrison (so not in fact much use as a watchtower) but is well stocked, and we now encounter another of the improbabilities with which *The Last Battle* is riddled. Rifling through the tower's supplies of arms and armour, Tirian pulls out a mail-shirt which Eustace comments is of a strange design.

> 'Aye, lad,' said Tirian. 'No Narnian Dwarf smithied that. 'Tis mail of Calormene, outlandish gear. I have ever kept a few suits of it in readiness, for I never knew when I or my friends might have reason to walk unseen in the Tisroc's land. And look at this stone bottle. In this there is a juice which, when we have rubbed it on our hands and faces, will make us brown as Calormenes.'[199]

Wait: Tirian is keeping suits of *Calormene armour* in a tower in *Lantern Waste*? I repeat: Lantern Waste is about as far away from Calormen as you can possibly get and still be in Narnia. To be of any use for Tirian's avowed purpose, this armour ought to be in some tower down on the southern

[199] *LB* 54

border. It makes zero sense, but when I was nine I accepted it, because things always work out well for the 'goodies' in adventure stories. (When the hero knocks out the enemy soldier and dons his uniform, the uniform always fits.) A sense of narrative familiarity, along with the sheer pace of the story, prevented me from noticing the unlikeliness of this convenient find.

Does it matter? I'm not sure. It depends how much it bothers you. If Lewis had been made to give the Narnia stories the same attention to detail that his friend Tolkien gave to Middle-Earth, they would never have been written. You can feel he just can't do it that way. Now it's true that the inconsistencies in the other books tend to be things like beavers who own sewing machines in a world without factories, or the appearance of Father Christmas, or the merry mixture of mythologies which made Tolkien wince. This seems of a different order, but perhaps the same logic applies: as a storyteller Lewis ruthlessly pursues what matters. It *matters* that Tirian and Jewel go off alone, so he makes the pageboy in the hunting lodge anonymous and forgettable. It *matters* that the story takes place in remote Lantern Waste, and not just because Shift's treason can unfold there away from the King's eye. For Lantern Waste is the place where Aslan first brought Narnia to life. Lantern Waste is where Lucy first stepped out of the Wardrobe. And it will be from Lantern Waste that Aslan brings this world to an end. Given all this, how much do we care how the Calormenes got here?

Disguised and armed, Tirian, Jill and Eustace venture under cover of darkness to rescue Jewel from Stable Hill, planning then to head east in hope of meeting Roonwit the Centaur leading his small relief force from Cair Paravel.

You might think Tirian, billed as 'an experienced warrior and huntsman', would prefer to find his reinforcements *before* risking everything on a night-time raid, but no: we are in a high-stakes adventure story and caution is again thrown to the winds.

> Out they went into the cold night. All the great Northern stars were burning above the tree-tops. The North-Star of that world is called the Spear-Head: it is brighter than our Pole Star.[200]

And there you are: Lewis is such a magician. I'm seduced already, objections melting away. Who cares about plot holes when you can steal through the Narnian woods on such a night? And, as so often with Lewis, with a girl in the lead. Jill knows the Narnian stars, has trained as a Guide, and is the best at finding a path. Tirian is amazed by her skilful, silent woodcraft.

> "By the Mane!" he whispered to Eustace. "This girl is a wondrous wood-maid. If she had Dryad's blood in her she could scarce do it better."[201]

How I glowed for her! Moreover, brilliantly, while Tirian in his Calormene disguise takes the sentry prisoner and releases Jewel who is tethered at the back of the stable, Jill goes *inside* on her own initiative. Her sudden absence frightens and angers Tirian and Eustace, who can hear the drums of marching Dwarfs approaching – whom for some

---

[200] *LB* 59
[201] *LB* 60

mysterious reason Tirian at once assumes will be hostile; have Narnian dwarfs acquired such a bad reputation? Then Jill reappears, bringing with her Puzzle the donkey — the false Aslan himself! It's a great coup. Jubilantly she explains how as soon as Tirian dealt with the sentry she decided to get into the stable to see what was really there, and striking a light in the darkness found only:

> '... this old donkey with a bundle of lionskin tied to his back. ... He was very fed up with the stable and quite ready to come — weren't you, Puzzle dear?'[202]

In fury at this evidence of treachery, maybe even of blasphemy, Tirian draws his sword to cut off Puzzle's head (!!!) but Jill defends him, flinging her arms around his neck — and the king suddenly realises that at last he and his friends have the upper hand over Shift and the Calormenes. They can parade Puzzle before the Narnians, irrefutable physical evidence of the Ape's treachery. His deceit unmasked, Tirian will 'hang that Ape on the highest tree in Narnia.'

It's a bit of a shock to discover the death penalty in Narnia (two threats in swift succession!) but let that pass. For the characters, the relief is palpable. 'Where are these honest Dwarfs?' Tirian demands, reversing his opinion of moments ago. 'We have good news for them.' It does not go as he expects.

Narnian dwarfs have never been comedy turns: they are stubborn, peppery characters descended from the Norse legends, and Alberich and Mime of *Das Rheingold*.

[202] *LB* 65

Obedient to what they believed were Aslan's orders, these have allowed themselves to be marched off as slaves to work in the Tisroc's salt mines. On being shown the fake Aslan, the disillusioned dwarfs revolt not only against their Calormene guards, but against Tirian and the real Aslan too. The king's attempt to rally them, appoint himself their leader and raise 'three cheers for Aslan' meets with sneers and growls as the Dwarf leader, Griffle, declares independence. From now on, the Dwarfs are for the Dwarfs. They trust nobody any more, not Aslan, not kings; and they certainly don't believe any nonsense about children from other worlds. When Eustace rudely calls them 'little beasts' and demands if they aren't at least grateful for being saved, Griffle ripostes with cynical accuracy that the King and his friends only rescued them because they wanted to make use of them — which if not the whole truth, contains enough truth to be difficult to answer. Tirian has made the great mistake of assuming he and the Dwarfs share a common mind-set and objectives.

I myself was dreadfully disappointed in these Dwarfs, and agreed with Eustace that people who'd been rescued ought to be grateful. Now though, I feel a good deal of sympathy. What reason have the Dwarfs to be grateful? Like Tirian, like Job, they have been confronted with a God, Aslan, who has apparently turned against them. That notion of Lewis's, that the infliction of suffering is God's attempt to wake us up and make us turn to Him — is all very well if it works. What if it doesn't? Unlike Job or Tirian, the Dwarfs did not ask questions. They obeyed what they believed to be a divine command: 'Aslan's orders. He's sold us. What can we do against *him*?' They represent, perhaps, the body of ordinary people who consider themselves believers without putting too much thought into it. On seeing that the Aslan whose command they have obeyed was a sham, they not unreasonably conclude that there is no Aslan. And why should they believe Tirian? For one thing they don't recognise him, and he's dressed like a Calormene soldier. For another, on the showing of this book, he's not been a very effective king. His job was to protect and govern his people, and here are the Calormenes invading the country, spreading fake news everywhere and enslaving people. There's a class thing going on too, made obvious in the dialogue: chivalrous king showing contempt for the workers. Jill cries that there *is* a real Aslan; she's seen him; he sent them here!

> 'Ah,' said Griffle with a broad smile. 'So you say. They've taught you your stuff all right. Saying your lessons, ain't you?'
> 'Churl,' cried Tirian, 'will you give a lady the lie to her very face?'[203]

'Churl', 'little beast': it's not the best way to talk when you want someone on your side ... The Dwarfs march off, but a single Dwarf, Poggin, catches up with the King and his companions and pledges loyalty. Cheered by this small addition, the party returns to the watchtower to regroup.

I must mention that during the rescue of the Dwarfs, Eustace kills one of the Calormene soldiers. No child in the Narnia books has ever killed a human being before, and it surprises me that the account is so perfunctory. Slashing wildly with his eyes shut, Eustace opens them to find the Calormene

[203] *LB* 72

dead at his feet. Lewis comments flatly, 'And though that was a great relief, it was, at the moment, rather frightening too.' I understand that Lewis is again deploying the adventure-story convention that the deaths of nameless baddies just don't count, and it's true the narrative hasn't room for an exploration of strong feelings at this point, but he should be able to do better than this emotional box-ticking. And a few pages later the killing is sanitised into a 'victory'. Jill is so impressed by what Eustace has done that she's tongue-tied and 'almost shy', which is quite distasteful: the implication seems to be that manslaying makes him a man ... When next morning Tirian inspects Eustace's sword, he finds that it's been put 'back in the sheath all messy from killing the Calormene. He was scolded ... and made to clean and polish it.' The dead Calormene is reduced to a 'mess' on Eustace's sword. It's a long way from the humanity of Sam Gamgee's reflections on the dead Southron, in *The Two Towers*, as he wonders what brought the man here so far from his home, 'and if he would not really rather have stayed there in peace ...'[204] And it's also a long way from the emotional aftermath of Peter's slaying of the Wolf, in *The Lion, the Witch and the Wardrobe*.

While they sit outside the watchtower waiting for breakfast to cook, Poggin tells his new friends how Shift is being manipulated by Ginger the Cat and the Calormene commander Rishda Tarkaan, and how Ginger has lied to the Beasts about Tirian's escape, claiming that Aslan appeared in a flash of lightning and gobbled him up. (Not one of the enemy seems at all interested in Tirian's whereabouts or possible actions, and they have no plan to find or intercept him. Lewis is keeping things simple.) Then with a shiver of unease the day changes, seeming cooler, cloudier. There's a

---

[204] Tolkien, J. R. R, *The Two Towers*, 269

foul smell, and something shadowy is moving on the other side of the clearing. Jewel scrambles to his feet and points with his horn, crying 'Look!' For just as the masquerading Ape of Spenser's poem called monsters to his aid, Minotaurs, Crocodiles and Dragons, so here. Tash has come to Narnia.

> At first glance you might have mistaken it for smoke, for it was grey and you could see things through it. ... It was roughly the shape of a man but it had the head of a bird; some bird of prey with a cruel, curved beak. It had four arms which it held high above its head, stretching them out as if it wanted to snatch all Narnia in its grip ... It floated on the grass instead of walking, and the grass seemed to wither beneath it.[205]

Pauline Baynes's marvellous illustration shows this sinister demon trailing a stippled shadow that looks like a cloud of flies; you can almost smell the stench. Where is the apparition heading? 'North into the heart of Narnia,' says Tirian. 'It has come to dwell among us.' Resonant though this sounds, the heart of Narnia is south-east of Lantern Waste, not north, and this actually *did* bother me when I was nine, for I knew the map of Narnia very well indeed. Perhaps 'Narnia' and 'the North' had become so synonymous that Lewis couldn't bring himself to write: '*South* into the heart of Narnia', but to me this looks a genuinely careless error and one piece of evidence that maybe Lewis didn't actually think very much about the map ... Anyway, as they recover from the sight, the six friends optimistically decide that Tash is more likely to bring trouble to their enemies than

[205] *LB* 79

THE LAST BATTLE

themselves. Poggin even chuckles and rubs his hands: what a shock it will be for the Ape and his confederates when they discover a real demon has come at their call!

In a common-sense decision that cheers everyone, the friends now set out to rendezvous with Roonwit and the 'little army' he must be bringing from Cair Paravel: no one wants to go near 'that horrible bird-headed thing which ... was now probably haunting Stable Hill'. (Nowhere near the heart of Narnia at all, then.) The humans remove their Calormene disguises and re-arm themselves with the straight Narnian swords and triangular shields which Lewis has ever contrasted with the curving Calormene scimitars as if the straightness stands for honesty and the curviness for deceit. Puzzle is still clothed in his uncomfortable lion-skin.

In the two pages of idyllic writing which follow, Lewis bids farewell to the old Narnia. The friends stroll through sunlit woods full of primroses and birdsong. Eustace and Poggin talk quietly of plant-lore and trees, while Jewel tells Jill tales of the long, mainly peaceful history of Narnia, crammed with whole centuries of happiness – tales I longed to hear and never will hear: of Swanwhite the Queen, and Moonwood the Hare, and King Gale who fought the dragon in the Lone Islands –

> And as he went on, the picture of all those happy years, all the thousands of them, piled up in Jill's mind till it was rather like looking down from a high hill on to a rich, lovely plain full of woods and waters and cornfields, which spread away and away till it got thin and misty from distance.[206]

[206] *LB* 85

It is ominous, this long view, this image of looking down at a beautiful country from a high hill: as if Jill is already standing on Aslan's holy mountain as she did at the beginning of *The Silver Chair* and will do again at the end of this book. She longs for the power of the Ape to end, and for the 'good, ordinary times' to return, but with foreboding we feel that her hope of Narnia's continuance is vain. 'All worlds draw to an end,' says the Unicorn, 'except Aslan's own country.' Moments later Farsight the Eagle swoops from the sky with terrible news. A Calormene fleet has invaded Narnia, Cair Paravel has been taken, and Roonwit the Centaur is dead: in his last words exhorting Tirian to seek a noble death, and repeating the Unicorn's elegiac phrase that all worlds come to an end.

> 'So,' said the King, after a long silence, 'Narnia is no more.'[207]

Turning to what can still be done, Tirian tries to persuade the children to return to their own land. Jill refuses at once, and Eustace points out that in any case they have no way of doing it. The children now face the fact that they may be killed and Eustace boldly speculates about the *consequences* of their possible deaths in Narnia: as a character he has always been someone who interrogates his circumstances. 'I mean, what will happen in our own world? Shall we wake up and find ourselves back in that train? Or shall we just vanish and never be heard of any more? Or shall we be dead in England?'[208] This is an intriguing way for the children to

[207] *LB* 88

[208] *LB* 92

engage with the seriousness of their situation, while also usefully reminding us of that train-journey and the possible significance of the 'awful jerk' that threw them into Narnia. Did they have a narrow escape?

There seems one final chance: go to Stable Hill, produce Puzzle in his lion-skin and proclaim the truth. Surely some of the Narnians will join them in fighting the Calormenes there? The plan fails from the start. Shift informs the Talking Beasts that Aslan (brilliantly renamed 'Tashlan') is angrier than ever and will no longer come out of the stable and show himself any more, because a wicked donkey has dressed itself in a lion-skin and impersonated him! If Puzzle is seen wearing it now, the furious Narnians will attack him, maybe even kill him.

By this time my nine year-old self was boiling with frustrated fury. Everything was so awful, so unfair! It was actually a relief to hear Griffle the Dwarf challenge Shift's version of events: he can't fetch Aslan out because there never was any Aslan except an old donkey dressed in a lionskin, and now he hasn't even got that!

It's the bare truth, but Shift and Rishda retaliate with an offer. Aslan won't come out, but anyone who likes may go *in* – touchingly, the Beasts almost rush the Stable in their longing to do this – but one at a time. Remember, Aslan is angry! He ate up the King! Who wants to be first? The Beasts hesitate, and Tirian whispers to Jill that in all likelihood what is really waiting in the Stable is a couple of armed Calormene soldiers. Then Ginger the Cat volunteers. We're sure it's a set-up, but all eyes are on the Cat as he strolls towards the Stable and through the door.

Since Jill has already been into the stable and seen nothing special, what happens next is truly shocking. With a frightful caterwaul Ginger streaks from the stable, knocking Shift over in his speed, and dashes up a tree where he turns around and hangs upside down with fur bristling, and eyes like 'saucers of green fire'. Worst of all, a thing of horror and terror: he is no longer a Talking Beast.

This is magnificent, edge-of-your seat writing. All this rapid bluff and counter-bluff, all these plans formed and re-formed, and failing as soon as formed — it's like watching blades flicker in a sword-fight. No wonder Tirian is 'dazed with the horrors' of the night, and it isn't over yet. Emeth, a young Calormene knight steps forward and asks permission to enter the Stable himself. On Rishda's hasty refusal ('Thou hast nothing to do with this stable. It is for the Narnians'), Emeth calmly replies that if his commander has spoken the truth, if Aslan and Tash are one deity and Tash is within the Stable, how can it be for the Narnians and not for him? Never mind the risk: 'For gladly would I die a thousand deaths if I might look once upon the face of Tash.'

With the sceptical Dwarfs jeering and hurling racial abuse, the Tarkaan can do no more to prevent Emeth from going in. Watching the boy walk shining-eyed towards the Stable, Jewel whispers to Tirian, 'I almost love this young warrior ... He is worthy of a better god than Tash.'

I too liked Emeth, whose name is derived from Hebrew *'emet*: truth.[209] But I now find it more difficult to accept what Lewis does with him. Like Aravis, he is depicted as not typical but exceptional: given Lewis's presentation of Calormenes throughout the books, this had to be the case. In *The Voyage of the Dawn Treader* they are slave-traders. In *The*

---

[209] I owe the information that *'emet* means 'truth' in Hebrew to Robert Alter's translation of The Book of Jonah, *Strong as Death is Love*, 135.

Horse and his Boy we see a hierarchical society of slaves, peasants and princes under a cruel and degenerate ruler. In *The Last Battle* the Calormenes who take Jewel and Tirian prisoner are a crowd of 'dark men ... smelling of garlic and onions, their white eyes flashing dreadfully in their brown faces'. It would be hard to cram more dog-whistle prejudice into a sentence than that. Even in the 1950s 'race prejudice' was a recognised thing, yet Lewis is relaxed about racial slurs and has nothing good to say about this Orientalist culture of his own creation.

More of this later. Emeth enters the stable. A moment later the door re-opens and a man falls out dead. Rishda claims the body is Emeth's, but Tirian and his six friends are close enough to see it is an unknown Calormene warrior. Believing the death to have gone according to plan, Shift gloats and jeers, picking out the Talking Boar as the next victim. Seeing the Boar preparing to fight for its life, Tirian has had enough. He whispers to the children and Poggin to draw swords, get ready to shoot, and follow him.

The friends leap out in front of the stable. Rishda Tarkaan jumps back calling on his men, but Shift is not so quick. Tirian grabs him and as Poggin opens the stable door, hurls the Ape through it into darkness. There's a blinding flash, followed by an earthquake and bird-like cackling. The Talking Beasts cower — Rishda Tarkaan changes his mind about Tash — and all the Talking Dogs in the crowd dash to Tirian's side, followed by the Boar and the Bear. Mice and squirrels scamper to gnaw through the ropes of the Talking Horses, tethered down slope. Yet these are the exceptions; most of the animals have not moved. They are afraid of 'Tashlan'.

It's interesting that apart from the Dwarfs there are no

human or human-shaped Narnians present in this crowd — no fauns, satyrs, nymphs or lesser gods; Roonwit the Centaur and the dryad who dies near the beginning of the book are the only representatives of what might be called the classical tradition. Maybe this is because we wouldn't easily believe that wise centaurs or bookish fauns could be taken in by Shift's trickery. (Remember Mr Tumnus's library?) The naivety of the Talking Beasts makes the crime committed against them seem worse, and we are more ready to excuse and forgive them.

Confused victims of fake news and toxic propaganda, these innocent Narnians have accepted the cynical invention 'Tashlan' as their god. Dry water and black suns: I well remember the anguished, helpless fury of reading all this when I was nine. But you know what? While writing this book I lived through the same rage, I recognised it: the horror and helplessness and bewilderment of living in a society broken down, divided and in conflict, with a fatuous, self-serving caricature in charge, who broadcast lies and claimed them as truths and called upon powers of darkness and violence. Here is a parable with relevance for our times. Tash walks through our world too.

Tirian orders his small force, and the Last Battle begins.

The first attack fails. Jill's arrows and Jewel's horn have done their work, leaving some Narnian traitors dead, but at cost: three Dogs are dead and the Bear is dying. The Dwarfs jeer the retreating Calormenes but refuse to join Tirian's side. No Kings! 'The Dwarfs are for the Dwarfs. Boo!' Now comes the worst atrocity. As the Calomene war-drum beats for reinforcements, and the great wave of Talking Horses gallops up the hill to Tirian's aid, the Dwarfs shoot them down. I'd been crying already over the death of the Bear. But this! 'Little *swine*!' Eustace shrieks as one after another the Horses tumble to the ground. 'Not one of those noble Beasts ever reached the King.'

What are we meant to think? Why do the Dwarfs do it? It's more than selfishness — more like hatred, or anarchy. Lewis seems to suggest that, loosed from an unexamined and purely conventional belief in God, the Dwarfs now have no moral compass and no anchor. Remember, they didn't ask questions when it seemed Aslan was acting as a tyrant rather than a guardian. Now they will have neither tyrant nor guardian. They will have nothing but themselves. Shown a black sun, they have chosen to disbelieve in *any* sun. (Shades of the Green Lady's attempt at gaslighting in *The Silver Chair*.) The end comes quickly. Jill is alone in front, twenty feet out from the others, shooting to cover her friends as they try to reach the protection of a white rock away from the stable. The Eagle helps: even in this extremity Lewis manages a touch of fun:

> Very few troops can keep on looking steadily to the front if they are getting arrows in their faces from one side and being pecked by an eagle on the other.[210]

And 'the Unicorn was tossing men as you'd toss hay on a fork': has there ever been a better description of a Unicorn fighting? All in vain. More enemy troops arrive. Eustace is thrown to some unknown fate in the Stable. There's a brief lull as the Dwarfs turn their bows on the Calormenes, but their arrows cannot pierce the Calormene mailshirts. They too are overcome and thrown alive into the Stable as offerings for Tash (no more talk of 'Tashlan'). In the final

[210] *LB* 118

onslaught, the friends go down one by one until Tirian is fighting Rishda Tarkaan in the very door of the Stable itself. With a sudden move he drops his sword, grabs his enemy and drags him into the Stable, shouting: 'Come in and meet Tash yourself!'

There's a bang and flash. The soldiers outside scream and slam the door shut. Rishda Tarkaan falls on his face as Tash appears, picks him up with a jerky, bird-like movement, and tucks him under one arm. The demon then turns its bird-head sideways to fix Tirian with a glaring eye, when a strong, calm voice speaks out, banishing Tash and his prey 'in the name of Aslan and Aslan's great Father the Emperor-over-the-Sea.' It is Peter the High King.

Tirian turns in amazement to see seven glittering Kings and Queens and recognises the two youngest as Jill and Eustace. Kissing him on both cheeks, Peter welcomes Tirian and makes courtly introductions to our old friends Polly and Digory, Edmund and Lucy. But someone is missing. Surely the High King has two sisters? Where, Tirian enquires, is Queen Susan?

'My sister Susan,' answered Peter shortly and gravely, 'is no longer a friend of Narnia.'[211]

This is where Lewis finally ditches Susan to make a theological point. At the very end of John Bunyan's *The Pilgrim's Progress*, Ignorance, who has followed the hero Christian from the City of Destruction (the world) to the Celestial City on top of Mount Zion (heaven), is refused entry. Instead of keeping to the King's Highway he has taken by-roads, dodging the

---

[211] *LB* 127

hardships and not learning the lessons, so when he comes to the gates he has no passport and is turned away:

> Then they took him up, and carried him through the air to the door that I saw in the side of the hill, and put him in there. Then I saw that there was a way to hell, even from the gate of heaven, as well as from the City of Destruction.

Susan is made an example of by Lewis to illustrate the same point. Her sins, according to her friends, are numerous. Eustace complains that she regards Narnia as a childish game. Jill says Susan's only interested in 'nylons and lipstick and invitations'. Polly — *Polly!* — snarkily accuses Susan of having wasted all of her time at school waiting to be the age she is now (is this really the sensible, responsible Susan who was so excellent at swimming and archery?) and predicts that she'll waste the rest of her life trying to stay that age.

It is a ludicrous prediction: Polly cannot possibly know how Susan will behave for the rest of her life. Even God doesn't judge you till you're dead. What Lewis clearly hopes to convey is that Susan has been lost to worldliness, but it's a sorry try. Nylons? What else did he think a young woman would put on her legs in 1955? The reference to lipstick may have worked (a bit) when I was a pony-mad nine year-old with no conception of ever wanting to use make-up or talk to boys, but it's poor evidence for the eternal damnation of a character who seems simply to have reached adolescence or committed what A.N. Wilson has called 'the unforgivable sin of growing up'.[212] Lewis has grafted all this on to Susan's

[212] Wilson, A. N., *C. S. Lewis: A Biography*, 228

character, and the whole thing is trivialised by the shocking indifference of her family and friends as they line up to drop a few catty remarks and dismiss her:

> 'Well, don't let's talk about that now,' said Peter. 'Look! Here are lovely fruit trees. Let us taste them.'[213]

Lovely fruit trees? Huh!

Till now we have been given no impression of Tirian's surroundings: Lewis has kept everything in close-up so there isn't too much to take in. Gone is the narrow dark stable. We are in the open air, under a blue sky, near a grove of trees covered with the delicious fruit with which they refresh themselves (as Christian and Hopeful refresh themselves in the 'goodly orchards and vineyards' below the Celestial City).

Eustace asks Peter how he and the others got here, and it becomes apparent there really was some kind of railway accident in England. Peter and Edmund saw the train coming in far too fast, and then with a roar and a bang '— we were here.' (I still thought that maybe by coming into Narnia, they'd escaped.) And the next thing that happens is that Tirian sees the Door.

The stable door by which they all came in from Narnia is now shown to be a portal, something already hinted at when from the outside Tirian described it as a doorway to death. The last time we saw anything like it was in *Prince Caspian* when Aslan opens a door in the air – two uprights and a lintel – to let the Telmarines pass from Narnia to their place of origin in our world, somewhere like Pitcairn Island. That doorway led from one mortal world to another. This one can be regarded

[213] LB 128

as the ultimate in the series of doorways discovered by the children in book after book: it leads from the mortal world to the eternal and opens the way to life after life, and room after endless room in the courts of Heaven.

The next few pages provide a much-needed rest from direct action as Lucy tells how the Battle of Stable Hill looked from the point of view of those inside it. Very significantly, Lucy has been silent so far. Lewis tells us this is because she has been 'too happy to speak', but personally I think she's been silent because he couldn't find any convincing way to write about her likely response to what's happened to Susan, and the criticisms of the others. It's hard to imagine Lucy not defending her sister, and even harder to imagine her joining in the catty blame-game. With interruptions from Edmund and Eustace she now describes to Tirian the Calormene sentry positioned to kill anyone who came in, the appearance of Tash to the terrified Cat, the fight between Emeth and the sentry (Emeth has wandered off looking for Tash) and the reappearance of Tash to peck up Shift. Edmund adds that about a dozen Dwarfs arrived after that, followed by Jill, Eustace and finally Tirian himself.

The Dwarfs. Sitting together in a close ring, facing inwards, backs turned, they are blind to what is 'really' around them, seeing not sky and trees and flowers but a 'pitch-black, poky, smelly little hole of a stable.' As Lucy and Tirian unsuccessfully try to persuade them that their perceptions are false, a great light flashes out behind them and Aslan appears at last. As Tirian falls at the Lion's feet, Aslan kisses him and says, 'Well done, last of the Kings of Narnia who stood firm at the darkest hour.'[214]

[214] *LB* 138

Well done, thou good and faithful servant. The praise is deserved. Tirian has been steadfast; he has grown during the course of the book.

Readers may still have questions about Aslan's role in all this. Why hasn't he appeared before? With a record of previous intervention in Narnian affairs, why hasn't he done so again? The answer of this book is going to be that all worlds end, and Aslan has much better in store for all his beloved: implicitly we are asked to apply this explanation to our world too. But not everyone will be saved, and even Aslan cannot change the Dwarfs' limited perceptions. When he places a banquet before them, the delicious food and wine tastes to them only like dirty water and raw turnips. As Mephistopheles explains in *Dr Faustus*, Hell is not a location but a state of being:

> Hell hath no limits, nor is circumscribed
> In one self place, but where we are is hell,
> And where hell is, there must we ever be.

This scene with the Dwarfs is a brilliantly clear elaboration of the concept reiterated by Milton's Satan ('Myself am Hell') that damnation is not a sentence prescribed by God, but something you do to yourself. There is no hope for the Dwarfs precisely because they have rejected hope. And Aslan has other work to do. The friends all follow him as he goes to the Door and roars:

> 'Now it is time!' then louder, 'Time!'; then so loud it could have shaken the stars, 'TIME.' The Door flew open.[215]

---

[215] *LB* 140

The chapter 'Night Falls on Narnia' defies paraphrase and you should really just go and read it again yourselves. In a night so deep you can barely tell where the darkness of the trees gives way to the darkness of the sky, a vast black shape rises against the stars. It is the giant Time, whom long ago Jill and Eustace saw sleeping in the deep caves under the northern moors. They watch him lift a horn to his mouth ... then, after a pause due to the slow speed of sound, they hear its note, 'high and terrible, yet of a strange, deadly beauty. Immediately the sky became full of shooting stars.'[216]

It will surprise no one to hear that there are allusions to the *Book of Revelation* here, specifically 6:12-15: 'The sun turned black as a funeral pall and the moon all red as blood; and the stars in the sky fell to the earth ... and every mountain and island was moved', and 8:7: 'all the green grass was burnt'. In Narnia the stars keep falling until a blackness spreads across the sky: not a cloud but an absence, an emptiness. At the very end, stars come raining down all around the children and Aslan: glittering silver people who 'made a hissing noise as they landed and burnt the grass.'

With the stars now serried behind us, we see miles of the Narnian landscape violently flood-lit, with huge dragons and lizards crawling down from the northern moors into the woods. Driven out by these monsters, every living thing in the Narnian world comes racing up the hill to the Door and each one looks in Aslan's face. Depending on *their* reaction to *him* — love or hatred — they come in by the Door or swerve away into shadow. Amongst those who

[216] *LB* 141

come in are some you wouldn't expect, like one of the Dwarfs who shot the Horses – this is a lovely touch which made me realise as a child that we can't always judge what's going on with people. But what I really loved was to see Jewel arriving, and Roonwit 'and Farsight the Eagle, and the dear Dogs and the Horses, and Poggin the Dwarf'. It's a joyful reunion, while on the other side of the Door, the monsters and lizards eat all Narnia's vegetation, leaving it barren. These too die, and a giant wave rises from the Eastern sea and crashes over Narnia, levelling it.

Here for the last time is the Atlantean image Lewis used in his autobiography as a metaphor for the death of his mother. The myth of Atlantis originates with Plato, who in the *Critias* describes the island of Atlantis and its people, offspring of the god Poseidon and a mortal woman, Cleito. While the divine nature remained strong in them, the people were happy, virtuous and prosperous, but 'when the divine portion began to fade away' they became more and more corrupt. As they descended into greed and unrighteousness, Zeus decided to punish them. This reason for the fall of Atlantis seems applicable also to Shift's Narnia; but Lewis's first encounter with Atlantis must have been in E. Nesbit's *The Story of the Amulet*, and his description of the fall of Narnia clearly owes much to her account. Nesbit writes:

> Across the smooth distance of the sea something huge and black rolled towards the town. It was a wave, but a wave a hundred feet in height, a wave that looked like a mountain ...
>
> The hills around were black with people fleeing from the villages to the mountains. And even as they fled thin

smoke broke out from the great white peak, and then a faint flash of flame. The earth trembled; ashes and sulphur showered down; a rain of fine pumice-dust fell like snow on all the dry land. The elephants from the forest rushed up towards the peaks; great lizards thirty yards long broke from the mountain pools and rushed down towards the sea ...

'Oh, this is horrible," cried Anthea, "Come home, come home!'[217]

Even to the lizards, the correspondences with *The Last Battle* are striking. Nesbit's children are able to escape through the portal of the Amulet, while in this book the children are able to look on in safety through the Door. As the sun rises, swollen and red and dying like the sun of Charn, the giant Time unforgettably stretches out an arm 'thousands of miles long' to squeeze it out. Darkness falls.

'Peter, High King of Narnia,' says Aslan, for of course it's Saint Peter who holds the keys of Heaven, 'Shut the Door.' Peter obeys, dragging it shut with difficulty over the rough ice which has already coated the ground beyond, and locks it with a golden key. No one will ever open it again. Narnia is gone.

Though Aslan turns playful, lashing his tail and shooting away crying to them, 'Come further up! Come further in!', Lucy is in tears and the other humans are pretty subdued as they walk away from the Door and the hapless Dwarfs. But the Dogs pick up a scent and lead them to Emeth, sitting beside a stream of clear water indicative of spiritual refreshment: 'Like as the hart desireth the waterbrooks, so

---

[217] Nesbit, Edith, *The Story of the Amulet*, 174

longeth my soul after thee, O God'. (Psalm 42). Emeth rises to greet them, and tells his story.

If Susan's interest in nylons is meant to illustrate that 'there is a way to hell even from the gate of heaven', Emeth is here to illustrate Lewis's on-the-face-of-it generous belief that there is truth in all religions and they all get something right even if Christianity gets top marks. (A concession dangerously close to condescension.) In a letter of January 1952 he wrote, 'I think that every prayer which is sincerely made even to a false god ... is accepted by the true God and that Christ saves many who do not think they know Him.'[218]

But who are we to judge whether the God someone worships is false or not? And who knows all the names of God? And if God accepts a prayer addressed to some other name (something not even possible to know), why is that name not rightly his? Quite apart from the dodginess of such speculations, it might be all very well if there was anything good or true about Tash, but there isn't. He is presented as an entirely evil and entirely loathsome demon, and though at many times and in many places people have believed in demons, and been afraid of them, to the best of my knowledge no world religion has ever *worshipped* a being from whom they expected to obtain nothing good. Visually, Tash is close to Nisroc or Nisroch, a winged Assyrian eagle-headed guardian spirit whose likeness is to be found in the British Museum. E. Nesbit uses the same figure in *The Story of the Amulet*, treating it with respect as an awesome but beneficent 'Servant of the Great Ones'. Tash's additional limbs are borrowed perhaps from Hindu imagery. Neither religion deserves the connection. In *The Horse and His Boy*, probably in

---

[218] Hooper, Walter (ed): *Letters of C. S. Lewis*, 428

an effort to differentiate Calormen from the Islamic culture of *The Thousand and One Nights* which it otherwise resembles, Lewis made it a polytheistic country. Aravis speaks of 'Tash and Azaroth and Zardeenah Lady of the Night'. *The Last Battle* forgets about Azaroth and Zardeenah and focuses on an Aslan/Tash dichotomy which is effectively Christ v Satan. How can Emeth possibly have found in Tash anything worthy of worship?

And sadly, on this re-reading I find that in spite of his courage and his courtly speech I don't like Emeth very much after all. If you actually read what he says, he comes across as a warlike, aristocratic snob guided largely by the rules of chivalry. He was keen to wage war, having longed to meet Narnia in battle, but he despises the lower classes, declaring that to go through Narnia disguised as a merchant is beneath him not only because it's a form of treachery, but because a merchant's garb 'is a shameful dress for a warrior and the son of a Tarkaan'.

Upon actually seeing Aslan he recognises the Lion as good and glorious, but his previous devotion to Tash remains inexplicable. Faithfulness to a truly detestable god suggests blinkered adherence to custom rather than a genuine desire for knowledge of the divine — and is a rather low bar for Aslan's approval. But this whole difficulty is entirely of Lewis's own making.

A comic exchange with the Dogs ends the interlude, and with Emeth one of the party, and picking up dear old Puzzle along the way, they all walk westwards, sensing a strange familiarity about the landscape. Those hills and mountains look very like Narnia ... Farsight the eagle takes to the air and sweeping around cries down that he can see everything — all the old landmarks! — even 'Cair Paravel still shining on the edge of the Eastern Sea. Narnia is not dead. This is Narnia.'[219]

Digory — the *Lord* Digory, the Professor of *The Lion the Witch and the Wardrobe* — launches into his favourite Platonic explanation: the old Narnia was but a copy of this greater, better, eternal Narnia which seems different only 'as a real thing is from a shadow or as waking life is from a dream.'

Here is Lewis as Apologist and Enchanter. Alas, his Farewell to Shadowlands doesn't work for me and it never has. And I'm not sure he quite convinced himself either, for he tries again, comparing this transfigured landscape to the depth and mystery of a reflection in a mirror (which seems the wrong way round) — and then the Unicorn restates it for a third time. It may be protesting a bit too much, so it's a relief when Jewel breaks into a gallop, neighing 'Further up and further in' — and they all follow, running faster and faster, swimming wonderfully and impossibly *up* the Great Waterfall with much comedy as the Dogs 'swarm and wriggle' and bark and get water in their mouths. If as I suspect, this watery episode parallels Christian and Hopeful's plunge into the River of Death, it's a most lovely and joyful take on that awesome experience. Much of what happens next is clearly modelled on Christian's approach to the Celestial City. I italicise the correspondences:

> ... the City *stood upon a mighty hill*, but the Pilgrims *went up that hill with ease,* because they had these two men [shining angels] to lead them by the arms: they had likewise *left their mortal Garments [their bodies] behind them*

[219] *LB* 159

in the river; for though they went in with them, they came out without them. They therefore *went up here with much agility and speed,* though the foundation upon which the City stood was *higher than the clouds;* they therefore went up through the Region of the Air, sweetly talking as they went ...

[The shining ones tell them:] You are going now to the Paradise of God, wherein you shall *see the Tree of Life* and eat of the never failing fruits thereof. *There you shall enjoy your friends again that are gone thither before you;* and there you shall with joy receive every one that follows into the holy place after you.

Now *while they were thus drawing towards the gate, behold a company of the heavenly host came out to meet them* ...[220]

Lewis tells how they run faster and faster until they are almost flying. A smooth green hill rises before them, topped with a green wall and orchard trees that we recognise from *The Magician's Nephew*. They charge up a slope as steep as a roof and find themselves facing great golden gates. A horn blows from within the garden, the gates open, and who should come out to welcome them but Reepicheep – oh, *Reepicheep!*

With him come Tirian's father, and Fledge the Flying Horse – there's a nice moment when Jewel is awed by his presence – and as they pass further into the garden, all the best characters from all the stories are there to meet them, right back to Mr and Mrs Beaver and Mr Tumnus the Faun, while in the centre of the garden under the Tree of Life sit King Frank and Queen Helen, like 'Adam and Eve in all their glory.'

[220] Bunyan, John, *The Pilgrim's Progress*, 276-7

It's a wonderful reunion. And yet I was not really happy. I didn't like it — I still don't — when Lucy, with her new telescopic vision, realises that the garden is itself another whole Narnia, and that there is 'world within world, Narnia within Narnia,' infinitely replicated one within another — 'like an onion,' says Mr Tumnus, 'except that as you go in, each circle is larger than the last.'

The effect for me was to make each one of them seem less: diminished, discardable, disposable. In which Narnia should one stay? Which is 'real'? Are some of them empty? Does what happens in one, happen in all? And — here was a bit I absolutely hated — Lucy suddenly sees, joined to Narnia, another peninsula jutting from the great, mountains of Aslan's country. England! Or rather, the eternal England of which the mortal one was but another shadow. And there are her mother and father waving at her as if from the deck of a great ship coming in to port. And then Aslan tells Lucy and the others the truth. They can stay here forever, because — and they rejoice to hear it — they and their parents were all killed in the railway accident. 'The term is over: the holidays have begun. The dream is ended: this is the morning.'[221]

My emotions as a child went like this: They're all dead? And that's supposed to be good? And nobody cares even a tiny little *bit* about Susan, left all alone and terribly unhappy? Don't even her *parents* care? And Narnia has turned into this complex onion-ring thing which connects to Britain? Worst of all, Aslan isn't even a lion anymore: 'For as He spoke He no longer looked to them like a lion ...'

[221] *LB* 171

I didn't like the new improved Narnia, I didn't want it and I didn't want to believe in it. I wanted the old Narnia, thank you very much, the same as it had always been. As for Lewis's assurance that the 'things that happened' next were 'so great and beautiful' he couldn't write them, I could see perfectly well that what he really meant was there weren't going to be any more stories. *Nothing* would happen. The adventures were over. If I wanted any more, I would have to write my own.

Maybe for some of you, perhaps for many of you, it does work. I can only report how it felt to me, how it still feels. Lewis's glimpses of Aslan's country have always worked best when they are just that – glimpses. The silence of the holy mountain with its bright birds at the eastern end of the world, the paradisal garden on the hill. The tingling smell and sound carried by the wind from beyond the great wave at the rim of the Silver Sea. The spell only works at a distance, because distance is the essence of that longing, that disturbance of 'unsatisfied desire which is itself more desirable than any other satisfaction'[222] which Lewis calls Joy.

In the earlier books, storytelling took precedence. I felt the mythic and emotional power of Aslan's death in *The Lion, the Witch and the Wardrobe* without at first the slightest notion that it was meant for a version of Christ's passion, and when eventually the connection dawned on me I did my best to forget it, because to say that Aslan *is* Christ spoils the story. We need to let the tale do its own work. Aslan is not Christ; his story is different in detail and affect: that is what fiction *is*. In *The Magician's Nephew*, Lewis imagined a Creation story with a lyrical and often even comic touch

---

[222] Lewis, C. S., *Surprised by Joy*, 23-24

which owes little to Genesis. *The Last Battle* — though it is richly, densely allusive, though it contains many powerful passages, though the chapter 'Night Falls on Narnia' has stayed with me all my life — is not so successful. Lewis is a genius at making ideas accessible to children. But in this book he pushes the message too hard. At the end he becomes a catechist rather than a storyteller, and for me at least, the spell breaks.

I spent half my childhood longing for Lewis's wonderful, magical, unattainable world. Not even he can tell me Narnia is a Shadowland.

Afterword

So what happened to her — the grumpy, passionate, imaginative little girl that used to be me, who wrote her own *Tales of Narnia* and badly wanted to own the complete boxed set of the Seven Chronicles with extra Pauline Baynes illustrations, but knew she never would, because she'd been given all the books separately already and the expense would have been unthinkable?

For one thing, she went on writing ...

There were no more Narnia stories. I'd seen it couldn't be done: you couldn't get into Narnia that way. The writer stays outside the book. Trying to fit inside it would be as uncomfortable as Alice, crammed into the White Rabbit's house with one arm out of the window and a foot up the chimney. However, I'd discovered that making up stories was a different kind of joy, and by the time I was fourteen I'd written a set of fairy tales — over a hundred pages of them, no less! — called *Mixed Magic*. One of the best was quirky and funny and well within my limits: it told the story of how and why Peter Piper picked that peck of pickled peppers. My father typed it out for me and sent it to a publisher, George G. Harrap & Co. A letter came back: 'Encourage your daughter to keep writing as it is quite possible that she may be able to produce something that would interest us at a later stage.' Whoopee! In fact I hardly needed the encouragement: I was certain that what I wanted in life (besides running my own riding stable) was to write books for children. So I went on reading, writing, and learning the craft. It took years longer than I thought it would, but I suspect a lot of children's authors write to keep faith with the uncompromising child who lives on inside us. When I was finally published, mine gave me a fierce nod of approval. So there was that.

But what about the other kind of faith?

If the Narnia books were really intended as subtle propaganda for brainwashing children into accepting the Christian message, then honestly, they don't work very well. For me, Aslan was Aslan, not Jesus, and he still is. However, ours too was a house of many books, and as I reached my teens I found other titles by C. S. Lewis on our shelves, such as *The Screwtape Letters* and some of his Christian apologetics including *Miracles* and *The Problem of Pain*. I read them because I'd loved Narnia, and I loved Lewis's 'voice', and because his books made me think. How *do* miracles happen – if they do? If God is good, why *is* there so much pain in the world? I searched out his literary criticism as well. I read his treatise on medieval and renaissance allegorical poetry, *The Allegory of Love*, well before I read any of the texts it examines – but then he made them sound so interesting I longed to read them, and now I knew about them, I could hunt them down. I'd been attending a small country grammar school run by a mainly elderly teaching staff with little interest in or ambition for the academic potential of their pupils: I got mediocre marks

Afterword

in everything but English, but there, with help from Lewis, I was educating myself.

C. S. Lewis changed my life. He certainly influenced the way I thought, though it didn't quite work out as you might imagine. I was brought up by C of E parents who took the truth of Christianity for granted but weren't regular church-goers. We went at Christmas and Easter, of course, and every school I ever attended held a religious assembly each morning so I knew plenty of Bible stories, and stories about Jesus, but no one ever talked about theology. The Trinity was a mystery. Father and Son were straightforward enough, but what was the Holy Ghost? When I wondered about it at all, I assumed it was Jesus risen from the dead. We used the old Prayer Book, and what else was a child to think?

Lewis's Socratic approach to Christian apologetics taught me that it was proper to ask questions about what you believe: in fact that you had a *duty* to ask questions. He seemed so sure there was this thing called the truth, which it was possible to pin down with logic. All fired up, I looked for it. I tried to get our vicar to tell me just who or what the Holy Ghost *was* (I'd learned to say 'the Holy Spirit' by now) but somehow he wasn't able to give me a really clear answer.

Still, aged eighteen I decided to be confirmed, feeling I'd learn more about my faith that way, and my mother decided to join me. She hadn't been confirmed before because *her* mother had never been confirmed, and she took the forthright Yorkshire view that if this meant her mother was going to hell (which I'm not sure anyone had actually suggested) then she was going to go there right along with her. The situation evolved into edgy comedy when the vicar asked my mother for her certificate of baptism and she didn't have one; it had been lost in the Sheffield Blitz. This worried him so much he suggested baptising her all over again to be on the safe side – upon which, nervous already and becoming upset, she snapped that if that was how he felt, he needn't bother: she would join the Methodists. She would have, too: most of our friends and neighbours went to the chapel ... He gave in ... and at the same time, in an earnest attempt to understand Holy Communion, I was begging the poor man to explain to me what made it different from a simple act of remembrance. My motives were sincere, but he couldn't provide a very clear answer for that either. Lewis, you had a lot to answer for.

This book has been about the Narnia stories, not my personal beliefs, but it's impossible to discuss Narnia and not talk about faith, and the reader may reasonably wonder where I now stand. Well, I stand with Puddleglum. I'll try to live as like a Narnian as I can even if there isn't any Narnia. I remained a practising Christian for many years, but in the end – with relief as well as regret, and regret as well as relief – I stopped believing in God. Each one of us has to make their own peace with this world. And if there is a God after all, I'll go with Job and say we can only wonder at the awesome power that made this amazing universe – and I'll go with Lewis, and say a loving God won't turn us away.

Appendix 1
Orphans in Narnia

Much of what follows has been inspired by a letter I received shortly after the publication of the first edition of *Spare Oom*. It was sent by a gentleman from Hertfordshire called Michael Baker, who pointed out something I hadn't noticed, close to the end of *The Last Battle*. It comes after Peter has shut and locked the Stable Door and 'Narnia is no more': Lucy is in tears, but Peter chides her, 'What, Lucy! You're not crying? With Aslan ahead, and all of us here?' Tirian replies for her, 'Sirs, the Ladies do well to weep. See, I do so myself. I have seen my mother's death. What world but Narnia have I ever known? It were no virtue, but great discourtesy, if we did not mourn.'[223]

Michael went on to say:

> 'I have seen my mother's death.' Narnia began with Digory seeking something to prevent his mother's death. The tree grown from the Narnian apple that

---

[223] Lewis, C. S., *The Last Battle*, 149,150

does so provides wood for the wardrobe that is the first way into Narnia. The death of Rilian's mother is the spring for the story of *The Silver Chair*, and now Narnia is mourned by Tirian as his dead mother. The cycle is complete. One might say that all his life Lewis was looking for his mother, though I don't place too much stress on that. But certainly, to me Narnia has the air of a land of lost content.

So it is that Narnia, the beloved land that nurtured him, is mourned by Tirian as if she were *his dead mother*. I found this and its implications very touching. One of the lovely things after the publication of *Spare Oom* has been the conversations it's provoked both on and off line, and Michael's letter prompted me to write something about orphans in Narnia.

Orphaned children, or children with absent or neglectful parents, are of course a recurrent theme in children's fiction and in fairy tales. Without adults to help them, these children have to solve their own problems and overcome danger: in narrative terms it gives them agency, and establishes an immediate bond of sympathy between reader and character. Think of Hansel and Gretel, Cinderella, Snow-White, Heidi – or Harry Potter, Lyra and Will... Orphaned or neglected children frequently appear in adult fiction too, like Jane Eyre, or Rudyard Kipling's Kim, or Cosette in *Les Misérables* – and are liberally scattered through the works of Dickens: David Copperfield, Little Dorrit, Pip, Oliver Twist, Jo the crossing sweeper, and so on.

Indeed, happy families are not easy to find in the Narnia books. The Pevensies' parents are remarkable mainly for their absence: we never even set eyes on them until Lucy sees them waving from a distant 'English' spur of Aslan's holy mountain — by which time all of them are dead. Eustace Scrubb's parents send him to boarding school at the ominously named Experiment House where he is bullied and made miserable. So do Jill's. All we learn of Polly's parents is that her mother sends her to bed for coming home late. Digory's father is far away in India, and he and his dying mother are forced to live with kindly but ineffectual Aunt Letty and dangerously 'mad' Uncle Andrew.

So much for the children from our world. What about those born in Narnia itself? Shasta (aka Prince Cor of Archenland) is stolen at birth and raised by an abusive foster-father who tries to sell him into slavery. Aravis escapes from a father who is pressuring her into a detestable marriage. Prince Caspian's father has been murdered by his usurping uncle, King Miraz, so that when his aunt, Queen Prunaprismia, gives Miraz an heir, Caspian's own life is in immediate danger. Whether true fathers or surrogates, father-figures in the Narnia books tend either to be absent, or else very much part of the problem.

There's a poignancy about Narnian orphans that probably comes from Lewis's loss of his own mother to cancer when he was nine years old. As was then common practice, she was nursed and even operated upon at home, and in his autobiography *Surprised by Joy* he describes how her illness affected him and his brother: '[O]ur whole existence changed into something alien and menacing, when the house became full of strange smells and midnight noises and sinister whispered conversations.'[224] He tells of desperately praying God for a miracle to save his mother,

---

[224] Lewis, C. S., *Surprised By Joy*, 24

and the terror of being taken into her bedroom 'to see her' when she had died.

Just a few weeks after this huge loss his grieving father, probably with no idea what better to do with his small son, sent him to the English boarding school his brother already attended, an establishment unfortunately run by a sadistic headmaster who might have come straight out of Dickens. No one can mistake the emotion with which Lewis paints himself and his fellow pupils as 'pale, quivering, tear-stained, obsequious slave[s].'[225] No wonder he never had a good word to say about schools in the Narnia series. He couldn't tell his father, partly because children often don't know how, but also because their relationship had suffered and, as he himself acknowledged, never really recovered, even after he was allowed to leave school to study with a tutor who recognised and encouraged his potential. Perhaps it's significant that (Aslan aside), Prince Caspian's tutor Dr Cornelius is the one Narnian father-figure whom Lewis depicts as entirely laudable.

It's clear that the painful series of events surrounding his mother's death remained vivid in Lewis's memory, for there are many other boys in the Narnia stories whose mothers have died. Shasta is separated from his mother when he is kidnapped as a baby, and then she dies long before he can be reunited with her. Yet there is no particular narrative reason why this should be so. It just *is* — perhaps Lewis couldn't visualise such a reunion. Caspian's parents are both already dead when we first meet him as a little boy: his father murdered by Miraz and his mother (perhaps) dying naturally and earlier. Youthful Prince Rilian of *The Silver Chair* loses his mother — Ramandu's daughter and Caspian's

[225] Lewis, C. S., *Surprised By Joy*, 36

Queen — when she is stung to death by a poisonous green serpent. This serpent is the Green Witch, who compounds her wickedness by enchanting and imprisoning Rilian, who loses ten years of his life with her, and is reunited with his father Caspian only on the old king's deathbed.

So, finally, for Tirian to describe the land of Narnia as his mother is a heartfelt expression of deep love for the country that bore him and which, as its king, he has ultimately failed to save — just as young Jack Lewis's prayers for his own mother failed. Yet Tirian's apparent loss is about to be transformed into a far greater victory. There is always something more to be said about Narnia.

Appendix 2
Of a Narnian Fish

After his first letter Michael wrote to me with another fascinating insight concerning the Narnian fish called a 'pavender'. It's mentioned in *Prince Caspian*, and also in *The Silver Chair* when Jill and Eustace enjoy one of the few good meals of their adventure, a royal feast in the great hall of Cair Paravel.

> The banners hung from the roof, and each course came in with trumpeters and kettledrums. There were soups that would make your mouth water to think of, and the lovely fishes called pavenders, and venison and peacock and pies, and ices and jellies and fruit and nuts, and all manner of wines and fruit drinks.[226]

I'd sometimes idly wondered if there really might be a fish called a pavender — after all, there are plenty of strangely named English fishes, such as gudgeon, chub, dace, roach, etc. — or whether Lewis had simply invented it. Well, the

[226] Lewis, C.S., *The Silver Chair*, 41

answer is neither and it's far more fun! Here is Michael to explain it all.

> In *Prince Caspian*, as you may remember, Trumpkin catches and cooks for the Pevensies some delicious little fish called pavenders.[227] This, I believe, is a private scholarly joke of Lewis's. It is a reference to a poem published originally in *Punch*,[228] called 'A False Gallop of Analogies' by one Warham St Leger. The conceit of the poem springs from a reference to 'the chavender, or chub' in Isaac Walton's *The Compleat Angler*. So it begins:
>
>> There is a fine stuffed chavender,
>> A chavender, or chub
>> That decks the rural pavender
>> The pavender, or pub,
>> Wherein I eat my gravender,
>> My gravender, or grub ...[229]
>
> And so on, with references to 'sweet lavender, or lub' and administering a 'snavender, or snub', to an intrusive young 'cavender, or cub', followed by 'the ravender, or rub' of having to return to town ...

Michael continues:

---

[227] Lewis, C. S., *Prince Caspian*, 36,37
[228] *Punch* was a satirical magazine founded in 1841. It ran until 1992, was revived in 1996 but closed again in 2002
[229] The whole poem can be found at this link: http://www.poetrynook.com/poem/false-gallop-analogies

Of a Narnian Fish

I am only aware of the poem through encountering it in the Festival of Britain[230] issue of *Punch*, which I was given by my father at the time. As well as topical items ... it contained an anthology of notable cartoons and other snippets, from issues over the past century. Lewis would no doubt relish the reference to the 'pavender, or pub' and have stored it away for future use.

I don't need to tell you how delighted I was to learn the origin of this obscure Narnian fish (or dish) and in the words of the other Lewis, Lewis Carroll, to have *un-dish-covered the fish and dish-covered the riddle.*[231] Thank you, Michael!

---

[230] The Festival of Britain was a national exhibition which took place in London in 1951
[231] From 'The White Queen's Riddle' in *Alice Through the Looking Glass*

Appendix 3

The Picture Portal in The Voyage of the Dawn Treader

A long time ago in my late teens I wrote a book with the rather unimaginative title *The Magic Forest* which quite rightly was never published. Although derivative (I was inspired by Walter de la Mare's strange and wonderful novel *The Three Royal Monkeys*) it was the closest I'd yet got to finding my own voice and I've still got a sort of *tendre* for it. It was a dream-quest story in which a girl goes through a picture into a magical world; the picture in question was a reproduction of Henri Rousseau's 'The Snake-Charmer' which hung on my bedroom wall. My heroine Kay looks at it and sees:

> ... the ripples of a lake reflecting the quick luminous afterglow of a sun's sinking. There were night-flowering reeds and a tall, heron-like bird, and standing in the darkness of the trees, partly in silhouette against the

night sky, was a human figure. It was wearing a dark cloak and piping on a flute. Answering the flute came snakes, great forest pythons pouring scarcely distinguishable from the branches and from the lake. Kay's feet sank into shallow mud. She heard the low, hollow-sweet notes, saw the snakes twist about the charmer's legs. A heavy, scaly body dragged over her foot. Midges stung and bit her, but a little coolness came breathing over the water.

So begins an adventure I won't bore you with; it's enough to say Kay goes on a quest with a yellow water-bird and a monkey, to find a sorcerer who has infested the forest with poisonous butterflies.

I knew that 'going into a picture' wasn't an original idea, since it had appeared in several of my favourite children's books. The earliest I'm aware of is Mrs Molesworth's *The Tapestry Room* (1879) in which two children find themselves able to enter, perhaps in dreams, the tapestry hanging in one of their bedrooms and find adventure in the world depicted there. John Masefield's young hero Kay in *The Midnight Folk* (1927) is able to climb up into a portrait of his great-great grandfather, to visit him in the past. In its sequel *The Box of Delights* (1935) the old Punch and Judy man, Cole Hawlings, escapes his enemies by bringing a painting of a Swiss mountain to life, and riding away into it on a mule. All these stories pre-date Lewis's book.

In *The Voyage of the Dawn Treader* Lucy and Edmund Pevensie, with their cousin Eustace Scrubb, tumble into a painting of what looks like a Narnian ship at sea. When Eustace asks Lucy why she likes it, she replies, 'because the ship looks as if it was really moving. And the water looks as

THE PICTURE PORTAL IN THE VOYAGE OF THE DAWN TREADER

if it was really wet. And the waves look as if they were really going up and down.'[232] She's right! The ship rises and falls with the waves, a wind blows into the room bringing a 'wild, briny smell' and, 'Ow!' they cry, for – 'a great, cold, salt splash had broken right out of the frame and they were breathless from the smack of it, besides being wet through.'[233] Eustace rushes to smash the painting – the other two try to pull him back – next moment all three are struggling on the edge of the picture frame, and a wave sweeps them into the sea.

I strongly suspect this passage was influenced by a Japanese tale, 'The Story of Kwashin Koji' from *Yasō-Kidan* (*Night-Window Demon Talk*), a book of legends collected by Ishikawa Kosai (1833-1918) and retold by Lafcadio Hearn in his 1901 book *A Japanese Miscellany*. It is certainly the sort of thing Lewis would have read. It tells of Kwashin Koji, a rather disreputable old fellow and a heavy drinker, who made a living 'by exhibiting Buddhist pictures and by preaching Buddhist doctrine'. On fine days he would hang a large picture – 'a kakemono on which were depicted the punishments of the various hells'[234] – on a tree in the temple gardens, and preach about it. The painting was so wonderfully vivid that onlookers were amazed.

Hearing this, Lord Nobunaga, ruler of Kyōto, commanded Kwashin Koji to bring the painting to the palace where he could view it. The old man obliged and Nobunaga was deeply impressed. Noticing this, his servant suggested Kwashin should offer the painting as a gift to the great lord. Since his livelihood depended upon the picture,

---

[232] Lewis, C. S., *The Voyage of the Dawn Treader*
[233] Lewis, C. S., *The Voyage of the Dawn Treader*
[234] Hearn, Lafcadio, *Writings from Japan*, 353

Kwashin asked instead for payment in gold. This was refused, so he rolled up the picture and left. But the servant followed him, killed him, and stole the picture for his lord. When the scroll was unrolled however, it was found to be totally blank, while Kwashin had mysteriously returned to life and was displaying his picture in the temple grounds as before. Not long after, Lord Nobunaga was himself murdered by Mitsuhidé, one of his captains, who invited Kwashin Koji to the palace, feasted him and gave him plenty to drink. The old man then pointed to a large folding screen depicting 'Eight Beautiful Views of the Lake of Omi', and said, 'In return for your august kindness, I shall display a little of my art'.[235] Way off in the background the artist had painted a man rowing a boat, a tiny detail less than an inch in length. As Kwashin Koji waved his hand, everyone in the room saw the boat turn and begin to approach them. It grew rapidly larger ...

> And all of a sudden, the water of the lake seemed to overflow out of the picture into the room, and the room was flooded; and the spectators girded up their robes in haste as the water rose above their knees. In the same moment the boat appeared to glide out of the screen, a real fishing boat, and the creaking of the single oar could be heard. Still the flood in the room continued to rise until the spectators were standing up to their girdles in water. Then the boat came close up to Kwashin Koji, and Kwashin Koji climbed into it; and the boatman turned about, and began to row away very swiftly. And as the boat receded, the water in the room began to lower rapidly, seeming to ebb back into

[235] Hearn, Lafcadio, *Writings From Japan*, 359

> the screen ... But still the painted vessel appeared to glide over the painted water, retreating further into the distance and ever growing smaller, till ... it disappeared altogether, and Kwashin Koji disappeared with it. He was never again seen in Japan.[236]

The lakewater flooding out of the painted screen corresponds to the 'great salt splash' of the wave bursting into the children's bedroom in *The Voyage of the Dawn Treader*. The creaking oar finds an echo in Lewis's description of 'the swishing of waves and the slap of water against the ship's sides and the creaking and the overall high steady roar of air and water'. And just as Kwaskin Koji is never seen again in Japan, the courtly Talking Mouse Reepicheep embarks on the Dawn Treader with the desire to find Aslan's own country. At the end of the voyage, where the ocean pours over the edge of the world in a huge standing wave, he gets into his coracle 'quivering with happiness':

> ... and the current caught it, and away he went, very black against the lilies. But no lilies grew on the wave; it was a smooth green slope. The coracle went more and more quickly, and beautifully it rushed up the wave's side. For one split second they saw its shape and Reepicheep's on the very top. Then it vanished, and since that moment no one can truly claim to have seen Reepicheep the Mouse.[237]

---

[236] Hearn, Lafcadio, *Writings From Japan*, 359
[237] Lewis, C. S., *The Voyage of the Dawn Treader*, 185

Acknowledgements

My thanks to Amanda Craig and Nicholas Lezard for their long-term encouragement of this project, and to Francis Spufford whose surprise email praising one of my blog posts on Narnia set me thinking seriously about rewriting them for publication. I'm also deeply grateful to Brian Sibley who generously offered to write the wonderful Foreword in which he shares some of his own childhood memories of Narnia, and to my friends Neil Philip, John Garth and Farah Mendlesohn whose experience and knowledge I could always rely upon. Grateful thanks also to Simon Bradshaw for advice about quotations, and to my agent Catherine Clarke for her support and encouragement over many years.

There was a moment when (with a thrilled shiver) I thought I might have been the first person to spot the connection between *The Last Battle* and Edmund Spenser's *Mother Hubberd's Tale*. On checking with Lewis scholars Professor Charles Huttar, and Arend Smilde, who owns the website *Lewisiana.NL*, I found that I wasn't; but they were able to assure me that all the same it hasn't been widely remarked upon. They couldn't have been kinder to this stranger writing to them out of the blue, and I'm most grateful.

Thanks also to Michael Ward, author of *Planet Narnia*, for kindly and patiently answering a whole variety of queries. Needless to say, all of the opinions and any mistakes to be found in these pages are down to me alone.

Finally, heartfelt thanks to all the readers of my blog *Seven Miles of Steel Thistles*, for without their sustained interest in children's literature, fairy tales, folklore, fantasy and of course Narnia, the book might never have been written.

BIBLIOGRAPHY

Aesop's Fables
Aesop's Fables: A New Translation by V. S. Vernon Jones with an Introduction by G. K. Chesterton and Illustrated by Arthur Rackham, Piccolo, Pan Books, London 1975

Alter, Robert
Strong as Death is Love: The Song of Songs, Ruth, Esther, Johah, Daniel, tr. with commentary by Robert Alter, W. W. Norton & Co, New York 2015

Andersen, Hans Christian
The Complete Fairy Tales and Stories, tr. Erik Hausgaard, Gollancz Children's Paperbacks, London 1994

Bourchier, John, Lord Berners
Huon of Bordeaux, retold by Robert Steele, George Allen, London 1895

Blishen, Edward (ed)
The Thorny Paradise: Writers on Writing for Children, Kestrel 1975

Bunyan, John
Grace Abounding and The Pilgrim's Progress, Cambridge UP 1907

Campbell, J. F.
Popular Tales of the West Highlands, Vol 2, Birlinn Ltd 1994 (originally published Edmonston & Douglas, Edinburgh 1860)

Carroll, Lewis
Alice's Adventures in Wonderland and Through the Looking Glass, Everyman's Library, Alfred A. Knopf, New York, London, Toronto 1992

Grahame, Kenneth
The Wind in the Willows, Methuen 1929

Gregory, Lady Augusta
A Book of Saints and Wonders, Put Down Here by Lady Gregory According to the Old Writings and the Memory of the People of Ireland, The Coole Edition, Oxford University Press, New York 1971

Grimm, Jacob and William
Grimms' Fairy Tales, tr. Margaret Hunt, Routledge & Kegan Paul, London 1948

Hooper, Walter (ed)
Letters of C. S. Lewis, Harcourt Brace, New York 1993

Hooper, Walter and Lancelyn Green, Roger
C. S. Lewis: A Biography, HarperCollins, London 2002

BIBLIOGRAPHY

Housman, A. E
Poetry and Prose: A Selection, F. C. Horwood (ed), Hutchinson Educational, London 1971

Jacobs, Joseph
English Fairy Tales, Dover Publications Inc, New York 1967

Jung, Carl
Memories, Dreams, Reflections, Collins, Fount Paperbacks, 1979

Kipling, Rudyard
The Day's Work, Macmillan, London 1898

Kipling, Rudyard
Just So Stories for Little Children, Macmillan, London 1950

Langley, Noel
The Land of Green Ginger, Puffin Books 1966

Lewis, C. S.
The Magician's Nephew, Collins & Son, London 1989 (first published 1955 by The Bodley Head

Lewis, C. S.
The Lion, the Witch and the Wardrobe, HarperCollins, London 1998 (first published 1950 by Geoffrey Bles)

Lewis, C. S.
The Horse and His Boy, William Collins Sons & Co, London 1989 (first published 1954 by Geoffrey Bles)

Lewis, C. S.
Prince Caspian: The Return to Narnia, HarperCollins, London 2009 (first published 1951 by Geoffrey Bles)

Lewis, C. S.
The Voyage of the Dawn Treader, William Collins Sons & Co, London 1989 (first published 1952 by Geoffrey Bles)

Lewis, C. S.
The Silver Chair, William Collins Sons & Co, London 1990 (first published 1953 by Geoffrey Bles)

Lewis, C. S.
The Last Battle, William Collins & Sons, London 1989 (first published 1956 by The Bodley Head)

Lewis, C. S.
The Screwtape Letters, Geoffrey Bles, London 1942

Lewis, C. S.
Spenser's Images of Life, ed. Alistair Fowler, Cambridge UP 1967

Lewis, C. S.
God in the Dock, Essays on Theology, ed. Walter Hooper, Fount, HarperCollins 1979

Lewis, C. S.
That Hideous Strength, Bodley Head, London 1976

Lewis, C. S.
The Problem of Pain, Geoffrey Bles, London 1944

Lewis, C. S.
Mere Christianity, Fount Paperbacks 1986

Lewis, C. S.
An Experiment in Criticism, Cambridge UP 1976

Lewis, C. S.
Selected Literary Essays, ed. Walter Hooper, Cambridge UP 1969

Lewis, C. S.
English Literature in the Sixteenth Century, excluding Drama, Oxford, Clarendon Press 1964

Lewis, C. S.
On Stories and Other Essays on Literature, ed. Walter Hooper, Harvest/HJB Books, Orlando Florida 1982

Lewis, W. H. and Hooper, W. (eds)
Letters of C. S. Lewis, HarperCollins, London 1993

MacDonald, George
Lilith, ed. Lin Carter, Ballantyne Books Ltd, London, New York 1971

MacDonald, George
The Princess and Curdie, Dent, London 1963

MacDonald, George
The Princess and the Goblin, Dent, London 1973

McGrath, Alister
C. S. Lewis: A Life, Hodder & Stoughton 2013

Miller, Laura
The Magician's Book: A Skeptic's Adventures in Narnia, Little, Brown & Co, New York, Boston, London 2008

Milton, John
Paradise Lost, Oxford University Press 2005

Malory, Sir Thomas
Le Morte d'Arthur, ed. Janet Cowan, Penguin 1969

Map, Walter
De Nugis Curialium, tr. M. R. James, Honourable Society Of Cymmrodorion 1923

Neilsen, Kay
East of the Sun, West of the Moon: Old Tales from the North, George H. Doran Company, NY 1920

Nesbit, Edith
The Magic World, Ernest Benn, London/NY 1959

Nesbit, Edith
The Story of the Amulet, Penguin Books, London 1967

Nesbit, Edith
The Story of the Treasure Seekers, Ernest Benn, London 1947

Oxford Book of Ballads, The
The Oxford Book of Ballads, selected & ed. James Kinsley, Oxford University Press 1969

Spenser, Edmund
Spenser: Poetical Works, ed. J. C. Smith and E. de Selincourt, Oxford University Press 1966

Sturlusson, Snorri
The Prose Edda, tr. Jean Young, University of California Press 1973

Temple, William
Readings in St John's Gospel, First and Second Series, Macmillan, London 1952

Tolkien, J. R. R. and Gordon, EV (Eds.)
Sir Gawain and the Green Knight, Second Edition revised by Norman Davis, Clarendon Press, Oxford 1972

Tolkien, J. R. R.
The Hobbit, or There and Back Again, HarperCollins, London 1991

Tolkien, J. R. R.
The Two Towers, George Allen and Unwin, London 1969

Twain, Mark
The Prince and the Pauper, Wordsworth Classics 1994

Ward, Michael
Planet Narnia, The Seven Heavens in the Imagination of C. S. Lewis, Oxford University Press 2008

Wilson, A. N.
C. S. Lewis: A Biography, HarperCollins, London 1991

White, T. H.
The Once and Future King, Collins, Fontana Books 1967

Wynne Jones, Diana
The Lives of Christopher Chant, Methuen, London 1988